MENTAL ILLNESS AND SOCIAL POLICY

THE AMERICAN EXPERIENCE

MENTAL ILLNESS AND SOCIAL POLICY

THE AMERICAN EXPERIENCE

HISTORY

OF THE

PSYCHOPATHIC HOSPITAL

BOSTON, MASSACHUSETTS

By

L. VERNON BRIGGS

ARNO PRESS
A NEW YORK TIMES COMPANY
New York • 1973

362.21
B854

Reprint Edition 1973 by Arno Press Inc.

Reprinted from a copy in
  The Medical Library Center of New York

MENTAL ILLNESS AND SOCIAL POLICY:
  The American Experience
ISBN for complete set: 0-405-05190-5
See last pages of this volume for titles.

Manufactured in the United States of America

———◆———

Library of Congress Cataloging in Publication Data

Briggs, Lloyd Vernon, 1863-1941.
    History of the Psychopathic Hospital, Boston,
Massachusetts.

    (Mental illness and social policy: the American
experience)
    Reprint of the ed. published by Wright & Potter
Print. Co., Boston.
    1. Massachusetts. Mental Health Center, Boston.
I. Title.   II. Series.   [DNLM: WM28 AM4 B7P9B
1922F]
RC445.M4B9 1973   362.2'1'0974461   73-2386
ISBN 0-405-05194-8

HISTORY

OF THE

PSYCHOPATHIC HOSPITAL

PSYCHOPATHIC HOSPITAL
74 Fenwood Road, Boston (front view)

HISTORY

OF THE

PSYCHOPATHIC HOSPITAL

BOSTON, MASSACHUSETTS

By

L. VERNON BRIGGS, M.D.

Member of the Massachusetts State Board of Insanity
1913, 1914, 1915, 1916

AND

COLLABORATORS

BOSTON
WRIGHT & POTTER PRINTING COMPANY
32 DERNE STREET
1922

Dedicated

TO THE MEMORY OF

ELMER E. SOUTHARD, A.M., M.D., Sc.D.

THE FIRST DIRECTOR OF THE BOSTON PSYCHOPATHIC HOSPITAL

AND EXPOUNDER OF THE

PSYCHOPATHIC HOSPITAL IDEA

FOREWORD

Part I of this volume describes how the Psychopathic Hospital came into existence as the result of an intolerable condition of the neglect of Massachusetts' mentally ill, and how this condition was put an end to in spite of the inactivity of the then State Board of Insanity, whose duty it was to protect and see that this class of our citizens had immediate hospital care and treatment.

It soon became evident that the first step necessary to compel the State Board to assume responsibility for the care of all of this large class of people was to place the Boston Insane Hospital patients and property in the care of the State.

The executive officer of the State Board, Dr. Copp, said it would not be possible at that time; that Boston was not ready — would not let go, etc. But we obtained the co-operation of the Mayor, of The Finance Commission, and others, and soon accomplished it.

The next great step was to prevent the mentally ill from being sent daily to the police stations, jails, to the Tombs or City Prison and the House of Correction.

The State Board had for years tolerated this condition of affairs even after the Legislature appropriated $600,000 to build the Psychopathic Hospital and to relieve this very situation. During the time the State Board was planning and building this hospital, they did not raise their hands to give *immediate* relief to these suffering and neglected citizens, and if they thought they lacked authority, the fact remains that they did not ask for it.

It was left for us, who could not bear it any longer, to act, in spite of discouragements and the obstacles the Board put in our way.

On February 21, 1910, the Legislature gave us a hearing and many prominent people testified as to the conditions and made statements of facts. I presented my bill, Senate No. 212, which read, in part, that "*on and after May 1, 1910,*" the "*State Board of Insanity shall provide*" suitable temporary quarters for these people "*until the Psychopathic Hospital shall be completed and ready to receive them.*"

Dr. Copp, the executive secretary of the Board, appeared before the committee and said, "*The first of May is out of the question,*" and he asked "*Who is to do it? The Board of Insanity is not an executive board.*" He acknowledged it would be at least two years before the Board could assume the care of these people.

The Legislature, after hearing my bill and the presentation of facts, passed almost unanimously a law which was promptly approved and signed by Governor Draper, which said, in part, that "*from and after May 1, 1910, the State Board of Insanity shall provide at the Boston State Hospital suitable temporary quarters for receiving and giving medical care and treatment to all persons suffering from the above-mentioned disorders who are now in the City Prison, House of Detention, or House of Correction,*" and that no more of our mentally ill shall be sent to these prisons.

The State Board of Insanity obeyed the mandate of the General Court. They suddenly found it was pos-

sible to immediately care for these mentally ill citizens.
We had obtained for them such authority as they had
not asked for themselves, and in the face of their opposition. Thus hundreds of our mentally ill citizens,
who would otherwise have been sent to prison, were
given humane hospital treatment in the same manner
as their fellows who were suffering from other diseases.

Part II of this volume is a history of what has been
accomplished in the Psychopathic Hospital since it
opened, and contains valuable suggestions from leaders
in this branch of medicine to assist any State which
contemplates establishing a similar institution.

Parts I and II will, I hope, serve as a guide to future
organizers.

INTRODUCTION

On August 15, 1912, Dr. Elmer E. Southard wrote to me that he proposed to write a history of the Psychopathic Hospital:

DEAR DR. BRIGGS: — I am going to write a history of the origin, establishment and scope of the Psychopathic Hospital in order to urge similar work in other institutions of Massachusetts and elsewhere. I know that various opinions are held as to your personal share in the development of psychiatry in Massachusetts. I propose, however, to write a truthful history of development *in re* the Psychopathic Hospital. Would you send me a brief, or even longer, account of your activities before legislative, official and other bodies in behalf of psychiatry in Massachusetts? I would be pleased to receive copies of letters or other documents touching these matters.

Sincerely yours,

E. E. SOUTHARD.

In answering his letter on December 30, 1912, I gave him substantially the outline set forth in this book, and received the following reply, dated January 20, 1913:

DEAR DR. BRIGGS: — I am exceedingly sorry that I failed to answer your note and enclosure of December 30, 1912. I have read the history over with interest and it will help me in my historical account of the development of the Psychopathic Hospital idea. You have succeeded in presenting an account which is objective and I should not suppose that many persons would dissent from your interpretation of the events.

I have not shown your letter to any one, but would like to show it some time to Dr. Copp in case you give me permission so to do. I should certainly like to have the sequel which you suggest in your note of September 30 might some time be written.

I question whether my history of the Psychopathic Hospital will be finished until late in 1913 or early in 1914, but any data which I can get will be of service.

Thanking you for the great pains which you have taken in the matter, I am

Sincerely yours,

E. E. SOUTHARD,

Director.

He added to his letter, " I have sealed up your history and put it away in my files."

I had many talks with Dr. Southard before his death, and he felt as I did that the history of the hospital could not be written until the object which we all sought had been realized, namely, a Psychopathic Hospital and not a mere department of a State Hospital for the mentally ill, both chronic and acute.

I gave him permission to show all my material to Dr. Copp. Whether he did so or not, I do not know, but a few weeks before he died he told me that he had had a long talk with Dr. Copp, and that Dr. Copp had told him that he was heartily in favor of separation, and that he was sorry he had ever advocated that the Psychopathic Hospital should be a department of the Boston State Hospital.

Dr. Southard died February 8, 1920, without leaving any written history of the Psychopathic Hospital, so far as has been ascertained. I have used his writings to a great extent, and they give a fairly good history of the Psychopathic Hospital from its beginning. To what he has written at different times, I have added an account of the activities of those who brought about the existence of the present hospital, — those who are directly and those who are indirectly responsible for it.

The care of the mentally ill in both public and private institutions in Massachusetts, after a slow process of development and improvement, had only reached what may be termed the perfected custodial stage at the beginning of the last decade. There was still a great discrepancy between the interest and intelligence mani-fested in the care of the physically ill on the one hand,

and the neglect and ignorance which was met in dealing with the mentally afflicted on the other.

Here and there, however, we find exceptions, as at the South Boston institution, which was opened in 1839, under the superintendency of Dr. Butler, with 104 patients. On that date it received 44 patients from the House of Industry and 21 from the House of Correction.

Charles Dickens in his "American Notes" records his impressions of the institution when he visited it in 1842:

At South Boston, as it is called, in a situation excellently adapted for the purpose, several charitable institutions are clustered together. One of these is the hospital for the insane; admirably conducted on those enlightened principles of conciliation and kindness which twenty years ago would have been worse than heretical, and which have been acted upon with so much success in our own pauper asylum at Hanwell.

Each ward in this institution is shaped like a long gallery or hall, with the dormitories of the patients opening from it on either hand. Here they work, read, play skittles and other games; and, when the weather does not admit of their taking exercise out of doors, pass the day together. In one of these rooms, seated calmly, and quite as a matter of course, amid a throng of mad-women, black and white, were the physician's wife and another lady, with a couple of children. These ladies were graceful and handsome; and it was not difficult to perceive at a glance that even their presence there had a highly beneficial influence.

Every patient in this asylum sits down to dinner every day with a knife and fork; and in the midst of them sits the gentleman whose manner of dealing with his charges I have just described. At every meal, moral influence alone restrains the more violent among them from cutting the throats of the rest; but the effect of that influence is reduced to an absolute certainty, and is found, even as a measure of restraint, to say nothing of it as a means of cure, a hundred times more efficacious than all the straight waistcoats, fetters and handcuffs that ignorance, prejudice and cruelty have manufactured since the creation of the world.

In the labor department every patient is as freely trusted with the tools of his trade as if he were a sane man. In the garden and on the farm they work with spades, rakes and hoes. For amusement they walk, run, fish, paint, read, and ride out to take the air in carriages provided for the purpose. They have among themselves a sewing society to make clothes for the poor, which holds meetings, passes resolutions, never comes to fisticuffs or bowie-knives as sane assemblies have been known to do elsewhere; and conducts all its proceedings with the greatest decorum. The irritability which would otherwise be expended on their own flesh, clothes and furniture is dissipated in these pursuits. They are cheerful, tranquil and healthy.

Up to the beginning of this century in most institutions the physical needs of the individual were looked after more or less efficiently, the standards varying in different hospitals. The State hospitals were undermanned by physicians and nurses, and it was a physical impossibility for the small staff of physicians to see and prescribe for each patient every day. The standards or requirements for nurses had never been high and thus the physicians had poor tools with which to work. Many of them were so inefficient and unintelligent that coercion instead of medical treatment was used even to the point of death at times. The standard of physical care and of housing gradually improved and in 1900 had reached a very satisfactory level; but the insane were still considered a class by themselves in so far as they were not treated like people suffering from other illnesses either by the public, by the authorities, or by most physicians. In a general way it may be said that to be mentally ill was considered a crime, punishable by imprisonment, following court procedure. The mentally ill were arrested and even sent to jails and prisons before being sent to the hospitals, and the public accepted this condition of affairs and apparently approved of it.

After the State Board of Insanity was organized they improved conditions materially in some directions, but it is almost inconceivable that they allowed other conditions to remain which we now look upon as only tolerable in the dark ages. Confused and mentally ill persons continued to be arrested on the streets of Boston or taken by the police from boarding houses and hotels, or even from their homes, to the City Prison in Pemberton Square, or first to one of the police stations from which, when it was found that they were delirious or irresponsible, they were removed to the City Prison. As late as 1906 I visited the City Prison and found that the kindly officer in charge quieted these people with the black contents of a bottle, which he kept in a drawer on the right-hand side of his desk. He gave this liquid, which had been furnished him by one of the city physicians, for all cases of delirium and confusion if the patient became noisy or violent. When I visited the cells, I found that these mentally ill persons were subjected to the gibes and the curses of the "drunks" in the cells near by. This excited them, and it was certainly "Bedlam let loose" until they were quieted with the black drops, the composition of which the officer did not know, but he was quite sure that it was quieting! If the maximum dose which the city physician had prescribed was reached and the black drops did not quiet, then the patient's clothing and everything in the cell was removed, that he might not commit suicide, and straw was thrown in to serve as a bed. The strait-jacket was resorted to when all other measures failed.

If any of these mentally ill persons happened to be arrested and locked up on a Saturday afternoon, thereby becoming prisoners instead of patients, they were obliged to remain in prison until Monday noon, as the court did not sit on Sunday and no legal commitment or other disposition could be made of them before. If Saturday or Monday was a holiday, or the court did not happen to be sitting, it became necessary to hold a patient prisoner several days, and it was not unusual for "drunks" and cases of delirium tremens to be placed in cells adjoining. Under these conditions the gibes of the drunken inmates and the howls of the insane were really too horrible.

This was only one of the unfortunate conditions which the authorities, including the then State Board of Insanity, allowed to exist for years. It seemed that something must be done to relieve this state of affairs. Leading alienists gave their opinion that a day or two under these conditions might be the turning point in the patient's illness, whereas, if it were possible to administer proper treatment, he might be saved. In New York the Psychopathic Department of the Bellevue Hospital had been established for some years, and to it were attached one or more ambulances so that when a man or a woman mentally confused or delirious was picked up on the street, the hospital was notified by telephone to send an ambulance, accompanied by a trained nurse, and the patient was removed to the hospital. There was no reason why Massachusetts should neglect her mentally ill when in New York they were given immediate care.

My pleadings were in vain as had been the pleadings of others before me.

I presented cases, dating as early as 1898, illustrating how our mentally ill were put in prisons instead of in hospitals. I did not go farther back than 1898, though conditions were the same before then. In that year I found recorded the case of the mother of George A. Phipps. He returned to his house in Boston at 7 A.M. and was told that his mother had had a shock the evening before and was unable to talk, that about midnight they had called an officer, who arrested her and took her to Station 1. From there she was sent to the Chardon Street Home, which refused to accept her on account of her mental condition, and she was then taken to the House of Detention or the City Prison in the Court House on Somerset Street, and locked in a cell. Visiting her, the son found her praying on her knees that she might be released. Her speech was defective and difficult but he could understand her. From there she was sent to Austin Farm Hospital, where she died. Later, Mr. Phipp's father, Bainbridge Phipps, who had for some years been mentally ailing, became worse, and Dr. W. H. Sawyer, the family physician, called in Dr. Parker. They decided and notified the police that Mr. Phipps was insane. A policeman from the station house called and told Mr. Bainbridge Phipps that he was wanted at the station house about a personal matter. He innocently went there and was immediately arrested and taken to the House of Detention, or, as it was called, "The Tombs," on Somerset Street, and kept there. On the following day he was examined by Drs. Jelly and Dewey, after which he was taken to the State Hospital in Mattapan. Another case was that of Mrs. Ellen Lucia of Lynn, who was taken from her bed at midnight and lodged in the police station on a warrant alleging that she was insane. After spending fourteen hours in a cell, the commission examined her, found her perfectly sane and her release was ordered.

Dr. M. S. Gregory of the Bellevue Hospital says:

One can readily appreciate the feelings of a sane person if he were summarily arrested and brought to a hospital by the police, but how infinitely more disastrous and exciting it must be to a mentally afflicted patient to be taken to a hopsital in a patrol wagon by several officers in uniform. Such treatment must make a patient who is already suspicious and apprehensive extremely excited, and it would intensify the delusion that he is being persecuted. It is not uncommon to hear patients say, "I have done no harm to any one. Why should I be brought here by a policeman? Why was I arrested in my home without any complaint?"

Only recently I heard that a wealthy woman was invited to go for a drive to a certain place which she was pleased to visit. Instead of taking her there, those in charge took her to a sanatorium. Imagine the feelings of the distinguished lady at being thus deceived, and what part of a cure could this be called?

To obviate the necessity of taking these mentally ill people to prisons and to give them early hospital care and treatment was the object for which those interested had been working for years. How it was finally brought about the reader can judge for himself after reading the following pages. That it was brought about was a cause for rejoicing not only among the victims but among their friends, and was another step in the path of progress in Massachusetts.

The history of the development of the Psychopathic Hospital up to the time it was opened to receive patients in its present building is told in Part I of this book.

Part II is its history from the time it was formally opened in 1912 until the next great step, — that of making it an independent unit.

Part II is written by members of its staff, who have been or are now heads of its different departments, and who through their efficiency and skill have been responsible for the successful development of this

pioneer work in Massachusetts.   I gratefully acknowl-
edge their valuable contributions to medicine, and their
assistance in making this volume a guide to those in
other States who wish to establish and conduct a
Psychopathic Hospital.

CONTENTS

PART I. CONCEPTION AND DEVELOPMENT.

CHAPTER   PAGE

I. THOSE FIRST IN THE FIELD OF MENTAL HYGIENE IN MASSACHU-
SETTS. — THOMAS HANCOCK, 1764. — EFFORTS IN 1810 TO
ESTABLISH "A HOSPITAL FOR LUNATICS AND OTHER SICK." —
CHARTER OBTAINED UNDER THE NAME OF THE MASSACHU-
SETTS GENERAL HOSPITAL, 1811. — EFFORTS TO ESTABLISH A
PRIVATE INSANE HOSPITAL, 1814–1818. — FIRST PATIENT AD-
MITTED MARCH 15, 1818. — STATE LUNATIC HOSPITAL AT
WORCESTER, 1833. — WRITINGS OF DR. NATHAN ALLEN. —
THE MASSACHUSETTS STATE BOARD OF INSANITY ORDERED
BY LEGISLATURE OF 1898 TO MAKE A REPORT BY JANUARY 1,
1900. — THE REPORT MADE JANUARY 3, 1900 . . . 3

II. NEEDS FOR AN OBSERVATION HOSPITAL RECOGNIZED AT THE BOS-
TON DISPENSARY IN 1900. — COMMITTEE ON NATIONAL CON-
FERENCE FOR CHARITIES AND CORRECTIONS ADVOCATE TREAT-
MENT OF MENTALLY ILL IN GENERAL HOSPITALS. — WORK
WITH THE FINANCE COMMISSION, CITY OF BOSTON, TENDS TO
BRING BOSTON'S INSANE UNDER STATE CARE. — DEPLORABLE
CONDITIONS REQUIRING IMMEDIATE CARE STILL FOUND TO
EXIST. — NO RELIEF IN SIGHT AND NO RESULTS FROM THE
STATE BOARD'S REPORT OF 1900 18

III. EFFORTS TO INCLUDE A PSYCHOPATHIC WARD IN THE PLANS OF
THE PETER BENT BRIGHAM HOSPITAL. — AUGUSTUS HEMEN-
WAY AND J. S. BILLINGS INTERESTED 27

IV. THE BOSTON CITY HOSPITAL REFUSES TO CARE FOR MENTAL
CASES. — TYLER STREET DAY NURSERY OFFERS ITS BUILD-
INGS FOR AN OBSERVATION HOSPITAL 32

V. THE CITY OF BOSTON CARING FOR ITS OWN MENTALLY ILL COM-
PLICATES ESTABLISHMENT BY THE STATE OF AN OBSERVATION
OR PSYCHOPATHIC HOSPITAL IN BOSTON. — EFFORTS TO OB-
TAIN THE CO-OPERATION OF THE FINANCE COMMISSION AND
THE MAYOR OF THE CITY OF BOSTON SUCCESSFUL, AND MAYOR
HIBBARD INTRODUCES A BILL FOR STATE CARE. — THE STATE
BOARD OF INSANITY AND OTHERS BECOME ACTIVE IN THE PASS-
ING OF BILLS BEFORE THE LEGISLATURE. — MAY 27, 1908,
THE JOINT COMMITTEE OF WAYS AND MEANS AND THE COM-
MITTEE ON PUBLIC CHARITABLE INSTITUTIONS REPORT RE-
VISED BILL FOR THE CARE OF INSANE OF BOSTON BY THE
COMMONWEALTH. — BILL PASSED AND SIGNED BY THE GOV-
ERNOR 38

CHAPTER PAGE

VI. On Motion of Senator Pickford, the Legislature passed a Resolve calling upon the State Board of Insanity to report not later than March 15, 1910, what Progress they had made toward establishing an Observation Hospital. — Dr. Briggs' Bill for Observation Hospital is passed. — Letters of Commendation. — Governor Draper influenced by the Board 60

VII. Contract for Psychopathic Hospital. — Still No Place for Delirium Tremens Cases. — City Hospital later obliged to receive them. — After Psychopathic Hospital opens, Dr. Southard accepts and treats Cases of Delirium Tremens 111

VIII. Psychopathic Hospital opens June 24, 1912. — First Year of Work. — Activities of State Board of Insanity in Relation to the Hospital. — Massachusetts State Psychiatric Institute established May 1, 1919. Psychopathic Hospital separated from the State Hospital and made an Independent Unit, December 1, 1920. . . . 126

PART II. ORGANIZATION AND OPERATION.

IX. The Administration Problem of the Psychopathic Department of the Boston State Hospital, by its Administrator, Elisha H. Cohoon, M.D., now Superintendent of the Medfield State Hospital, Medfield, Massachusetts . 145

X. The Out-Patient Department of the Psychopathic Hospital, by Douglas A. Thom, M.D., Chief of the Out-Patient Department, Boston Psychopathic Hospital; Instructor in Psychiatry, Harvard Medical School; Advisory Consultant, United States Public Health Service; Director of Children's "Habit Clinic," South Bay Union Settlement; Director of the Section of Mental Hygiene in the Department of Mental Diseases of Massachusetts 154

XI. The Social Service, 1913 to 1918, of the Psychopathic Hospital, by Mary C. Jarrett, formerly Chief of Social Service, Psychopathic Department, Boston State Hospital; now Associate Director, Smith College Training School for Social Work, Northampton, Massachusetts . . 172

XII. The Alcohol Club, by A. Warren Stearns, M.D., late of the Medical Staff of the Psychopathic Hospital, now Assistant Professor of Neurology, Tufts Medical School; Chief of Clinic, Department of Nervous and Mental Diseases, Boston Dispensary 184

CHAPTER PAGE

XIII. SURVEY OF THE WORK OF THE DIRECTOR OF THE PSYCHOPATHIC HOSPITAL, BY MYRTELLE M. CANAVAN, M.D., ASSOCIATED WITH DR. SOUTHARD AS ASSISTANT PATHOLOGIST TO THE STATE BOARD OF INSANITY; NOW PATHOLOGIST TO THE MASSACHUSETTS DEPARTMENT OF MENTAL DISEASES 187

XIV. NURSING AND OCCUPATIONAL DEPARTMENTS, BY HELEN B. HOPKINS, TRUSTEE, PSYCHOPATHIC HOSPITAL . . . 194

XV. THE WORK ON SYPHILIS AT THE PSYCHOPATHIC HOSPITAL, BY H. C. SOLOMON, M.D., CHIEF OF THERAPEUTIC RESEARCH, PSYCHOPATHIC HOSPITAL; INSTRUCTOR IN NEUROPATHOLOGY, HARVARD MEDICAL SCHOOL 205

XVI. THE FUNCTIONS OF TRUSTEES, BY ALBERT EVANS, M.D., SECRETARY-TREASURER OF THE MASSACHUSETTS STATE HOSPITAL TRUSTEES ASSOCIATION 216

LIST OF ILLUSTRATIONS

PSYCHOPATHIC HOSPITAL, 74 FENWOOD ROAD, BOSTON (FRONT
VIEW) . . . . *Frontispiece*

FACING
PAGE

DR. CHARLES W. PAGE, AN ARDENT ADVOCATE FOR NON-RESTRAINT . 72

DR. JAMES J. PUTNAM, A FRIEND OF THE MENTALLY ILL WHO DURING
HIS LIFE SUPPORTED ALL PROGRESSIVE MEASURES FOR THEM . 93

DR. ELMER E. SOUTHARD, FIRST DIRECTOR OF THE BOSTON PSYCHO-
PATHIC HOSPITAL 119

DR. COHOON, DR. FROST, DR. ADLER AND DR. SOUTHARD ON THE
STEPS OF THE PSYCHOPATHIC HOSPITAL 126

MAJOR ELMER E. SOUTHARD, AS DIRECTOR OF THE TRAINING COURSE
CONDUCTED AT THE BOSTON PSYCHOPATHIC HOSPITAL FOR THE
UNITED STATES ARMY 136

DR. GEORGE M. KLINE, COMMISSIONER OF MENTAL DISEASES, WHOSE
INTEREST AND CO-OPERATION IN SOLVING THE PROBLEMS OF THE
MENTALLY ILL HAVE DONE MUCH TO EXTEND THE USEFULNESS OF
THE PSYCHOPATHIC HOSPITAL OVER THE STATE, AND DEVELOP
THE PSYCHOPATHIC HOSPITAL IDEA THROUGHOUT THE COUNTRY . 140

PSYCHOPATHIC HOSPITAL (REAR VIEW) 145

MAJOR L. VERNON BRIGGS, CAPTAIN DOUGLAS A. THOM AND MAJOR
JAMES V. MAY AT CAMP DEVENS, MASS., OCTOBER, 1917. DR.
MAY SUCCEEDED DR. FROST AS SUPERINTENDENT OF THE BOSTON
STATE HOSPITAL AND ITS PSYCHOPATHIC DEPARTMENT IN 1917 . 156

DR. SOUTHARD PRESIDING AT THE REGULAR DAILY STAFF MEETING
AT THE PSYCHOPATHIC HOSPITAL 189

PSYCHOPATHIC HOSPITAL STAFF 193

DR. SOUTHARD AND DR. SOLOMON IN THE OFFICE OF THE DIVISION OF
RESEARCH IN BRAIN SYPHILIS 205

xxiii

PART I

CONCEPTION AND DEVELOPMENT

HISTORY OF
THE PSYCHOPATHIC HOSPITAL

CHAPTER I.

THOSE FIRST IN THE FIELD OF MENTAL HYGIENE IN MASSACHUSETTS. —
THOMAS HANCOCK, 1764. — EFFORTS IN 1810 TO ESTABLISH "A HOSPITAL
FOR LUNATICS AND OTHER SICK." — CHARTER OBTAINED UNDER
THE NAME OF THE MASSACHUSETTS GENERAL HOSPITAL, 1811.
— EFFORTS TO ESTABLISH A PRIVATE INSANE HOSPITAL,
1814–1818. — FIRST PATIENT ADMITTED MARCH 15,
1818. — STATE LUNATIC HOSPITAL AT WORCESTER,
1833. — WRITINGS OF DR. NATHAN ALLEN. —
THE MASSACHUSETTS STATE BOARD OF
INSANITY ORDERED BY LEGISLATURE
OF 1898 TO MAKE A REPORT BY
JANUARY 1, 1900. — THE
REPORT MADE JAN-
UARY 3, 1900.

The earliest record of any legislation regarding the
insane in Massachusetts was made in 1676, when the
following law was passed:

Whereas, There are distracted persons in some tounes, that are unruly,
whereby not only the families wherein they are, but others, suffer much damage
by them, it is ordered by this Court, and the authoritie thereof, that the
selectmen in all tounes where such persons are are hereby impowred and in-
joyned to take care of all such persons, that they doe not damnify others.

In 1694 an act was passed, entitled "An Act for the
Relief of Idiots and Distracted Persons," in which the
care of the insane is given to the selectmen and overseers of the poor.

In 1764 Thomas Hancock, the uncle of Governor John Hancock, died. In his will he says:

I give unto the Town of Boston the sum of six hundred pounds lawful money towards erecting and finishing a convenient House for the reception and more comfortable keeping of such unhappy persons as it shall please God, in His Providence, to deprive of their reason, in any part of this Province; such as are inhabitants of Boston always to have the preference.

This legacy was declined by the selectmen of Boston for the reason that there were not enough insane persons in the province to call for the erection of such a house.

In 1798 the law permitted the commitment of such lunatics as were "furiously mad so as to render it dangerous to the safety or the peace of the good people to be at large" to the House of Correction.

In 1827 the law was changed in regard to the safe-keeping of "lunatic persons furiously mad" so that they were committed to the hospital or lunatic asylum instead of to the jail.

In 1829 Horace Mann was chairman of a committee in the Massachusetts House of Representatives to which was referred an order for them "to examine and ascertain the practicability and expediency of erecting or procuring at the expense of the Commonwealth an asylum for the safekeeping of lunatics and persons furiously mad." In 1830 they made their report and in it stated that returns had been received from 114 towns, comprising less than one-half the population of Massachusetts, and that in 25 of these towns there were no insane persons; that in the remaining 89 towns there were 289 lunatics or persons "furiously mad;" and that 161 of that number were confined as follows: In poor houses and houses of industry, 78; in private houses, 37; in jails and houses of correction, 19; in insane hospitals, 10; in other places of confinement, 17; and at least 60 in the insane hospital at Charlestown (McLean); that these persons had been confined from one to forty-five years each. They also reported that in some towns it had been the practice to make private contracts with the keeper of the jail or house of correction to take the insane poor at a low price and to imprison them in unoccupied cells, without assuming any responsibility for their proper treatment or any authority to examine into it. Other towns, it was said, had annually offered the keeping of their insane poor at auction and struck them off to the lowest bidder, by whom they were treated with various degrees of kindness or cruelty, according to the character of the individual, whose object in bidding for them was generally solely to make a profit by keeping them. The language used by this committee, of which Horace Mann was chairman, is most interesting. They complained that the incarceration of persons "furiously mad" in jails and houses of correction really placed them beyond the reach of recovery, for the commissioners had never heard of more than three or four instances of restoration among those who had been subjected to the rigors of confinement in jails or houses of correction. Continuing, they say:

To him whose mind is alienated, a prison is a tomb, and within its walls he must suffer as one who awakes to life in the solitude of the grave. Existence and the capacity for pain alone are left him. From every former source of pleasure or contentment he is violently sequestered. Every former habit is abruptly broken off. No medical skill seconds the efforts of nature for his recovery, or breaks the strength of pain when it seizes him with convulsive grasp. No friends relieve each other in solacing the weariness of protracted disease. He is alike removed from all the occupations of health, and from all the attentions everywhere but within his homeless abode bestowed upon sickness. The solitary cell, the noisome atmosphere, and unmitigated cold, and the untempered heat are of themselves sufficient soon to derange every vital function of the body, and this only aggravates the derangement of his mind.

Can the reader conceive, after such a report from our legislative body, that it would be nearly one hundred years before Massachusetts ceased sending her insane to prisons and jails instead of to hospitals?

The second report of the "Prison Discipline Society," issued just prior to 1830, states that there are 30 lunatics in Massachusetts prisons, and says:

The sheriff and jailers complained that they were compelled to receive such patients and had no suitable accommodations for them. In one prison where there were ten, one was found in an apartment in which he had been nine years. He had a wreath of rags around his body and another around his neck. This was all his clothing. He had no bed, chair or bench. Two or three rough planks were strewed around the room; a heap of filthy straw, like the nest of swine, was in the corner. He had built a bird's nest of mud in the iron grate of his den. His wretched apartment was a dark dungeon, having no orifice for the admission of light, heat or air, except the iron door, about two and one-half feet square, opening into it from the prison. The other lunatics in the same prison were scattered in separate cells which were almost dark dungeons. It was difficult, after the door was open, to see them distinctly. The ventilation was so incomplete that more than one person on entering them has found the air so fetid as to produce nauseousness and sometimes vomiting. The old straw on which they were laid and their filthy garments were such as to make their insanity more hopeless, and at one time it was not considered within the province of the physician's department to examine particularly the condition of the lunatics. In these circumstances any improvement of their minds could hardly be expected. . . .

In the prison in which there were six lunatics their condition was less wretched. But they were sometimes an annoyance and sometimes a sport to the convicts, and even the apartment in which the females were confined opened into the yard of the men. . . .

In the prison or house of correction, so called, in which were ten lunatics, two were found about seventy years of age, — a male and a female, — in the same apartment of an upper story. The female was lying on a heap of straw under a broken window; the snow in a severe storm was beating through a window and lay upon the straw around her withered body, which was partially covered with a few filthy and tattered garments. The man was lying in the corner of the room and was in a similar situation except that he was less exposed to the storm. The former had been in this apartment six and the latter twenty-one years.

Another lunatic in the same prison was found in a plank room on the first story, where he had been eight years. During this time he had never left the room but twice. The door of this room had not been opened for eighteen months. The food was furnished through a small orifice in the door. The room was warmed by no fire; and still the woman of the house said "he had never froze."

In the light of these conditions, the commissioners recommended that, since the hospital at Worcester had been prepared for the reception of the insane, the statutes of 1797 and of 1816 be so modified that such patients should be committed to the hospital at Worcester instead of to any jail or house of correction, and that any insane persons who were confined to any jail or house of correction be removed to State hospitals.

In spite of this recommendation it was nearly one hundred years before this plan was fully carried out.

On November 12, 1798, Thomas Boylston, Esq., by his will, which was proved after his death in 1800, made the town of Boston his residuary devisee in trust, among other objects, to erect a smallpox hospital and a lunatic hospital. The testator, unfortunately, became insolvent before his death.

In August, 1810, a long circular letter was prepared by Drs. James Jackson and John C. Warren, addressed to several of our wealthiest and most influential citizens, which contained the following:

It has appeared very desirable to a number of respectable gentlemen that a hospital for the reception of lunatics and other sick persons should be established in this town. By the appointment of a number of these gentlemen, we are directed to adopt such methods as shall appear best calculated to promote such an establishment. . . . It is unnecessary to urge the propriety and even obligation of succoring the poor in sickness. . . . It may be said that instances are rare among us, where a man, who labors, with even moderate industry, when in health, endures privations in sickness. They are not, however, rare among us who are not industrious. . . . In a well-regulated hospital, they would find a comfortable lodging in a duly attempered atmosphere; would receive the food best suited to their various conditions, and would be attended by kind and discreet nurses, under the directions of a physician. In such a situation, the poor man's chance would be equal perhaps to that of the most affluent, when affected by the same disease. . . . Journeymen mechanics commonly live in small boarding-houses, where they have accommodations which are sufficient, but nothing more than sufficient, in health. . . . Persons of this description would do well to enter a hospital, even if they had to pay the expense of their own maintenance. In most cases they would suffer less and recover sooner by so doing. . . . Not uncommonly, a young girl is taken sick in a large family, where she is the only servant. She lodges in the most remote corner of the house, in a room without a fireplace. . . . Persons of these descriptions would not be disposed to resort to a hospital on every trivial occasion. But, when afflicted with serious indisposition, they would find in such an institution an alleviation of their sufferings, which it must gladden the heart of the most frigid to contemplate. . . . There is one class of sufferers who peculiarly claim all that benevolence can bestow, and for whom a hospital is most especially required. The virtuous and industrious are liable to become objects of public charity, in consequence of diseases of the mind. When those who are unfortunate in this respect are left without proper care, a calamity, which might have been transient, is prolonged through life. The number of such persons, who are rendered unable to provide for themselves, is probably greater than the public imagine; and of these a large proportion claim the assistance of the affluent. The expense which is attached to the care of the insane in private families is extremely great; and such as to ruin a whole family that is possessed of a competence under ordinary circumstances, when called upon to support one of its members in this situation. Even those who can pay the necessary expenses would perhaps find an institution, such as is proposed, the best situation in which they could place their unfortunate friends. It is worthy of the opulent men of this town, and consistent with their general character, to provide an asylum for the insane from every part of the Commonwealth. But if funds are raised for the purpose proposed, it is probable that the Legislature will grant some assistance, with a view to such an extension of its benefits. . . .

It is possible that we may be asked whether the almshouse does not answer the purposes for which a hospital is proposed. That it *does not*, is very certain. The town is so much indebted to the liberality of those gentlemen who, without compensation, superintend the care of the poor, that we ought not to make this reply without an explanation. The truth is that the almshouse could not serve the purpose of a hospital without such an entire change in the arrangements of it as the overseers do not feel themselves authorized to make, and such as the town could not easily be induced to direct or to support.

The almshouse receives all those who do not take care of themselves, and who are destitute of property, whether they be old and infirm, and unable to provide means of assistance; or are too vicious and debauched to employ themselves in honest labor; or are prevented from so employing themselves by occasional sickness. This institution, then, is made to comprehend what is more properly meant by an almshouse, a bridewell or house of correction, and a hospital. Now, the economy and mode of government cannot possibly be adapted at once to all these various purposes. It must necessarily happen that in many instances the worst members of the community, the debauched and profligate, obtain admission into this house. Hence it has become, in some measure, disreputable to live in it; and, not unfrequently, those who are most deserving objects of charity cannot be induced to enter it. To some of them death appears less terrible than a residence in the almshouse.

It is true that the sick in that house are allowed some greater privileges and advantages than are extended to those in health; yet the general arrangements and regulations are, necessarily, so different from those required in a hospital, that the sick — far from having the advantages afforded by the medical art — have not the fair chance for recovery which nature alone would give them Most especially they suffer for the want of good nurses. In these officers must be placed trust and confidence of the highest nature. Their duties are laborious and painful. In the almshouse, they are selected from among the more healthy inhabitants; but, unfortunately, those who are best qualified will always prefer more profitable and less laborious occupations elsewhere. It must, then, be obvious that the persons employed as nurses cannot be such as will conscientiously perform the duties of this office.

The only medical school of eminence in this country is that in Philadelphia, nearly 400 miles distant from Boston; and the expense of attending that is so great, that students from this quarter rarely remain at it longer than one year. Even this advantage is enjoyed by very few, compared with the whole number. Those who are educated in New England have so few opportunities of attending to the practice of physic, that they find it impossible to learn some of the most important elements of the science of medicine until after they have undertaken for themselves the care of the health and lives of their fellow-citizens. This care they undertake with very little knowledge, except that acquired from books, — a source whence it is highly useful and indispensable that they should obtain knowledge, but one from which alone they can never obtain all that is necessary to qualify them for their professional duties. With such deficiencies in medical education, it is needless to show to what evils the community is exposed.

To remedy evils so important and so extensive, it is necessary to have a medical school in New England. All the materials necessary to form this school exists among us. Wealth, abundantly sufficient, can be devoted to the purpose, without any individual's feeling the smallest privation of any, even the luxuries of life. Everyone is liable to suffer from the want of such a school; every one may derive, directly or indirectly, the greatest benefits from its establishment.

A hospital is an institution absolutely essential to a medical school, and one which would afford relief and comfort to thousands of the sick and miserable. On what other objects can the superfluities of the rich be so well bestowed?

A charter was obtained on February 25, 1811, under the name of the Massachusetts General Hospital. The War of 1812 delayed the plans for buying land and building the hospital.

On February 23, 1813, the first meeting of the trustees was held at the house of Col. T. H. Perkins; the draft of an address to the public was read and adopted. At the next meeting, March 9, 1813, the committee reported favorably on the site which had been contemplated, and suggested for consideration the Winthrop estate in Cambridge, or the made land at bottom of the Common, since known as the Public Garden.

On January 9, 1814, an address to the public having been approved by the overseers of the poor, it was adopted, and committees appointed to solicit subscriptions. This address was in pamphlet form, signed by the twelve trustees, and shows the urgent need of such an institution for the relief both of the "sick and the insane."

On May 18, 1814, a communication from Dr. George Parkman was received, stating that he proposed to erect a hospital for the insane "for accommodation of such patients as shall be able to pay their own expenses." This was, so far as I know, the first private hospital for the insane in Massachusetts.

On October 4, 1816, Dr. Parkman had a private institution for the insane on the Magee place of 16 acres in Roxbury, which he said "can be bought for $16,000, and if the institution will pay $5,000 I will procure to be given to this institution the remaining $11,000." The proposal was accepted and a committee appointed to complete the purchase. Dr. Parkman was appointed superintending physician of this institution, "whenever the Magee place shall be purchased, as provided in the preceding vote." Further in the records is a memorandum: "The Board subsequently considered that it was inexpedient to purchase the Magee place." This estate was later occupied by the widow of Governor Eustis.

The Board of Trustees caused to be made a house-to-house solicitation with such success that within a week $93,969 was subscribed, of which $43,997.47 was contributed specifically for the asylum. In all 1,047 different persons subscribed, — residents of Boston, Salem, Plymouth, Charlestown, Hingham, Chelsea and elsewhere.

On December 17, 1816, the Massachusetts Humane Society subscribed $5,000 for an insane hospital, and in December of that year the Board of Trustees purchased the Joy or Joseph Barrell estate on Cobble Hill or Poplar Grove in Charlestown, where in 1775 General Putnam and Colonel Knox had laid out a fort. At the foot of the hill flowed a small stream called Miller's River, which emptied into the Charles, over which there was erected a footbridge.

On February 2, 1817, an address to the public was adopted to obviate the impression that the insane hospital was designed exclusively for the wealthy. On the estate stood a colonial dwelling designed by Charles Bulfinch and erected in 1792 by Joseph Barrell. The final passing of the papers took place on March 16, 1817, and the deed of Benjamin Joy was put in a tin box. At the same time, Mr. Bulfinch presented a ground plan for an insane hospital, and Mr. Lowell reported the rules and regulations for the hospital. Dr. George Parkman offered himself as candidate for physician of the institution. The Joy estate and the additional buildings and alterations cost, in 1818, $89,821.16. The residence was used as the administration house of the asylum for seventy-seven years.

On March 15, 1818, the Board decided that it was expedient to unite in one person the offices of physician and superintendent of the asylum, and Dr. George Parkman withdrew his application; and on March 23, 1818, Dr. Rufus Wyman was unanimously elected and authorized to visit hospitals in New York and Philadelphia.

The first patient was admitted on October 6, 1818, — a young man whose father made the request. The committee spent three hours in conversing with him and finally decided to receive him. The father said he believed his son to be one of those spoken of in the Bible as "possessed of the devil;" and when asked what remedial measures he had adopted, replied that he was in the habit of whipping him. The young man was completely cured at the hospital and subsequently became a peddler, in which vocation he acquired a property of $10,000 or $12,000. At the end of the first year 13 patients had been admitted.

The hospital was named McLean on June 12, 1826, for John McLean who had bequeathed a large sum of money to it.

On April 11, 1826, 4 incurable patients were removed from the asylum to make room for curable cases; and in 1828 Thomas B. Wales and others subscribed $825 apiece for free beds for life in the General Hospital. In the early days the patients under care in the asylum equaled, and at times exceeded, the number at the General Hospital.

The early reports show that attendants were carefully chosen and were instructed to treat their patients with kindness and gentleness. In 1833 Dr. Wyman writes that "chains or strait-jackets have never been used or provided in this asylum," and that "no attendant is allowed to put the smallest restraint upon a patient without the direction of the supervisor, who enters the fact in a book and reports it to the physician;" also that "no person is ever allowed to strike a patient, even in self-defence."

In the very first published report, in 1822, Dr. Wyman speaks of the advantages of occupation and says that the "amusements provided, as draughts, chess, backgammon, ninepins, swinging, sawing wood, gardening, reading, writing, music, etc., divert the attention from the unpleasant subjects of thought and afford exercise both of body and mind. . . . . Exercise, work and rest have a powerful effect in tranquilizing the mind, breaking up wrong associations of ideas and inducing correct habits of thinking as well as acting." Outdoor exercise was insisted upon, and in 1828 the first carriage and pair of horses for the use of the patients were bought.

During the year ending in April, 1828, 218 free patients were discharged from the asylum. In 1832 the number of patients at the General Hospital was 52, and in the asylum 51.

On November 9, 1850, a communication received from William Appleton, Esq., president of the corporation, announced his donation of $20,000 for the erection of buildings at the McLean Asylum, designed "especially for such patients as shall have previously dwelt in residences of spacious and cheerful character and with a view to affording, as far as possible, to this, the wealthiest class of our inmates, the accustomed comforts and conveniences of home." He had previously given a fund of $10,000, the income of which was forever after to be applied to aid the poorer patients.

Following the reports of the legislative committee, of which Horace Mann was chairman, and of the "Prison Discipline Society," both prior to 1830, Massachusetts awoke to the fact that the mentally ill must have better medical and more humane care. Beginning with the erection of the State Lunatic Hospital at Worcester in 1833, the Commonwealth continued to build hospitals for the housing of the mentally ill, but it was not until the resolves and orders of the Legislature, stimulated by public opinion, made action obligatory that the State Board of Insanity took definite steps, and the Butler Building of the Boston State Hospital was opened in 1910.

There was one physician of Massachusetts who has not been given the prominence that he should have had for his work for the mentally ill, and that is Dr. Nathan Allen, who was born at Princeton, Massachusetts, on April 25, 1813, and whose essay, when he graduated from the medical school, was entitled "Connection of Mental Philosophy with Medicine." This attracted much attention at the time and resulted in a department of scientific investigation in which he became distinguished. In 1864 he was appointed a member of the State Board of Charities. His biographer quotes him as saying:

No fact is better established in science than that there is a most intimate mental as well as physical relation between the parent and the child — between each generation and the succeeding one. This relation has been well expressed by the proverbs: "What is bred in the bone cannot be whipt out of the flesh," and "Like begets like."

In 1875 he wrote a paper on "State Medicine and its Relation to Insanity." In the same year he was one of two commissioners appointed by the Governor and Council under an act passed June 23, 1874, whose duty it was to examine carefully the laws touching lunacy; to critically examine into the condition of the several lunatic asylums, — the treatment, freedom allowed, diet, and all matters pertaining to the care and comfort of their inmates; and to make a report to the next Legislature. This report covers the number of insane in Massachusetts; the distribution in the various hospitals; support; private patients; acute and chronic cases; treatment; restraint and freedom allowed; relations of lunatic hospitals to the public; suggestions and improvements; future policy of the State, etc.

A paper which Dr. Allen read before the Conference of Charities at Cincinnati, May 22, 1878, was entitled "The Prevention of Disease, Insanity, Crime and Pauperism." In this he says:

In the history of disease and insanity, while there has been an immense expenditure of labor and means to cure these evils, little, comparatively, has been done to prevent them. The same holds true in respect to crime and pauperism. For the prevention of insanity the same course must be pursued as with reference to other diseases, — ascertain its causes, diffuse information on the subject. This may be accomplished in a variety of ways, — enlisting the press, through journals and books, by family and educational training, by legislation and associated action. It should be the settled policy of all legislative bodies and the executive officers of every State to carry on some systematic measures for the prevention of insanity, and unless such provision is made by legislative action, the work, we fear, will never be done.

In a paper on "The Prevention of Insanity," 1883, he brings out the facts "(1) that insanity is a disease and can be prevented as other diseases are. (2) For this purpose similar means must be used as are employed to prevent diseases generally. (3) The public must be better educated and trained in respect to the laws of health." He adds that "by this means only can we expect a diminution of the disease. Lunatic hospitals will never do it. One of the most marked evidences of progress in the knowledge of insanity is that its primary causes are traced more and more directly to the body. If the preservation of good health checks the growth of insanity, let the principles of sanitary science be cultivated more and more and be brought to apply in every possible way for improving the health of people. No fact connected with insanity is more firmly established than that it usually originates directly from inherited tendencies."

He stresses the importance of early treatment and of sending the person at once to a lunatic hospital as soon as any marked symptoms have appeared. He urges the medical profession to study the nervous system more carefully so as to detect the first symptoms. "Then," he says, "they could treat them intelligently and in many cases successfully." He quotes the superintendent of one of the largest hospitals in the State:

The more we see of mental disease in its various forms, the more we are convinced that the study of its prevention is infinitely more important than even the study of its cure; and that the dissemination of more correct views of the true way of living and a more rigid observation of the laws of health and nature would greatly diminish its frequency.

At the close of this paper he says:

Almost any amount of money has been expended in building and managing lunatic hospitals but nothing to prevent insanity. How long will it take the public and legislative bodies to learn the truth of the proverb, "An ounce of prevention is worth a pound of cure?"

In 1880 he also wrote a paper in regard to insanity, entitled "The Supervision of Lunatic Hospitals," from which I should like to quote. We may well call Dr. Nathan Allen the father of mental hygiene.

CHAPTER II

NEEDS FOR AN OBSERVATION HOSPITAL RECOGNIZED AT THE BOSTON DIS-
PENSARY IN 1900. — COMMITTEE ON NATIONAL CONFERENCE FOR
CHARITIES AND CORRECTIONS ADVOCATE TREATMENT OF MENTALLY
ILL IN GENERAL HOSPITALS. — WORK WITH THE FINANCE COM-
MISSION, CITY OF BOSTON, TENDS TO BRING BOSTON'S
INSANE UNDER STATE CARE. — DEPLORABLE CON-
DITIONS REQUIRING IMMEDIATE CARE STILL FOUND
TO EXIST. — NO RELIEF IN SIGHT AND NO
RESULTS FROM THE STATE BOARD'S
REPORT OF 1900

When I began my service in the Mental Department
of the Boston Dispensary in the year 1900, I felt the
great need of an observation ward or detention hospital for acute cases of mental disease.

I learned from Dr. George F. Jelly, who was examiner for the Public Institutions Department, that he
had advocated a detention hospital for twenty years,
and later I found many other people who had advocated similar action, but no one had made any efforts
to put through any definite plan.

The thirty-fourth National Conference of Charities
and Corrections, held in 1900, received a report from
a committee of fourteen physicians (members of a previous conference) on the "elements of an adequate
system of public care and treatment for the insane."
This report was not unanimous, three members dis-
sented, and one was absent in Europe, but its recommendations were excellent. The most valuable part of
the report is as follows:

Prior to the necessity of forcible detention of a mental patient, his exclusion
from a special department of the general hospital for acute physical disease is

neither necessary nor justifiable.   Initial derangement of the mind of short
duration should not bear the stigma of confirmed insanity. The aversion of
the patient and his friends to the idea of insanity precludes his early treatment
so long as it necessitates association with an insane hospital regime, however
enlightened. Humanitarian as well as economic reasons impel to such relief
of the poor. Thereby the student of medicine might become familiar with mental disease as he will meet it in general practice. The general practitioner might
become competent to treat it, but would find it impracticable to do so with
such public facilities. Early treatment would avert many insane commitments.
Often the treatment would be limited to the voluntary period, while the patient
is willing or may be tactfully persuaded to co-operate with his caretakers. The
special hospital for acute and curable insanity is not to be supplanted nor the
functions of the general hospital perverted. This work is supplementary to
both, and otherwise, largely remains undone.

In May, 1906, while still physician of the Mental
Department of the Boston Dispensary, I wrote an
article for the "Boston Medical and Surgical Journal"
on "Treatment of Mental Disease caused by Auto-
Intoxication."   In the light of present-day knowledge,
it is interesting to note that there was much adverse
criticism by the men who were also opposing my efforts
to establish an observation hospital.   This article in-
stanced many cases of mental disturbance whose
symptoms were caused by auto-intoxication and successfully treated at the Boston Dispensary.

In the meantime, in the Albany Hospital, in New
York, Pavilion F was set aside for an observation ward
for mental cases.   Much adverse criticism was heard
in Massachusetts of Dr. Mosher's accounts of the work
done at his hospital, but they were most inspiring to
those who were progressive.   Dr. Mosher encountered
opposition in establishing this ward, and two years
before he succeeded he wrote:

All attempts at separate care of acute cases had been premature and have
failed, because prior to the development of the large modern state hospital
its possibilities and limitations have not been revealed. Hospitals for the

insane are not always available; the natural reluctance of patients and their friends to commitment often prevents this step until the disease has reached a stage at which the chances of recovery are jeopardized.

On June 21, 1906, I wrote an article for the "Boston Medical and Surgical Journal," entitled "Observation Hospital for Mental Diseases," setting forth "some reasons why there should be one in Boston, or at least an observation ward; statistics of those at Albany and Glasgow." An extract from the article follows:

For some years the project of an observation hospital for mental disorders in the city of Boston has been discussed, but no concerted movement among physicians has ever taken place, owing to various discouragements, and to their difference of opinion as to the best plan for bringing relief to the class of patients who in the early stages of mental disorder have now no place to go for treatment. Quite a large number of physicians consider that the present hospitals for the insane are sufficient, and they answer those who favor a special hospital by saying that the present institutions for the insane are able to take care of all people in all stages. . . . In the first place, most of the present institutions for the insane are situated at inconvenient points, and have so many chronic cases that most people in the early stages are not willing to go to them. The internes who are in insane hospitals as a rule see only the chronic cases, and have no opportunity of observing or studying the early stages of mental diseases. There is no provision at the present time for systematized study of mental disease in its early stages by physicians or students, except in the one department of the Boston Dispensary which has the only strictly mental clinic in the city, and, so far as I know, in any other city in the United States, most of the clinics being mixed, — nervous and mental (1906). It is the study of the incipient cases which seek relief at the Dispensary that impresses one with the necessity of an observation hospital, where patients in the early stages may be sent, and their disease often aborted; where the officer may send the lunatic arrested on the street, for immediate care and treatment, and where the physician or student may have an opportunity of studying these early cases which is now denied him. The cases which find their way to the hospitals for the insane are usually so far advanced that they are committed as insane. Seldom a day passes during which clinics are held in the Mental Department of the Boston Dispensary when one of the three physicians to that department, Dr. A. C. Jelly, Dr. L. A. Roberts or myself, does not feel the crying need for such a hospital. Many patients come to the Dispensary to-day, or are attended at their homes by physicians, who have to remain in their present surroundings, which often are the cause of their trouble, until such time as they are insane enough to commit, for no treatment can be carried out in the homes of these patients, and the physician is powerless to do anything but wait for them to get insane enough to commit to a large insane hospital. . . . So far, the general hospitals have refused to take apparently insane patients even for a day, unless they have injured themselves and require surgical treatment. There is no place where you may send such cases, excepting to the insane hospitals, and many of them are not insane, for their mental disorders are often the result of disturbed metabolism or acute auto-intoxication, or of disturbed habits of mind and body, brought about by their surroundings, or improper food and sleep. I do not believe that a separate building on the grounds of any insane institution is going to give relief to these people. They would prefer to wait until nature reacts and they recover, or become worse and are obliged to be sent to the main building of such an institution. The class that would go to an observation hospital connected with an insane institution will be of two kinds: *First*, The voluntary patient, who is often a patient who has been there before, and feels a recurrence of his disease coming on and applies for relief. *Second*, The occasional patient who is incapacitated, but not seriously ill, whose family find his support burdensome, or his care confining and urge him to go, or send him to the hospital instead of keeping him until he recovers, or is insane enough to commit. . . . I know that this advance in the treatment of those mentally ill will meet with a great deal of opposition, as every new movement does. One physician, president of one of our neurological societies, told me the other day that he did not believe in such a hospital, that it was not necessary, that he did not believe in the Haymarket Square Relief Hospital; he thought the general hospitals could take care of all the patients without loss of time sufficient to endanger the life of the patient; that if I asked for an observation hospital, I might as well ask for a temporary hospital or stand on every corner of the street, with physicians stationed there to take particles out of people's eyes; that there would be no limit to the number of hospitals, if things kept on.

About 1906 I started actively to bring about what up to this time the State Board had failed to accomplish, — the purchase of the Boston Insane Hospital by the State and the taking over of its patients, thus for the first time placing all of the institutional cases of mental disease under State care.

I drew up a petition and asked the Finance Commission to present it to Mayor Hibbard on economic grounds, stating that the city of Boston would benefit financially by such a transfer. With this transfer of the Boston insane, the argument for a psychopathic hospital in Boston was sure to carry more weight.

This petition was signed by many of our leading physicians and citizens, and resulted in another petition being drawn up this time by the Finance Commission under date of December 24, 1907, which set forth a mass of figures and among other things said:

Chapter 433, section 25, Acts of 1898, directed the State Board of Insanity to report to the Legislature, on or before the first Wednesday in January in the year 1900, such method or methods as in its opinion will most effectually provide for the care and support of the insane poor, who, under existing laws, are cared for or supported at the expense of the cities and towns of the Commonwealth. In compliance with these instructions, the State Board of Insanity issued a report, January 3, 1900, recommending such legislation as will provide that all insane persons who are now or may hereafter become public charges shall be supported at the expense of the Commonwealth on and after January 1, 1904. To enable this recommendation to be put into effect, a bill in accordance therewith was presented to the Legislature of 1900 and was passed, but at a later reading in the Senate, the Boston Insane Hospital was exempted through the votes of the Boston Senators. Thus, under the provisions of chapter 451, Acts of 1900, the State assumed control of all its insane population, except those of the Boston Insane Hospital.

The considerations which eight years ago convinced both the State Board of Insanity and the Legislature, except for the intervention of the Senators from Boston, that such a complete transfer should be made are even more operative to-day. From a humanitarian point of view, it is clearer than ever that each institution in the State should bear a harmonious relationship with every other, and that they should all be near the centers whence the inmates are drawn, that friends may visit with the least possible expenditure of time and money.

At present the State cares for almost two-thirds of the insane of Boston, the city for hardly more than one-third, while about one-half of the insane population of the State comes from the so-called metropolitan district. Yet the State has no hospital nearer Boston than Taunton, Worcester and Westborough, except an asylum for chronic cases at Medfield. To-day all persons in Boston who become suddenly insane, and are so poor that they cannot be cared for at their homes, are sent of necessity to the City Prison, the House of Detention or Deer Island. At these places they are humanely treated, but the stigma should be avoided and better medical care provided at a critical period. The needs are:

1. An emergency hospital within the city.

2. Enlargement of the Boston Insane Hospital to bring back to the city the insane population now scattered in hospitals comparatively distant.

3. A colony for chronic cases within comfortable reach of trolley lines.

In justice, unless Boston is to suffer permanently for the mistaken judgment of its Senators eight years ago, the State should assume the burden.

To-day Boston pays its share, some 37 per cent, of the State's care of all its insane. In addition, it supports its own hospital.

In the transfer of ownership hereby proposed the State will be able to formulate an all-embracing plan for the care of its insane, a consummation devoutly to be wished but hitherto impossible. It will also be taxing Boston no more proportionately than the other cities and towns within its borders.

For humanity, justice, and a great saving annually to Boston taxpayers, the Finance Commission invite Your Honor to join it in a petition to the Legislature, etc.

Following this petition, the "Boston Medical and Surgical Journal" of January 2, 1908, printed an editorial, entitled "State Care for the Boston Insane," in which it said:

It is a great satisfaction to all who have at heart the best interests of our dependent insane, that a determined movement has at last been inaugurated to include all of the insane of Boston among the wards of the State, thereby securing to them the advantages of nearness to their relatives which the rest of the insane of the Commonwealth now enjoy, and enabling the State to formulate a comprehensive and harmonious system of care for the entire insane population, under public supervision. . . . Another advantage to come of the care of the local insane under State management would be the establishment of an emergency station and observation hospital, a matter which concerns not only the city but the entire metropolitan district as well. By the report of the State Board of Insanity of 1904, it appears that from *one-third to one-half of the patients in Boston committed to insane hospitals are obliged to go temporarily to the House of Detention, the City Prison or Deer Island, prior to their transfer to the State Hospitals.* Aside from the impropriety of associating the insane with criminals, whose rights also may be infringed by the turbulence of violent cases of insanity, provision for medical attention and nursing is wholly inadequate in such places of detention. There are, moreover, frequent cases of transient or obscure mental disturbance which may quickly clear up or be arrested in development and thus escape treatment in an insane hospital. . . . We cannot too strongly urge upon the profession throughout the State their hearty and practical co-operation in the concerted effort that is now being made to secure early and wise legislation on this important measure.

Conditions had not improved and I could learn of no active steps to change the situation of the emergency case. I give below a few selected cases out of many which could be quoted:

On April 6, 1906, one Mrs. Augustina Eckurberg, a Swedish woman forty years old, of 5 Forest Hill Avenue, frightened her neighbors by walking backward into several houses, and was taken to the police station where she stood against a wall for six hours. Later she was returned home, her delirium having been decided to be the result of a recent illness.

On July 9, 1907, Richard Finnerty went "insane" while in the Municipal Criminal Court. He was adjudged insane but was not committed immediately to an institution but was allowed to remain in the House of Detention for several days. A paper of July 10, says:

"Finnerty was removed to the House of Detention, where he was placed in a strait-jacket. He should not have been brought to the Court House yesterday. It is said that the officials of the City Prison should have had him removed from there Monday, and that he should not even have been kept there Monday night.

"Many complaints are heard about insane prisoners at the Court House. All day long the sessions of the court are disturbed by the howling, singing and jeering of maniacs in the padded cells below. It has been said that the House of Detention and the Tombs are the only places available for the keeping of insane prisoners pending the disposition of their cases in court."

George McMullen, 50 years of age, was arrested on a Saturday night and placed in a cell at Station 4. Being delirious, he was transferred to the Tombs shortly before midnight. He received no medical attention, and at 4.40 on the morning of January 14, 1907, he was found dead in the cell. The autopsy of the same date gave as the cause of death "œdema of brain; contributing cause, alcoholism." So after all, this man was not mentally ill except so far as alcoholism was the cause, and should have been immediately sent to a hospital and treated.

On March 30, 1907, Frederick H. Terry, aged 39, was taken from his house on Lynde Street, West End, to the Tombs, pending an examination into his sanity. According to the patrolman in charge of Terry, he seemed to be in as good physical health as could be expected when he was removed; but shortly before 10 o'clock on the same morning, he found Terry lying on the floor of the cell unconscious. A physician was then called, but Terry was dead when he arrived. There was no autopsy, but the cause of death was given as "probably alcoholism."

On July 31, 1907, William C. Smith, aged 48, of New York, crazed by the heat, jumped into the water from the ferryboat "Brewster." Rescued by members of the crew, he was taken to the City Prison, where he was held pending examination regarding his sanity.

One of the most pathetic cases was that of Thomas H. Mulrennan, who had a wife and six children, and who became delirious and was taken to the Cambridge Relief Hospital, where, becoming violent, they sent him to Station 2 for "safekeeping." He was put in a cell, where they reported he was comparatively quiet until about 8.30, when, after a few outbreaks, there was a complete silence, which caused the guard to go to the cell, where he found Mulrennan hanging to the door by his suspenders. He was almost unconscious but soon recovered, and was put into a strait-jacket and placed in a padded cell. Here was a case of the hospital sending a delirious man, probably suffering from some acute mental disease, to the prison.

There are innumerable records of the mentally ill having been confined for days in this prison, and the newspapers exploited their behaviors in a sensational manner not tending to allay the fears of the nervous individual who has apprehensions of becoming mentally ill. A newspaper article, in January, 1908, tells of an Italian taken to a padded cell in the City Prison, where he tore his clothes into strips and constructed elaborate designs by sticking the shreds on the cell wall. These included a head of President Roosevelt, an Italian and a United States flag, and flocks of birds of brilliant plumage.

A newspaper account on May 31, 1908, tells of a case of a man who was "nabbed" by policemen in front of the City Prison and put in a padded cell for safekeeping. One of his stunts was to walk on his hands and feet and try to bark like a dog.

On June 1, 1908, a Mrs. Annie Daley of Locust Street became crazed with the heat; and, fearing she might become violently insane, threw herself into the water. She was rescued and taken to the Tombs.

Another case similar to that of Mulrennan, and just as flagrant a disgrace to medical men, was that of

John F. Naven, 35 years old, of 11 Linden Park, Boston, who was taken to the Relief Station of the Boston City Hospital in Haymarket Square on Wednesday, suffering from pneumonia. They said insanity developed, which was probably delirium; so on Saturday night he was taken to the City Prison, where it was claimed no medical attention was given him; and when Dr. Dunn finally called to see him, on December 9, 1907, he was lying dead in his cell. There was an autopsy; and the official cause of his death, as rendered by the medical examiner, was "acute lobar pneumonia." Could anything be more brutal?

The Sunday "Globe" of November 21, 1907, gives a very striking account of the handling of women prisoners and the mentally ill. It says:

The House of Detention on Somerset Street is a receiving depot for all the female prisoners of the police stations. . . . In addition to this, all women under arrest, suspected of insanity, are transferred to the House of Detention for keeping until they have been observed by alienists and dispositions are made of their cases. Besides the added responsibility of deranged women, the police matrons must be ever on the alert for attempts at self-destruction. Experience makes them apt at sizing up such persons at first glance and the hearing of a few words, and they can tell of some exciting instances of the value of their quick brains and quick hands in saving life. The physical health of the prisoners, too, they must bear in mind. In the chief matron's room is a good-sized case containing all the requisites for "first aid to the injured." Dr. Dunn of the Hanover Street police station can be summoned, as a general rule, inside of ten minutes to attend any patient under the matron's care.

For deranged prisoners a one-piece canvas garment, called a camisole, is used instead of what bears the general and somewhat mysterious title of a "strait-jacket." A contrivance of wristlets and belts is preferred by the chief matron to the camisole, since it is not so likely to impede the circulation of the blood. This leather contrivance has the wristlets lined with some sort of soft material so they do not cut the flesh, yet when the present writer was confined in it he found himself unable to make much use of his hands. Said he: "What if a mosquito lights on my nose?" "Bow your head a little and spread your fingers out." This proved to be the solution of the riddle.

CHAPTER III

In 1905 I made an effort to have the trustees of the
Peter Bent Brigham Hospital include a psychopathic
ward in their plans, which would make it the first
hospital in Massachusetts to establish such a ward.
I first appealed in December, 1905, to my wife's uncle,
Augustus Hemenway, who was one of the trustees.
On January 5 he wrote me a letter in which he said:

When you spoke to me last year about the matter in which you are interested, — I brought it before the Brigham trustees, and handed your letter
to Dr. Billings, who told us, after considering your proposition, that he thought
perhaps something might be done in this direction. If you can see Dr. Billings, you might explain to him further what your ideas are. He is now considering the preliminary plans for the hospital, but I am afraid that at present
he is not very well and is unable to do a great deal of work.

On February 5, 1906, a month later, Mr. Hemenway
wrote me:

There is to be a meeting of the trustees of the Brigham Hospital in a few
days, and I will inquire whether there is any prospect of their considering
your proposition. We can only do a very little at present in the way of
planning for the future, as we are still in the hands of the courts.

I was in correspondence with Dr. Billings, who had
been selected by the trustees to study and prepare
plans for the new hospital. A year after the above
correspondence, I received a letter from Dr. Billings,
dated January 31, 1907, in which he said he had
taken under consideration the matter of a psychopathic
ward in the proposed Brigham Hospital, and had con-

ferred with physicians and others on the subject.   He
added:

> I am of the opinion that a ward for this purpose should be provided in the
> Brigham Hospital and am including it in the sketch block plans which are now
> under way, and which I hope to submit to the Board of Trustees some time in
> March next.   The subject has never been discussed in the Board of Trustees,
> and I am at present unable to say what view they will take of the matter.
>
> Dr. Cowles promised to send me a sketch plan for such a ward, but has
> never done so.   I do not suppose I shall be able to obtain it from him.   If
> you have any ideas as to the arrangement of such a ward, I should be glad to
> have a pencil sketch showing it.
>
> I shall be glad to see you on your return from the South, by which time I
> hope to have some block plans ready for consideration.
>
> Faithfully yours,
>
> J. S. BILLINGS.

Two weeks later, on February 16, 1907, Dr. Billings
wrote me as follows:

> I have your note of February 14, with enclosed sketch, for which please
> accept my sincere thanks.   I do not need any more at present.   What you
> send me is sufficient to indicate on the sketch plan which is to be submitted
> to the trustees in March what is considered desirable.   It is not worth while
> to go into further detail until the trustees have signified their approval of this
> feature of the sketch.

Persisting in my efforts, I sent another letter to
Augustus Hemenway, which he answered on March
28, 1907, as follows:

> I have received your letter of the 20th regarding the plans for the Brigham
> Hospital, and am writing a line to say that I shall be glad to talk with you
> regarding the matter.

I later ascertained that during the time I was in
correspondence with Mr. Hemenway, the trustees had
decided to consult Dr. Muir (?), who was an authority
on hospital buildings for mental cases.   They sent Dr.
Billings abroad to study plans for a general hospital,
having in mind the possibility of an observation ward

for mental cases.   On January 7, 1908, Dr. Billings
wrote me as follows:

Your note of January 5 is received.   I did not get to Scotland last summer.   I went to Paris, Rome, Vienna, Dresden, Berlin, Hamburg and London.
In the sketch which I submitted to the trustees of the Brigham Hospital I have included the possibility of *an observation ward for psychopathic patients*, which,
however, may be used for other cases, in case the final conclusion is not to
establish a psychopathic ward.   In my judgment the *solution of this question
will depend mainly on whether the faculty of the Medical School desire to have
such a ward established and obtain a man qualified to take charge of it and do the
requisite teaching.*
Wishing you the compliments of the season, I remain,
Yours very sincerely,
J. S. BILLINGS.

About this time there was a contest over the
Brigham bequest for the hospital, which involved
about $8,000,000.   It was stated at a hearing that
the fund was bequeathed for the care of the indigent
sick of Suffolk County, and that the funds were being
diverted for the benefit of the Harvard Medical
School.

Dr. Billings told me that after he had presented his
plans to the trustees, they changed them a good deal,
in fact that his plans were not accepted in a manner
satisfactory to him, and that a surgeon was allowed to
draw his pencil through the psychopathic wards, with
the remark, "We need all these wards for surgery."
It was a pity that there was not a trustee on that
Board who would have erased those pencil marks and
said, "We need a psychopathic department to make
this hospital complete and carry out the purposes of
the testator that this hospital should be for the poor of
Suffolk County.   You have surgical wards; let us take
care of *all* the different forms of illness with which the
poor people may be afflicted."

On April 9, 1908, I wrote an article for the "Boston Medical and Surgical Journal" on "Observation Hospital or Wards for Early Cases of Mental Disturbance." It was intended to encourage physicians and to put before them how far-reaching our efforts had been and what effect the publicity given our work was having in other cities. A quotation from it may not be amiss:

The long-continued and persistent efforts by a few individuals for observation wards or hospitals now seem to be about to bear fruit. This is certainly a satisfaction to those who have watched the conversion of the doubting minds, who have striven to pry these doubters out of the ruts they have been in so long and show them how they should have relieved many sick people who have been neglected and who have had no voice or recognized rights in their own treatment. A general active movement in this direction is now apparent in many of the large cities of this country. In and about Boston, committees have been formed in times past, recommendations made, and many other fruitless efforts have been attempted to bring about that which a few well-directed efforts give hope of accomplishing this winter. I have contributed several papers on this subject, and cannot add much to what has already been said, but should like to bring before the profession further evidence in favor of this movement from other sources than those before mentioned, and some new evidence from the same sources. In view of the favorable attitude shown at the hearings this winter before the Massachusetts legislative committees on bills along this line, many physicians who heretofore have considered an observation hospital or ward a remote possibility of doubtful expediency, now seriously consider the subject. At the above hearings no opposition appeared. Such unanimity would not have been possible a few years ago. We are not going to stop at an observation hospital, but within a very few years all of our largest general hospitals will realize the value to themselves of observation wards (under whatever name they choose to give them) as a part of their system for clinical instruction and the training of their nurses. The public are now becoming educated to this crying need as rapidly as the average practitioner, and they are demanding such wards. While I am writing this paper, the information comes to me that an effort is being made to equip by private subscription a ward at the Massachusetts General Hospital for early cases of neurasthenia. This is a move in the right direction, and whether it is called by one name or another does not matter, so long as relief is afforded in these early cases. The first wards for this purpose were put in operation in Germany, and to Griesinger belongs the credit of the first plan for establishing these wards. Scholtz established observation wards in connection with the Bremen general hospitals in 1870, and about the same time Reijers organized similar wards in Würtzburg. The first clinic for these cases was opened by Furstner at Heidelberg in 1878, where later Kraepelin did such excellent work. A little later Fleichsig opened the second clinic at Leipsic. From time to time these clinics have increased until now in each of the twenty German universities, or in general hospitals, or in buildings in their neighborhood, there are clinics and patients under observation. At Blockley Hospital in Philadelphia, the municipal almshouse and the general and insane hospitals are grouped under one management and have four wards for the observation and detention of early cases. In Pittsburgh the General Hospital of St. Francis has four well-equipped wards, which are under charge of Dr. Theodore Diller, where mental cases were first received fifteen years ago in a small wooden building serving as an annex to the hospital, and which was so successful that three years ago a brick pavilion was constructed containing one hundred beds. Bellevue Hospital in New York has a separate pavilion, which is nominally a distribution station.

CHAPTER IV

In reaching out for help early in 1906, I appealed to the Boston City Hospital and the Massachusetts General Hospital to establish observation wards for mental patients, but both hospitals turned deaf ears.

As treasurer of the Tyler Street Day Nursery, I appealed to the corporation (who had decided to discontinue their activities) for the use of one or both of their buildings for an observation hospital. I wrote Dr. Councilman my plan for the Massachusetts General Hospital and received, on February 15, 1906, his answer in a few words. He said, "I am much interested in the plan you suggest and hope that something may be done."

Alice N. Lincoln was then quite active in public affairs, and in March I conferred with her, telling her of my plans. On March 14, 1906, she wrote to me as follows:

I was especially interested in what you said about an observation hospital. . . . A number of years ago some of the ladies with whom I was associated asked for a hearing before the Board of Aldermen in regard to the establishment of such a hospital. The aldermen treated us with much consideration, but did not grant us the hospital.

A more serious attempt was made a few years later, through a conference in the mayor's office between the persons interested in the establishment of such a hospital and the trustees of the Boston City Hospital, who were unwilling to assume the charge of such wards, believing they would be used largely for cases of delirium tremens. Thus both attempts met with no positive result.

I urged Mrs. Lincoln to get the ladies who were interested together again for the purpose of bringing about the desired object. On March 23, 1906, she wrote me:

> I think you will be interested to know that, at a meeting of the Committee on Council and Co-operation, held last Wednesday, the ladies were much interested in reviving the project for observation wards or an observation hospital. The ladies represent a number of thousands of individuals (perhaps 6,000 or 8,000), and the central body is composed of delegates from these various organizations. I have already spoken to two friends of the mayor concerning it, and am surprised that we encountered *no opposition except in regard to lack of funds.*

Fearing some move which might result in failure, as had all previous efforts, I hastened to answer Mrs. Lincoln's letter, urging her to be sure to keep in touch with what different ladies were doing, and stated that we did not want any newspaper notoriety until we had something definite to offer the papers. On March 24 she answered as follows:

> I hasten to allay your very natural anxiety concerning the observation hospital.
> The ladies of the C. C. C. are only anxious to help where help is needed, and if you feel that they can help best by remaining quiet, I am sure they will be glad of the suggestion.

After referring to the differences of opinion among the ladies as to the proposed site on the vacant land adjoining the Relief Hospital near Haymarket Square, she continued: "You can see how immediately I turned to you. There was no thought of any public appeal or newspaper notice."

In March, 1906, I appealed to Dr. George H. M. Rowe, superintendent and resident physician of the Boston City Hospital. His answer I quote in full:

MARCH 16, 1906.

Dr. L. V. BRIGGS, *208 Beacon Street.*

DEAR DR. BRIGGS: — I have been obliged to delay answering your letter of February 3, with numerous others asking for statistics, plans, opinions, etc., on account of some extra writing I have had to do.

I do not believe there is any probability of there being established in this hospital a ward for the observation of the insane such as they have in Albany. You say you would like to talk the matter over with me. I have talked this subject and discussed it, until I never want to hear it mentioned again while I am here. I admit all the arguments in favor of having an observation ward somewhere, but I feel the same about the matter as some one at the Massachusetts General Hospital, who said, "Oh, yes, I thoroughly agree that there should be an observation ward in connection with some hospital, but I want that hospital to be yours, and not mine." If this were a privately incorporated hospital outside of city control, I might favor it, but an observation ward would simply end in being a ward for recovery from drunkenness, delirium tremens, etc. You can count on me as being opposed to such a scheme here, and I think the trustees, to an individual, are of the same opinion.

Yours very truly,

GEORGE H. M. ROWE,
Superintendent.

In the meantime, I was urging the State Board of Insanity to establish an observation hospital. They counseled delay, giving as their reason, lack of funds, Legislature not ready to appropriate money, etc. I appealed to Dr. Herbert B. Howard, chairman of the State Board, who was also resident physician of the Massachusetts General Hospital, and after a long delay he sent me a note on April 12, 1906, saying he was in his office every morning between 9 and 10 o'clock, excepting Monday, and would be glad to see me. But my interviews with him did not bring any results.

Mrs. Lincoln continued her activities, interviewing many officials and physicians, and all seemed favorable but did nothing. She also made an attempt to have an old building, then unoccupied and belonging to the House of the Good Samaritan, set aside for temporary use, but was unsuccessful. She wrote to me she was afraid that I was anxious to start on too large a scale.

The public through the papers were becoming interested, and for the next two years the interest grew until the State Board of Insanity were obliged to begin to recognize the public, who were demanding that more should be done for the mentally ill of the State.

On February 29, 1908, the Rev. Herbert Robbin wrote to the "Boston Herald" in favor of the establishment of a psychopathic hospital for acute and doubtful cases of insanity, and said that such a building would be endorsed by every "psychopathist" and many other humane people.   He further said:

For two years I have been conducting, in my church, a class studying carefully and scientifically experimental psychology for the purpose of intelligent clinical work in this and similar fields.

and winds up his communication as follows:

By all means, Mr. Editor, let Massachusetts establish a psychopathic hospital.

About this time, 1908, Dr. John Macpherson, High Commissioner of Insanity of Scotland, wrote me:

I have often thought of your aims and objects toward erecting a mental hospital in Boston, and wondered with what measure of success or failure your efforts have been crowned.

No relief being in sight, and no results from the State Board of Insanity's report of 1900, the Legislature of 1908 directed the Board to make another report with recommendations before May 1, 1908.

I received the following letter: —

MARCH 20, 1908.

L. VERNON BRIGGS, M.D., *208 Beacon Street, Boston.*

DEAR DOCTOR:— The Board of Insanity is required to make a report to the present Legislature, according to the terms of the enclosed Resolve, Senate No. 211. The Board would appreciate the favor of your counsel and suggestion in the matter and invites you to a conference with other physicians on Wednesday, March 25, at 2 P.M., in Room 34, State House.

Cordially yours,

OWEN COPP,
Secretary.

At this conference at the State House, March 25, 1908, much was said about the lack of funds and the impossibility of finding a building or any quarters for an observation hospital. It was urged that the conference consider taking a part of the Tyler Street Day Nursery to use as an experiment until permanent quarters could be established. Dr. H. R. Stedman and one or two others visited the Nursery on Harrison Avenue with me, and all seemed unanimous in the opinion that to start an observation hospital there would be a step in the right direction, but that was all it ever amounted to. Nothing more was heard about that plan. Mary Morton Kehew, of sacred memory. who established and was president of the Women's Educational and Industrial Union, who was instrumental in placing the New England Hospital for Women and Children on its feet when it most needed help, and who established and was president of the Tyler Street Day Nursery, was a strong supporter of my plans for the use of the Tyler Street buildings.

Denison House was making a strong plea for the use of these houses for itself, and one or two of the directors favored selling out the property, as the Nursery had already decided to move elsewhere. But Mrs. Kehew remained firm, and the trustees voted to offer the building to the State at a nominal rent of $1 a year.

I was asked to confer with the directors on March 30, 1908, at that time being one of them, as well as the treasurer, and immediately received from the secretary, Mary S. Rousmaniere, a copy of the vote "to give preference to the possible plans for an observation hospital over the several schemes which had been suggested." On April 1, I received the following letter from Mrs. Kehew:

MY DEAR DR. BRIGGS: — Miss Rousmaniere has probably reported that the Tyler Street Day Nursery directors "give preference" to the Observation Hospital. This may seem much or little, as we put meaning into it. The attitude of the directors is the Biblical one of "almost thou persuadest me" and there is still more "persuading" to be done if they are to adopt the plan enthusiastically. I venture to advise that you telephone or see Mrs. Mack, and stimulate *her* interest — *Verbum sap.!* I shall be out of town for a week or two, but on my return I shall be glad to have an opportunity to ask a few questions, that I may be a bit more intelligent as to ways and means.

Yours sincerely,

MARY MORTON KEHEW.

Dr. Theodore Diller of Pittsburgh, who had been instrumental in establishing a psychopathic department in St. Francis Hospital in that city, wrote me on April 23, 1908:

Nobody has taken any notice of my writings except you and a Toronto doctor, who came down to examine St. Francis; but I feel strongly that at least one large general hospital in every large city should provide a psychopathic department, and especially in cases where hospitals are attached to medical schools. For example, I would like very much to see the hospital of the University of Pennsylvania (my Alma Mater) add such a department. It ought to be done; don't you agree with me?

CHAPTER V

The City of Boston caring for its own Mentally Ill complicates Establishment by the State of an Observation or Psychopathic Hospital in Boston. — Efforts to obtain the co-operation of the Finance Commission and the Mayor of the City of Boston successful, and Mayor Hibbard introduces a Bill for State Care. — The State Board of Insanity and Others become active in the Passing of Bills before the Legislature. — May 27, 1908, the Joint Committee of Ways and Means and the Committee on Public Charitable Institutions report Revised Bill for the Care of Insane of Boston by the Commonwealth. — Bill passed and signed by the Governor

Up to January, 1908, I was still urging the State Board of Insanity to be prepared to give early care and treatment to Boston's mentally ill, but as the Board took no definite action I asked Mayor Hibbard to introduce the following bill:

HOUSE . . . . No. 619

Bill accompanying the petition of G. A. Hibbard, mayor, for legislation to provide for the establishment of an emergency hospital for insane and delirious persons in the City of Boston. Cities. January 21.

The Commonwealth of Massachusetts

In the Year One Thousand Nine Hundred and Eight

AN ACT

To provide for the Establishment of an Emergency Hospital for Insane and Delirious Persons in the City of Boston

Be it enacted by the Senate and House of Representatives in General Court assembled, and by the authority of the same, as follows:

Section 1. There shall be established in the city of Boston an emergency hospital for insane and other persons in a delirious state needing restraint or supervision, under the control of the State Board of Insanity, to be devoted to the care of persons temporarily detained by the local authorities of said city on the charge of insanity or delirium from any cause. The location of said emergency hospital for observation of mental disturbances shall be determined by the said Board of Insanity with the approval of the mayor of said city. The entire charge and management of said emergency hospital shall be under the direction of said State Board of Insanity, and the entire expenses for the maintenance of said emergency hospital shall be borne by the Commonwealth.

SECTION 2. This act shall take effect upon its passage.

This was the result of many drafts made during the previous year which it would be a waste of space to publish.

On February 5 Mayor Hibbard held a public hearing at his office in City Hall, on the subject of "Observation Wards." About twenty persons attended the hearing. Chairman Clark of the Board of Aldermen was present. Among those who spoke in favor were Drs. Jelly, Charles P. Putman, Walter Channing, Phillip C. Knapp, Mrs. Lincoln and Messrs. Charles F. Gaynor, John B. Martin, Robert Treat Paine and myself. Drs. Copp, Francis X. Corr, James J. Putman and Henry R. Stedman also supported the bill.

About this time Alice N. Lincoln petitioned the Legislature in House Bill No. 792, but her bill was permissive only. On February 14 the legislative Committee on Cities gave a hearing, at which Mrs. Lincoln stated her bill did not in any sense conflict with the one presented by Mayor Hibbard, which put the emergency hospital under the State Board of Insanity. Her bill, which was supported by Drs. Putman, Channing, Stedman and Copp, provided that the city of Boston *might* establish an observation ward. I could not understand Dr. Copp and his friends supporting a bill which would take the insane from city to State care, and at the same time supporting another bill which would create another hospital for the insane to be established by the city of Boston and controlled by them. However, this was the situation. Dr. Channing said that there was one of three ways the work could be performed: patients might be sent to the City Hospital; they might be handled by some individual institution; or they might be cared for by the State.

A strong ally came forward about this time in the person of Dudley M. Holman, editor of the "Taunton Herald-News," who not only wrote in his own paper, but sent a communication to the "Boston Herald." Among other things, he said:

We seem to think that the State's duty is done when it has segregated the insane from their fellows, has given them good food, shelter and medical attendance. The real work of these institutions ought to be scientific research into the causes, prevention and cure. Our insane hospitals have become merely boarding houses for the chronic insane and places where the acutely insane soon become chronic. It is a disgrace to our State that there is one hospital that is not equipped with a pathological laboratory, and scientists properly trained. Massachusetts does not want to be simply a training school for other States. They should be given every opportunity to do what they can here and furnished the power to make their work effective. Why should Massachusetts have allowed Meyer to go to New York, Barret to Michigan University, Diefendorf to Middletown? If Harvard or Yale should lose professor after professor in an important department, we should know that something was radically wrong. We are behind the times and apparently making no effort to catch up. Our hospitals have been overcrowded for years, and are to-day. The scientific study of insanity is not receiving the attention it deserves, nor are the pathologists being properly recognized and backed up by those responsible for the management of this branch of the State work.

These statements were very true and they give a good idea of conditions at that time.

A hearing on my bill, No. 619, which Mayor Hibbard introduced to the Legislature, was held May 25, 1908, before the Public Charitable Institutions Committee of the Legislature. Alice Lincoln's bill, No. 792, was heard at the same time. The Tyler Street Day Nursery Corporation again offered its two buildings to be used for a psychopathic hospital or observation wards, at a rental of $1 a year. Mrs. Lincoln spoke in favor of our original plan, as did William P. Fowler, registrar of institutions of the city of Boston. Dr. Walter Channing favored the mayor's bill. Dr. George F. Jelly, who had been examining cases of mental disease for the city for twenty-seven years, favored State care and the mayor's bill. Mrs. G. T. Perkins gave an account of a significant case who would have been benefited had a psychopathic hospital been available, but who died in consequence of lack of treatment in a police station. Dr. George T. Tuttle of the McLean Hospital thought that an observation hospital would be a great help to medical students, and favored an institution to which the whole metropolitan district would have access.

Drs. Copp and Howard of the State Board threw cold water on the meeting by talking at great length in their efforts to show that the State Board of Insanity's report covered the whole subject and that this legislation was not needed; in other words, that the State Board was planning to do this very thing and had so planned for years. It was plain to the members of the Legislature that these plans had not materialized, and that no obstacle should be put in the way of immediate action. Dr. Copp said:

The State cannot at present adopt temporary quarters. The theory of the State Board is that these institutions should be established; and the method of doing it has already been planned.

It was immaterial who should bring about immediate action and establish a hospital so long as it was done, but in the meantime the people whose relief we were seeking were being neglected and were suffering.

Alice Lincoln spoke of two persons with mental trouble who had died in prison since the last hearing.

Dr. Jelly stated that for twenty-seven years his efforts had been in this direction, and he had been a member of the State Board of Insanity for several years. Just for a moment, pause and think that a member of the State Board of Insanity for many years had favored the very thing that we were after, but had not been able to accomplish it!

Senator George H. Garfield of Brockton, who was a member of the Public Institutions Committee, was most co-operative and active. He had early in January, 1908, introduced a resolve, as follows:

SENATE   .   .   .   . No. 211

RESOLVE

To provide for an Investigation and Report by the State Board of Insanity as to the Best Method of Provision for the Insane

Resolved, That the said Board of Insanity is hereby directed to investigate and report to the general court not later than the first day of May of the present year, with such recommendations as it may deem necessary or expedient, as to what it deems to be the best method of provision for the insane, including Boston and its vicinity, in locations convenient to the interested friends of such insane persons, with special reference to (1) first care and observation of mental cases; (2) the early treatment of mental diseases; (3) the treatment of acute and curable cases of insanity.

On May 1, 1908, the State Board of Insanity in obedience to the Senate Resolve No. 211, as above, made its report, which was signed by Drs. George F. Jelly, Michael J. O'Meara and Herbert B. Howard and Messrs. Henry P. Field and William F. Whittemore. It was an exhaustive report, dealing with all phases of the care of the insane. It was one of the most enlightened and progressive reports which had been published on the care of the insane up to the time of its filing. It recommended that the Boston Insane Hospital be immediately acquired by the State; a psychopathic hospital be established in Boston with a voluntary or convalescent branch in the suburbs where patients should be accessible to their relatives; that this psychopathic hospital should be located near a general hospital and medical school; that the medical director should supervise the medical and scientific work of all hospitals of the Commonwealth, under the direction of the State Board; that the Psychopathic Hospital should be made attractive to physicians, scientists and students of the first order; that all State hospitals be permitted to receive for temporary care, not exceeding five days, voluntary cases and others, and authorizing the committal to the State hospitals on the certificate of two qualified physicians of all persons in such mental condition that committal is necessary for their medical care and observation pending the determination of their insanity; psychopathic wards in general hospitals; that there should be out-patient departments similar to that in general hospitals; that all cases should be received in the psychopathic hospital, exclusive of alcoholics, for first care and observation, and that it should be the center of investigations into causes of insanity.

Following the report of the State Board, Senator Garfield introduced Senate Bill No. 382:

SENATE . . . . No. 382

AN ACT

To provide for the Preparation of Plans and the Location of a Hospital for Acute and Curable Mental Patients in the Metropolitan District

Be it enacted by the Senate and House of Representatives in General Court assembled, and by the authority of the same, as follows:

SECTION 1.   The State Board of Insanity shall, with the approval of the governor and council, select, and secure option on, land in the city of Boston suitable for the establishment of a hospital conveniently located for the first care and observation of mental disease. Said board shall prepare and submit to the legislature, not later than March one, nineteen hundred and nine, preliminary plans, general specifications and estimates of the cost of constructing and equipping, for the use of said hospital, buildings sufficient to accommodate one hundred and twenty patients and the necessary officers, nurses and employees, and to furnish adequate provision for the treatment of acute and curable mental diseases and scientific research into the nature, causes and results of mental diseases. Said board shall in like manner select, and secure options on, land in or near said city suitable for the establishment of a branch of said hospital for the treatment of voluntary mental patients, and shall prepare and so submit to the legislature such plans, specifications and estimates for buildings sufficient to accommodate one hundred patients and the necessary officers, nurses and employees.

SECTION 2.   A sum not exceeding ten thousand dollars may be expended to carry out the provisions of this act.

SECTION 3.   This act shall take effect upon its passage.

Senator Garfield told me recently that he introduced the above bill on his own initiative because he became impatient at the delay and inactivity of the State Board in relation to their own reports and recommendations.

The next day after the above bill was introduced, I wrote the following letter to Senator Garfield:

MY DEAR SENATOR GARFIELD: — After seeing you this morning, I feel that I should put to you in writing the main points of a bill, in which you and I are interested, for the *immediate* relief of the emergency cases.

Bill No. 792 if changed from the "city of Boston *may*" to "the State of Massachusetts *shall*" might still be objected to by the State Board as not meeting the full requirements. If this objection is raised, could not a bill be drawn and substituted something as follows:

"The State Board of Insanity is hereby directed to secure immediately after the passage of this bill temporary accommodations for the examination and immediate care of all cases of suspected insanity, who would otherwise be sent to the City Prison or House of Detention; and for the better protection of themselves and the public, the State Board shall have authority to detain such persons, pending a determination of their mental status, and in fact all persons who if allowed their liberty might in the opinion of physicians in attendance be a menace to the public or themselves; the State Board to have full power for the maintenance and care of such hospital or wards and of the persons admitted to them; an appropriation to be made the first year of, say, $3,000 for furnishings; $2,000 for salaries; $15,000 for running expenses and care."

The State Board's report covers much of the above, and I do not see how they can oppose the immediate care of these unfortunates. No one else will do it, the city has not done it and will not.

The State Board in their report on pages 8, 9, 10, 11, 13, 28, 29, 32 and 36 recommend and evidently intend to eventually put through some bill which will cover the above ground and that it will be so worded as to meet the objections of the Board and not be an elaborate plan which might be defeated in the Ways and Means Committee or elsewhere. All that is asked now is a place where these sick people may temporarily be put to bed and nursed until the State Board are ready to receive them in a more elaborate hospital. If it is desirable to follow their reports in the matter of giving the resident physician power to reject any applicant who in his opinion is suffering only from alcoholism, it may be well to do so.

If the State Board allows the present intolerable condition of affairs to continue for three or four more years, we must be the ones to bring about provision for small temporary quarters at least until the Board perfects their more splendid plan for the future.

I hope you will in some way help these demented people, who would certainly appear for themselves if they could. It can be done. I believe you can and will help. How can the State Board refuse them immediate care?

Very truly yours,

L. VERNON BRIGGS.

The Tyler Street Nursery again offered their property, and the two houses necessary to carry out the purpose of a bill, which was as follows:

SECTION 1. The city of Boston shall within one year from the passage of this act establish and maintain within its limits a suitable building or special wards for the reception, medical observation and temporary care of those persons suffering from sudden delirium, mental disturbance, transitory excitement or other kindred disorders, who are now classed as "observation cases," and owing to the lack of such a building or wards are at present placed in the City Prison, the House of Detention, or the House of Correction at Deer Island, pending medical examination or treatment.

SECTION 2. Until the time when such building or wards shall be established, the mayor of said city is authorized and directed that such persons shall be placed for observation and treatment in the care of any general hospital belonging to the city.

SECTION 3. This act shall take effect upon its passage.

On account of the State Board's opposition — they did not seem willing to further this movement at this time — the bill was drawn so that the city of Boston should establish a hospital, and I determined that before it was passed it should be amended so that the Commonwealth would care for all the institutional insane. The above form had to be acceded to in order to get any compromise bill introduced. It was the State Board of Insanity that really defeated Mayor Hibbard's and Mrs. Lincoln's bills. Many executive sessions were held by the executive officer and his friends with the committees. Senator Garfield, Mrs. Lincoln and I appeared for the new compromise bill. It was making headway and there appeared little chance of our being able to amend it. We feared that the object we were seeking — State care of all insane — might be defeated, so decided it was best to work for a law forbidding Boston to establish such a hospital.

Our efforts to prevent Boston erecting a hospital resulted in a law which became chapter 613, section 1, Acts of 1908, which contains the following:

The city of Boston shall not hereafter establish any asylum or other institution for the care of the insane.

Since early in the fall of 1907 I had been often in conference with Mayor Hibbard, the corporation counsel of the city of Boston, the Finance Commission of the city, and with the State Board of Insanity and its executive officer, Dr. Copp. The Finance Commission saw the advisability of State care for financial reasons, and also from a progressive point of view. As early as January 2, 1908, Mr. John F. Moors of the Finance Commission wrote to me:

My Dear Dr. Briggs: — I enclose a draft of my report on the transfer, suggested by yourself, of the Boston Insane Hospital to State ownership.

It does not differ in essentials from the report finally adopted by the Finance Commission and published.

Yours very truly,

John F. Moors.

On January 15, 1908, he wrote to me:

Mr. Spring of the city law department would like to have you get in touch with him about the Insane Hospital bill.

It seems as if the mayor's public support of the bill might be very helpful, and I shall be grateful if you and Mr. Spring can take the matter entirely off my hands.

Mr. Spring is very busy as Saturday approaches and hopes that you can make the advances to him.

Conference with Mayor Hibbard and with the corporation counsel, Mr. Spring, resulted in a bill, the first draft of which was as follows:

An Act to provide for the Care of the Insane of the City of Boston by the Commonwealth

Section 1. The Commonwealth from and after the first day of January in the year nineteen hundred and nine shall, by the officers and boards authorized thereto, have the care, control and treatment of all insane persons who are now cared for by the city of Boston or by any board of officers thereof, and said city of Boston shall not hereafter establish any asylum or other institution for the care of the insane, nor after said date maintain any such institution, or be liable for the board, care, treatment or act of any insane person. As soon as possible after the first day of January in the year nineteen hundred and nine the said Board of Insanity may transfer all insane persons who are cared for by the said city of Boston or by any board of officers thereof and who are not cared for in any hospital, asylum or receptacle maintained by the Commonwealth, to such a hospital, asylum or receptacle so maintained as the said Board of In-

sanity may deem expedient, provided that the Boston Insane Hospital hereafter to be transferred to the Commonwealth shall be used by said board for
the care and support of citizens of said city.

SECTION 2. The State Board of Insanity is hereby authorized with the
approval of the governor and council in the name and behalf of the Commonwealth, to take by purchase or otherwise, the lands and buildings now con-
stituting the Boston Insane Hospital in said city of Boston. In the event of
the taking of said land and buildings by said board, said board shall file in the
registry of deeds for the county of Suffolk descriptions of the lands and buildings so taken with a statement signed by said board or a majority thereof that
the same are taken under the provisions of this act in the name and behalf of
the Commonwealth, and the act and time of filing thereof shall be deemed to
be the act and time of taking of such lands and buildings, and shall be sufficient notice for all persons that the same has been so taken. The title to all
the lands and buildings so taken shall vest absolutely in the Commonwealth
and its assigns forever. The Commonwealth shall be liable to pay all dam-
ages sustained by said city of Boston by reason of the taking of said lands and
buildings and said State Board shall have full power, subject to the approval
of the governor and council, to settle with the mayor and board of trustees of
said Boston Insane Hospital, the value of the lands and buildings taken as
aforesaid, and if said value cannot be so agreed upon by them, said value shall
be assessed by a jury at the bar of the superior court in said county of Suffolk
upon petition to be filed in the office of the clerk of said court by said city of
Boston within one year after said taking and not afterward.

SECTION 3. The provisions of section two of chapter four hundred and
fifty-one of the acts of the year nineteen hundred and the last paragraph of
section six of chapter fifty-seven of the Revised Laws in so far as they make an
exception in the case of the city of Boston in the provisions of said acts respectively, are hereby repealed. All acts or parts of acts inconsistent herewith
are hereby repealed.

SECTION 4. This act shall take effect upon its passage.

This resulted in House Bill No. 724, 1908, being a
redraft which petitioned the Legislature to provide for
the care of the insane of the city of Boston by the
Commonwealth. This draft was introduced by Mayor
Hibbard on January 21, as follows:

The Commonwealth of Massachusetts

In the Year One Thousand Nine Hundred and Eight

AN ACT

To Provide for the Care of the Insane of the City of Boston by the
Commonwealth

*Be it enacted by the Senate and House of Representatives in General Court
assembled, and by the authority of the same, as follows:*

SECTION 1. The Commonwealth, from and after the first day of January
in the year nineteen hundred and nine, shall, by the officers and boards authorized thereto, have the care, control and treatment of all insane persons
who are now cared for by the city of Boston, or by any board of officers thereof,
and said city of Boston shall not hereafter establish any asylum or other institution for the care of the insane, or after said date maintain any such institution,
or be liable for the board, care, treatment or act of any such person.   Said
Boston Insane Hospital shall from and after said date be subject to all existing
laws governing other state insane institutions.

SECTION 2. The State Board of Insanity is hereby authorized, with the
approval of the governor and council in the name and behalf of the Commonwealth, to take, by purchase or otherwise, the lands and buildings now con-
stituting the Boston Insane Hospital in said city of Boston.   In the event of
the taking of said lands and buildings by said board, said board shall file in the
registry of deeds for the county of Suffolk, descriptions of the lands and buildings so taken, with a statement signed by the said board, or a majority thereof,
that the same are taken under the provisions of this act in the name and behalf
of the Commonwealth, and the act and time of filing thereof shall be deemed
to be the act and time of the taking of such lands and buildings, and shall be a
sufficient notice for all persons that the same have been so taken.   The title of
all lands and buildings so taken shall vest absolutely in the Commonwealth
and its assigns forever.   The Commonwealth shall be liable to pay all dam-
ages sustained by said city of Boston by reason of the taking of said lands and
buildings, and said state board shall have full power, subject to the approval
of the governor and council, to settle with the mayor and board of trustees of
said Boston Insane Hospital, the value of the lands and buildings taken as
aforesaid, and if said value cannot be so agreed upon by them, said value shall
be assessed by a jury at the bar of the superior court in said county of Suffolk,
upon petition to be filed in the office of the clerk of said court by said city of
Boston, within one year after said taking and not afterward.

SECTION 3. The provisions of section two of chapter four hundred and
fifty-one of the acts of the year nineteen hundred, and the last paragraph of

section six of chapter fifty-seven of the Revised Laws, in so far as they make an exception in the case of the city of Boston in the provision of said acts, respectively, are hereby repealed.

SECTION 4.   This act shall take effect upon its passage.

This was a great step; and the consent of the city of Boston was not won without an immense amount of work and unceasing vigilance. The State Board of Insanity did little to assist; in fact their inactivity seemed to be interpreted by some members of the Legislature as opposition to the bill. They, however, did send out a notice reading as follows:

JANUARY 31, 1908.

DR. L. VERNON BRIGGS, *208 Beacon Street, Boston.*

DEAR DOCTOR: — There will be a hearing in Room 440 before the Public Charitable Committee on Wednesday, February 12, at 10.30 A.M., concerning the taking of the Boston Insane Hospital by the State.

Very truly yours,

OWEN COPP,
Executive Officer.

I obtained the assistance of the Massachusetts Civic League, several other societies and many prominent people in efforts to put through legislation which would bring about the new laws we desired. The Massachusetts Civic League, by its representative, Edward T. Hartman, presented an appeal on April 24, 1908, and incorporated in his appeal much of the report of the Finance Commission favoring the transfer. The league also stated in its appeal:

This bill (House, No. 724), put in on the petition of Mayor Hibbard, has been reported leave to withdraw by the committee and the report has been accepted by the House. The plan is to have the bill substituted in the Senate where it comes up on Monday.

The bill has the support of the trustees of the hospital, of the State Board of Insanity, of Mayor Hibbard, of the Finance Commission, and of the medical profession.

In favor of the bill are two principal considerations. *First*, it is more humane in caring for the Boston insane near their homes, a matter of great importance not only to the happiness of many of them but as affecting their chance of recovery. *Second*, it will do away with the obvious injustice of the present arrangement under which Boston pays its full share of the cost of all the insane, and a considerable part of the cost of its own insane over again. The situation is well described in the report of the Finance Commission.

The next step was by the Senate as follows:

SENATE   .   .   .   . No. 381

The Commonwealth of Massachusetts

SENATE, April 28, 1908.

The Committee on Ways and Means, to whom was referred the Senate Bill to provide for the care of the insane of the city of Boston by the Commonwealth (printed as House, No. 724), report that the same ought to pass, in a new draft, herewith submitted.

For the committee,

ELMER A. STEVENS.

The new draft which was the same as House Bill No. 724 up to the word "aforesaid" in section 2, then read:

and if said value cannot be so agreed upon by them, the superior court upon application of either party within one year after said taking and notice to the other, shall appoint three commissioners who shall determine said value, and whose finding when accepted by the court shall be final. Only one of the said commissioners shall be a resident of the county of Suffolk. The commissioners shall receive any compensation as may be determined by the court, which shall be paid by the city of Boston if the value of the said lands and buildings as determined by the commissioners, exclusive of interest, does not exceed the amount which the Commonwealth offered to pay therefor prior to the application for the appointment of the commissioners; and otherwise the compensation of the commissioners shall be paid by the Commonwealth.

Section 3 was not materially changed.

The legislative committee held a hearing at the State House on Thursday, May 14. The main plea was made by corporation counsel, Thomas M. Babson, who appeared before the Ways and Means Committee and the Committee on Public Charitable Institutions at this joint hearing. He quoted liberally from the report made by the State Board and made a fervent and eloquent plea himself. This carried the day; and Senate Bill No. 348, under a new draft numbered 381, was reported favorably by these two committees. A committee of the Boston Society of Neurology and Psychiatry, composed of Drs. Henry R. Stedman, Walter Channing, George T. Tuttle and W. N. Bullard, interested themselves actively in getting people before this committee to plead for the cause. The bill passed the several stages of legislation; and the State paid $1,000,000 to the city for the Boston Insane Hospital, the Governor and Council approving the final settlement in June, 1909.

Senate Bill No. 381, in section 1, changed the date on which the Commonwealth should take over the care of the insane in the Boston Insane Hospital from January 1, 1909, to December 1, 1908, and instead of referring to it as "said Boston Insane Hospital," provided that —

The institution or asylum in which such insane persons are cared for shall from and after said date be called the Boston State Hospital and shall be subject to all laws so far as applicable governing state insane hospitals. The government of Boston State Hospital when established shall be vested in a board of seven trustees to be appointed by the governor with the advice and consent of the council, five of whom shall be men and two of whom shall be women. One member shall annually in January be appointed by the governor with the advice and consent of the council for a term of seven years from the first Wednesday of the February following. The members of the Board may be removed for cause. The members of the Board first appointed by the governor shall hold office from the time of their appointment for terms expiring one, two, three, four, five, six and seven years respectively from the first Wednesday of February in the year nineteen hundred and nine, the length of their terms to be designated at the time of appointment.

Section 2 remained unchanged.

In section 3, the words "paragraph of section six of chapter fifty-seven" were changed to "sentence six of chapter eighty-seven."

Thus the care of the insane passed entirely into the hands of the State of Massachusetts. An editorial in the "Boston Medical and Surgical Journal" of October 15, 1908, said:

It is not to be questioned that through the admirable work of the Massachusetts State Board of Insanity a grasp of the present situation and of future needs has been secured which will render the solution of the problems in the future far simpler than have been those of the past. It should, however, be understood that the Board's relation to institutions and their inmates is essentially advisory and that in this capacity it may exert a very wide influence in promoting uniformity of administration and efficiency. In order that the exact relation of the State Board to institutions and their inmates may be generally known, we quote the following statement: "It has no direct control over local administrations and internal regulations of institutions. Its direct powers relate to general relations between institutions, the classification and transfer of patients between them, discharge on appeal, investigation as to claims for support in institutions, collections for support if private funds are available for the purpose of deportation out of the State of those who have such claim elsewhere. Family care of the harmless insane is under the control of the Board."

On January 13, 1909, the State Board of Insanity filed a special report as to locations for a hospital for the first care and observation of mental patients and for the treatment of acute and curable mental diseases, and a branch thereof for voluntary mental patients. Following this, the bills which were filed for a branch hospital in Lexington for convalescents and voluntary cases failed in the Legislature, mainly because of the opposition of 900 citizens of Lexington who signed a petition against it, and arguments by Dr. J. O. Tilton, practicing physician; James P. Monroe of the School Committee; Mrs. Charles H. Masheury, president of the Daughters of the American Revolution; Representative Bayley and others. Those who favored it before the legislative committee were Mr. Field, Dr. Copp, Dr. Edward W. Taylor, Dr. Walter Channing and others. We did not feel enthusiastic about this branch hospital until the Psychopathic Hospital or observation hospital was in commission. We therefore concentrated our efforts against the opposition to the present site of the Psychopathic Hospital. In March, 1909, Dr. Albert Evans became actively interested, and proved to be a most helpful ally to all who were working for the immediate care and treatment of the mentally ill and the improvement of the conditions that existed at this time.

On April 20, 1909, another special report of the State Board of Insanity was filed with the Legislature, in compliance with chapter 626 of the Legislature of 1908, requiring the preparation of preliminary plans, general specifications and estimates of the cost of constructing and equipping (1) an observation hospital in Boston; (2) a branch thereof for the treatment of voluntary mental patients, in the vicinity of Boston; and the Board recommended "$100,000 for the purchase of land for an observation hospital in Boston, and the authorization of the expenditure of $500,000 for building and equipment."

No bill and no recommendation had yet been drawn specifically for the care of the confused or mentally ill persons who were arrested on the streets or sent to the prison or tombs. Conditions for these unfortunates remained the same, and again from a large number I give a few typical instances.

A newspaper of August 11, 1909, gives an account of one Augustus Hollander, aged 74 years, of Sudbury Street, who had been missing for over three days and was found in the Taunton Insane Hospital, after a long search by policemen and firemen. It was later learned that he was picked up in Charlestown suffering from heat prostration, taken to the Chardon Street Home, from which, having shown signs of insanity, he was taken by an officer of Station 3 to the Tombs. Later he was committed and sent to Taunton.

In April, 1909, Patrick Lyons was taken to the City Prison in an unconscious condition. Dr. Dunn was called, but the man was dead when he arrived, and the autopsy showed cause of death "acute lobar pneumonia."

Patrick Welch, aged 35, in September, 1909, was found on the sidewalk on Lincoln Street, acting as though intoxicated. He was booked for insanity. Later he was sent to the City Prison and confined in a padded cell, where he was found by one of the guards a short time after, groaning upon the floor. Dr. Dunn, the prison physician, was summoned and advised the man's removal to the City Hospital, at which place the doctors found him suffering from a fractured skull. He lived but a few hours.

It was claimed that Welch was first booked on a charge of intoxication, and that the entry was later changed to one of insanity. Medical Examiner Magrath received his first notice of the death from a "Traveler" reporter. An editorial in the "Transcript" of September 29, says:

"The death at the City Hospital of a man whose skull had been fractured, and whose case had been diagnosed as drunkenness, calls for some explanation. The police are not expected to be able to make medical diagnoses, but that any man with a fractured skull could be handed about from hospital to police and to another hospital, suggests unpleasant things. . . . Presence of traces of alcohol upon a helpless person is not conclusive proof that there is nothing else the matter with him."

The record of autopsy states the cause of death to have been "fracture of the skull, with associated contusions and hemorrhage of the brain. Sustained under circumstances unknown."

November 28, 1909, William J. Mulhern, aged 28 years, was taken to the City Prison from the Relief Station, and the next day was found dead in his cell. An autopsy was performed, and the cause of death was given as "œdema of the brain; dilatation of the heart; chronic tuberculosis of the lungs."

Efforts were made to obtain statistics of the numbers of mentally ill persons who had been sent to the Tombs in the last two years; inquiries were made as to how many had died while in the Tombs, or after arrest before arriving at the Tombs; how many were committed to State hospitals; how many were found to have delirium tremens or were unsuitable for insane hospitals; what was the disposition of those who were not transferred to State hospitals; how many were sent to Deer Island or the House of Correction; how many were discharged without being committed elsewhere. Police Commissioner Stephen O'Meara answered these inquiries under date of January 20, 1910, that "to answer the above questions would require the examination of the records of more than 32,000 persons and was next to impossible."

In the midst of the fight for these unprotected people I received a request on May 12, from the President of the American Association of Medical Examiners, to read a paper on this very subject at the meeting of the association to be held at Atlantic City June 7, 1909, which I did. Just prior to May 20, 1909, the Ways and Means Committee of the Legislature reported favorably on a bill giving the Boston State Hospital authority to acquire, by purchase or otherwise, land for establishing a hospital in the city of Boston for the first care and observation of mental diseases, and for acute and curable cases. The feature that this hospital should be a part of the Boston State Hospital I at first opposed, but withdrew my opposition to that part, feeling that the first thing was to get an observation hospital, if necessary to be attached, as was the plan of Dr. Copp of the State Board, to a State hospital, but later I intended to bring about a separation and make it an independent hospital for the first care and treatment of the mentally ill. It seemed to me that the purpose of a psychopathic hospital was defeated when it became attached to a State hospital. If the Psychopathic Hospital was to be a department of the Boston State Hospital, then patients were at once under the care of the State hospital, and the original purpose of the Psychopathic Hospital was partly defeated. After years of patient work, this condition was corrected and the Psychopathic Hospital was separated from the Boston State Hospital and made an independent unit.

It was now in the summer of 1909, and nothing had been done to relieve the deplorable conditions which existed at the City Prison. On July 29, 1909, I received the following notice:

CITY OF BOSTON, INSTITUTIONS REGISTRATION DEPARTMENT.
OFFICE OF THE REGISTRAR, 28 COURT SQUARE.

BOSTON, July 29, 1909.

DEAR SIR: — During the month of *August*, hearings for the commitment of insane will be held by the judge of probate at the regular hour (12 o'clock) on Tuesdays and Fridays of each week, and on no other days during that month, with the two following exceptions:

Monday, August 9, is substituted for Tuesday, August 10.
Thursday, August 19, is substituted for Friday, August 20.

I am

Yours respectfully,

CHARLES F. GAYNOR.

This meant that persons arrested and sent to the City Prison·pending determination of their mental condition might be held from Monday until Thursday, or from Thursday until Monday, without medical care or treatment. This was an added stimulus to my friends to protect these people and see that they had immediate and proper care.

In November, 1909, the site of the present Psychopathic Hospital was purchased on Fenwood Road, five minutes' walk from Harvard Medical School.

Up to December, 1909, in the messages of the Governors, the mentally ill had received little attention.

References made to this class bore strongly on economy in care and housing rather than preventive, scientific or even efficient treatment. Interviews with Governor Draper only resulted in his conferring with the State Board and assuming a negative attitude. In his message he was only willing to say, "while economy should be constantly in our minds this year, we ought to provide well for the care of our unfortunate insane and erect such additions to our institutions as are necessary for this purpose." This was seen to be only a housing proposition and showed how far his education had been carried by the officials upon whom he depended.

I urged that the State Board present bills covering the class of persons who should be sent to the Psychopathic Hospital, and also endeavored to find out from them what progress they were making in the matter of providing a hospital for these patients to be sent to. Failing to get action I presented Senate Bill No. 212.

SENATE   .   .   .   . No. 212

AN ACT

Relative to Persons suffering from Certain Mental and Other Disorders or Diseases in the City of Boston

Be it enacted by the Senate and House of Representatives in General Court assembled, and by the authority of the same as follows:

SECTION 1. All persons suffering from the disorders hereinafter referred to, now under arrest or who may come under the care and protection of the police of the city of Boston and who, owing to lack of suitable buildings or wards, are at present placed in the City Prison or the House of Correction at Deer Island, pending a medical examination and transference, shall be taken directly to the Psychopathic Hospital for examination when said hospital has been completed and is ready for the reception of patients, in the same manner as other persons afflicted with other diseases are taken to the Massachusetts General Hospital. If after examination the physician in charge of the Psychopathic Hospital decides the case to be one of delirium tremens, he shall not be obliged to admit patient to said hospital, but otherwise said hospital shall admit and observe or care for all persons suffering from delirium, mental con-

HISTORY PSYCHOPATHIC HOSPITAL 59

fusion or delusions and hallucinations until such persons can be transferred to the hospitals or institutions appropriate in each particular case, unless the patient should recover before the transfer is made.

SECTION 2. From and after the first day of May in the current year and until such time as a psychopathic hospital shall be completed and ready to receive persons suffering from the disorders referred to in section one, the State Board of Insanity shall provide suitable temporary quarters for receiving and giving medical care and treatment to all persons suffering from sudden delirium, mental disorders or kindred conditions, who are at present placed in the City Prison, House of Detention or the House of Correction at Deer Island, pending medical examination and transference. To provide for defraying the cost of such quarters, medical care and treatment there shall be paid annually until the completion of said Psychopathic Hospital a sum not exceeding. . . .

SECTION 3. On and after the first day of May in the current year no person suffering from mental confusion, mania, delirium, hallucinations or delusions shall hereafter be harbored or confined in any penal institution within the city of Boston for a period exceeding twelve hours.

This was the first bill presented to the Legislature for the protection and care of persons arrested in the streets and placed in police stations or the Tombs.

CHAPTER VI

The Senate was becoming impatient at the delay in establishing an observation hospital. Senator Pickford of Worcester, a member of the Public Charitable Institutions Committee, which passed upon bills for the dependents of the State, offered the following resolve:

SENATE . . . . No. 264

Introduced on leave by Senator Pickford of Worcester. Public Charitable Institutions.

The Commonwealth of Massachusetts

RESOLVE

Relative to the Hospital for Observation of Mental Patients and the Treatment of Acute and Curable Mental Disease

Resolved, That the State Board of Insanity is hereby requested to report in detail to the general court as soon as practicable, and not later than the fifteenth day of March, nineteen hundred and ten, what progress has been made by the board toward the establishment in the city of Boston of a hospital for the first care and observation of mental patients and the treatment of acute and curable mental disease, what contracts have been made by the board relative thereto, what provision has been made by the board for the care and treatment of such patients until the completion of said hospital, and when the hospital can reasonably be expected to be ready for the reception and treatment of patients.

The "Boston Evening Transcript" was also getting impatient, and the following appeared on the editorial page of the issue of January 22, 1910:

"First aid" for the mentally unbalanced is what is sadly lacking among all our public provision for succoring the unfortunate. Something partaking of the spirit of the "whips-and-the-cell" prescription for the insane that prevailed up to within three-quarters of a century, even in parts of New England, still survives in the police regulations of the city of Boston and in the policy of the State Board of Insanity. "If you or I were found wandering about the streets," says a well-known Beacon Street physician, "either picturesquely or dramatically exhilarated, or simply dazed and confused, you or I would be taken to the nearest police station, and thence to the Tombs. There we should be put through the privations and hardships of what is practically solitary confinement, that is, in a bare cell without even the poor arrangements for creature-comfort of the ordinary cell, on the theory that the insane might destroy them or harm himself with them. Cautiously at last, if you were very still, the attendants might introduce a mattress upon the floor, and, perhaps, a stool; but if you were at all excitable, you would be allowed to stand around between padded walls or stretch yourself for rest on the bare floor. If your seizure happened on a Friday afternoon, this would be your treatment until Monday afternoon. . . .

"What the doctors who have seen too much of this sort of thing, to rest content with 'things as they are,' wish to see inaugurated here, is either an observation ward in one of the existing hospitals, or a small emergency hospital for the insane, where all suspected cases may be taken, put to bed and cared for the same as are those who are ill with disorder in any other organ of the body besides the brain. The State Board, it seems, deems it not to be the policy of the State to take care of demented people until their insanity has been passed upon by the courts. It has a $600,000 psychopathic hospital under consideration, to be completed some four years hence. But meanwhile, unless some other provision is made, the average unfortunate, in his first days of mental alienation or confusion, must be thrown into prison with criminals, amid surroundings and privations that increase his bewilderment; till the mind which has been hanging, perhaps on the ragged edge, goes over the precipice. It is estimated that nearly one-third of the insane committed to the State hospitals arrives there via the Tombs, and, thereafter, each becomes a charge of about $5,000 annually upon the State. Every year, to be sure, some unfortunate relieves the State to the extent of passing away with pneumonia or exhaustion while at the Tombs; but there are more humane and scientific methods of anticipating and lightening the burden of the State from its insane than exposure to cold and mental suffering which has equally fatal possibilities."

On January 25, 1910, I appealed to our new mayor in the following letter:

> 64 BEACON STREET, BOSTON,
> January 25, 1910.

The Hon. JOHN F. FITZGERALD, *Mayor, Boston, Mass.*

MY DEAR MR. FITZGERALD: — In 1908 when the State of Massachusetts assumed the care of all of its insane, Mayor Hibbard signed and put in a bill that the State should also give immediate medical attention and hospital care to those insane and mentally disturbed persons who are now arrested on the streets or taken from their families and thrown into the police stations and the Tombs, pending medical examinations and commitment.

In 1909 the Commonwealth went still further and forbade the city of Boston or any other city to care for these sick people, saying they are now wards of the State. They have been given no relief and apparently the State Board does not intend to relieve them for some years to come.

I have been told that you are interested, and I am therefore writing to you. I believe that action in this matter should be in accordance with your plans as expressed in your letter addressed to myself and other physicians. I have put a bill in the Legislature which I hope will result in something being done immediately.

I should like to talk it over with you, for, as the mayor of the city of Boston, I am sure you will want to see the people who come from the poorest parts of the city have as good care as those who can afford to go to private sanatoriums, and that the $600,000 appropriated for this purpose last year, and the $358,000 that the State Board asked for this year for the same hospital in addition to the $102,900 which the State Board of Insanity asked for their own expenses and salaries this year, ought to be enough to provide for these people who are in their charge according to the law of to-day, but who, as yet, have received no benefits from the $600,000 which was asked especially for them last year.

You may not remember me, but I sat beside you in Jackson's class in the Boston Latin School when you, Foster, McCleary, Alexander and myself were vying for first place.

I will not make any definite appointment for Thursday or Friday of this week until I hear from you.

> Very sincerely yours,
> L. VERNON BRIGGS.

Before answering, Mayor Fitzgerald evidently made inquiries of the State Board, for under date of January 25, he answered:

I am informed that the State has bought land for the purpose indicated in your communication in the vicinity of the Harvard Medical School, in Roxbury. I think if you will make some inquiries about this, you will find it to be true.

My bill was coming up for a hearing and I sent a notice to many prominent people asking them to support it if they were in sympathy with it. In answer, many came to the hearing; others who were not able to attend wrote letters. Prof. William James of Harvard University wrote as follows:

95 IRVING STREET, CAMBRIDGE,
February 14, 1910.

DEAR DR. BRIGGS: — I wish I might be present at the hearing of your bill for immediate care of the insane, pending their commitment. It is a shocking injustice that such unfortunates should be handled by the police and pass through penal institutions, — enough, I doubt not, to materially lessen the chance of recovery in many cases of melancholic and delusional type. The State should have expert treatment of helpless patients at the outbreak of the attack, organized not only for humane but for eventual economic reasons. After-care and previous care of cases of insanity is now recognized as an imperative part of the economic burden. Much is to be hoped from the psychopathic hospital; but a much larger movement should be organized in Massachusetts, similar to the "social service" work planned by the Connecticut Society for Mental Hygiene, which numbers the chief asylum superintendents among its directors, and is ready to begin operations. Our State should not fall behind, and the remedying of the present scandal of police co-operation in medical work can't be removed too early.

The fact must be faced that insanity is a tremendous public burden. But these softening measures, expensive at first, will lessen State outlays in the end.

Sincerely yours,

WM. JAMES.

Dr. James J. Putman, Professor of Neurology at Harvard Medical School wrote:

106 MARLBOROUGH STREET,
February 16, 1910.

DEAR DR. BRIGGS: — I have your postal and am very sorry that I neglected to answer your first communication.

I think your plan is an excellent one, and I will try to be on hand at the State House on Monday, February 21.

Yours very truly,

JAMES J. PUTMAN.

EMMANUEL CHURCH, 15 NEWBURY STREET,
BOSTON, February 16, 1910.

DR. L. VERNON BRIGGS, 64 Beacon Street.

DEAR DR. BRIGGS: — I know that we are both very busy, but if you are in this part of the city during any of my office hours, I should be very glad to talk with you on the subject of your bill.   I am much interested in your statement, and believe that you are undertaking an important and very unselfish piece of work, and it will give me pleasure to be of any assistance, if I could be instructed as to how I could serve you.   I am at the office every morning, except Saturday, from 10 to 1.

Yours sincerely,

ELWOOD WORCESTER.

BOSTON CHILDREN'S AID SOCIETY,
GENERAL SECRETARY, CHARLES W. BIRTWELL

BOSTON, MASS., February 18, 1910.

L. VERNON BRIGGS, M.D., 64 Beacon Street, Boston.

MY DEAR DR. BRIGGS: — You do not need to see me about the matter referred to in your letter of the 16th inst.   Just tell me how I may be of any help.   Of course, I am working myself to pretty nearly the limit, but the matter appeals to me strongly.   For years I have wished that something might be done to meet the situation.

Yours sincerely,

CHARLES W. BIRTWELL.

The following is a list of those who either wrote or gave their names in support of the bill, other than those already mentioned in this chapter:

Dr. Joel E. Goldthwait, 372 Marlborough Street.
Dr. Robert B. Osgood, 372 Marlborough Street.
Arthur Dehon Hill, 53 State Street.
Warren F. Spaulding, Massachusetts Prison Association, 56 Pemberton Square.
Prof. Wm. T. Sedgwick, Massachusetts Institute of Technology.
Robert A. Boit, 40 Kilby Street, President Boston Dispensary.
Augustus Hemenway, Clarendon Street.
Dr. Chas. Hammond, Secretary, Plymouth County Medical Association.
A. Shuman, President Boston City Hospital Board.
Miss Crocker, Treasurer, Colonial Dames, 352 Marlborough Street.
Mrs. F. S. Watson, 263 Clarendon Street.
Mrs. Henry Dalton, 181 Beacon Street.
Mrs. Richard Bradley, Longwood Avenue.
Miss Rose Lamb, 129 Mt. Vernon Street.

Mrs. Henry Parkman, 30 Commonwealth Avenue.
Mrs. Roland Gray, 83 Marlborough Street.
Mrs. Mary Morton Kehew, 29A Chestnut Street.
E. H. Clement, 10 Concord Avenue, Cambridge.
Hon. David P. Keefe, House of Representatives.
Miss Alice L. Higgins, Associated Charities.
Dr. W. M. Knowlton, Channing Sanitarium, Brookline.
George Noble, 21 West Cedar Street.
Senator Melvin S. Nash, Plymouth County.
Hon. H. C. Mervin, House of Representatives.

The Massachusetts Civic League had been "seen" by those opposed to the measure. From a letter which was addressed to Mrs. Mary Morton Kehew, it was evident that they had been influenced against the measure by or through the State Board or their friends, who wished every one to wait until they should build the Psychopathic Hospital. I quote from the above-mentioned letter the following:

There is also to be a hearing on Dr. Briggs' bill, and you may be interested in a statement I have just received from Mr. Koren to the effect that he feels the passage of this bill will not expedite the development of the Psychopathic Hospital, and that he thinks our energies ought to be headed in that direction. He apparently believes that the situation is not as serious as we think, and that most of the people whom we are considering are ordinary, or perhaps I should say extraordinary, cases of delirium tremens.

E. T. HARTMAN,
Secretary.

Dr. George A. Gordon of the New Old South Church wrote that he was not able to give attention to any more things, "not even the cause of humanity that you have at heart."

No one seemed able to interest Major Henry L. Higginson or the Rev. Mr. Gordon in the cause of the mentally ill. For years relatives and friends endeavored to obtain Major Higginson's sympathy for and interest in this unfortunate class, but without avail.

In the meantime the State Board still permitted sick people to be thrown into jails and prisons. Although I could give many, many more cases, I select three to illustrate this:

In January, 1910, James B. Hand, aged 31 years, was arrested as intoxicated; and when, the next morning, he was lined up with others to go to the City Prison, the officer in charge discovered that he was bleeding from the ears. He was taken to the Relief Hospital, where it was found he was suffering from a fractured skull.

On January 16, 1910, Daniel P. Harrington, aged 22 years, of East Boston, attempted suicide by attaching an outlet to the gas jet in his room and inhaling the fumes. Tenants, smelling the gas, broke the door down. Harrington was taken to the Relief Hospital, and by the doctors at that hospital he was sent to the City Prison, pending investigation as to his sanity.

In November, 1911, Mrs. Catherine Zappavigna, aged 21 years, was found to be sick and was removed to the almshouse, from which she was sent to the police station and placed in a padded cell. But the next day she was so rational that Judge Bosworth refused to commit her. Later she was sent to the hospital; but what she went through in the process, no one knows.

I again appealed to the State Board in the following letter:

FEBRUARY 18, 1910.

MY DEAR DR. COPP: — As you probably know, my bill, No. 212, comes before the Committee on Public Charitable Institutions, Monday, February 21, at 11 A.M.

I hope as executive officer of the State Board, you will not in any way oppose it at the hearing or *afterward;* but if you have any intention of bringing any influence to bear on the bill, I hope it will be at the hearing, as the public wants to know, and has a right to know, the reasons, if any, the Board has for not taking care of all of the classes of people now that it intends to take care of when the Psychopathic Hospital is built. I hope and trust that every member of the State Board of Insanity, including its executive officer, will lend his hearty support to my bill and relieve the present deplorable situation not six months or a year hence, but now.

Very truly yours,

L. VERNON BRIGGS.

The hearing of my bill, Senate, No. 212, was held on Monday, February 21, 1910, at 11 A.M. at the State House.   The petition on the bill was as follows:

To the Honorable Senate and House of Representatives of the Commonwealth of Massachusetts in General Court assembled:

The undersigned petitioners, citizens of Massachusetts, respectfully petition for legislation relative to persons now arrested, or coming under the care and protection of the police of the city of Boston, suffering from mental disturbance or disease or disorders, to persons affected with mental confusion, mania, delirium, hallucinations or delusions, and for the care of such persons in the Psychopathic Hospital in the city of Boston.

L. VERNON BRIGGS.
JOEL E. GOLDTHWAIT.
VINCENT Y. BOWDITCH.
E. F. MERRIAM.
MARY MORTON KEHEW.
AUGUSTUS HEMENWAY.
CHARLES F. PAINTER.
ROBERT B. OSGOOD.

Copy of the bill, as presented with the petition, is as follows:

SENATE   .   .   .   . No. 212

To accompany the petition of L. Vernon Briggs and others that persons suffering from certain mental disorders in the city of Boston shall be treated at the Psychopathic Hospital.   Public Charitable Institutions.

The Commonwealth of Massachusetts

In the Year One Thousand Nine Hundred and Ten

AN ACT

Relative to Persons suffering from Certain Mental and Other Disorders or Diseases in the City of Boston

Be it enacted by the Senate and House of Representatives in General Court assembled, and by the authority of the same, as follows:

SECTION 1.   All persons suffering from the disorders hereinafter referred to, now under arrest or who may come under the care and protection of the police of the city of Boston and who owing to lack of suitable buildings or wards, are at present placed in the City Prison, the House of Detention or the House of Correction at Deer Island, pending a medical examination and transference, shall be taken directly to the Psychopathic Hospital for examination when said hospital has been completed and is ready for the reception of patients, in the same manner as other persons afflicted with other diseases are taken to the Massachusetts General Hospital. If after examination the physician in charge of the Psychopathic Hospital decides the case to be one of delirium tremens, he shall not be obliged to admit patient to said hospital, but otherwise said hospital shall admit and observe or care for all persons suffering from delirium, mental confusion or delusions and hallucinations until such persons can be transferred to the hospitals or institutions appropriate in each particular case, unless the patient should recover before such transfer is made.

SECTION 2.   From and after the first day of May in the current year and until such time as a psychopathic hospital shall be completed and ready to receive persons suffering from the disorders referred to in section one, the State Board of Insanity shall provide suitable temporary quarters for receiving and giving medical care and treatment to all persons suffering from sudden delirium, mental disorders or kindred conditions, who are at present placed in the City Prison, House of Detention or the House of Correction at Deer Island, pending medical examination and transference.   To provide for defraying the cost of such quarters, medical care and treatment there shall be paid to the State Board of Insanity from the treasury of the Commonwealth annually until the completion of said psychopathic hospital a sum not exceeding . . . dollars.

SECTION 3.   On and after the first day of May in the current year no person suffering from mental confusion, mania, delirium, hallucinations or delusions shall hereafter be harbored or confined in any penal institution within the city of Boston for a period exceeding twelve hours.

The hearing follows:

The Commonwealth of Massachusetts

COMMITTEE ON PUBLIC CHARITABLE INSTITUTIONS

A public hearing on Senate Bill No. 212 relative to persons suffering from certain mental and other disorders or diseases in the city of Boston.

STATE HOUSE, BOSTON, MASS.,
February 21, 1910.

Senator Turner, Presiding

The opening statement was made by Dr. L. Vernon Briggs, as follows:

Mr. Chairman and Gentlemen, Members of the General Court of Massachusetts: We petitioners appear to you to-day to plead the cause of a goodly number of our citizens who cannot speak for themselves and we pray that you will pass some law for their immediate relief. In 1907 Mayor Hibbard petitioned the Legislature in Bill No. 619 for the State to establish an emergency or observation hospital, having for its purpose the care and treatment of the incipient insane who were then and are still sent to the City Prison, etc. The result of this agitation was the passage of a bill in 1908, appropriating $10,000 for plans, etc., and in May, 1909, the passage of a bill appropriating $600,000 for the site, construction, equipment, etc., of a psychopathic hospital. The State Board of Insanity in *May, 1908*, made a special report to the Legislature, Senate Document No. 358. On page 26 of that report they urge that something must be done as the general hospital managers are obdurate in their refusal to accept these cases.

On page 13, in speaking of the location of the institutions being near the center, they say: "Thus would be minimized the exhaustion of a long journey to the feeble patient, the disturbance in transporting the excited, the delay in emergency cases, and the present regrettable necessity of detention over-night, over Sunday and holidays or longer, during the infrequent sittings of courts, owing to vacation periods in some localities, in police stations, city prisons and other receptacles for criminals, where not only are associations objectionable, but adequate medical attention and nursing are not available nor reasonably to be expected. Conditions existing throughout the State necessitate such detention, pending the completion of legal formalities, in about one-third (28.7 per cent) of all commitments to our insane hospitals."

And on page 31, they say, "the hospital stage has been reached," and speak of the "ineffectual attempt of the city of Boston to care for its own insane."

On page 33, they say: "It is not less discreditable to the Commonwealth than to the city that one-third of Boston's insane are lodged temporarily in the City Prison and House of Detention, because State insane hospitals are so far away as to prohibit their prompt reception. The insane are now wards of the State."

Since the Legislature has voted authority for Massachusetts to build a psychopathic hospital, New York has further relieved its situation, has secured a location and built a hospital which is now in commission and receiving nervous and mental cases. In speaking of this hospital the editor of the "Boston Medical and Surgical Journal" said, two months ago: "The need is not so much for those who have distinctly passed beyond the bounds of sanity, for whom ample provision is already made, but rather for the great and probably increasing number of border-line cases who may be restored to lives of usefulness if proper methods are employed in their early treatment. Such patients are not welcome and no doubt do not belong in the wards of our general hospitals. They certainly should not, even did the law permit, be committed to institutions for the insane."

The State of Illinois on April 16 last opened its fourth new psychopathic hospital after a campaign which was begun by Governor Deneen only two years ago, and in other States rapid progress is being made to the same end. Because Massachusetts has not taken care of its incipient insane and provided for the prevention of insanity, it has now a hoard of chronic insane people on its hands, increasing every day, at an enormous expense to the State and a loss of intelligence to our community. If the State does not assume this care before its Psychopathic Hospital is completed, it is asking you to jeopardize the minds and lives of 500 of your citizens each year, a good proportion of whom will be added to the chronic insane and become a burden for many years. Since I came before you with Mayor Hibbard's bill of 1907, 1,000 people have gone through the mill, have been arrested, thrown into prison behind bars, left there to suffer or die alone without proper medical care and, if alive, finally committed to insane institutions where the chronic, acute and all types mingle together. At that time the bill was defeated because the State did not support it. Dr. Copp, the executive officer of the State Board of Insanity, appeared before you and made this statement. He said: "No obstacle should be put in the way of immediate action, but the State cannot at present adopt temporary quarters. The theory of the State Board is that these institutions should be established, and the method of doing it has already been planned." I have heard within a few days that the policy of the State might be one of delay, that they saw no reason why the city should not assume the care of these people and provide a place for them in their general hospitals until such time as a psychopathic hospital was ready to receive them. It would be preposterous to believe that my informers had understood this statement correctly if I had not been told it myself only three months ago by the one man in the State to whom insanity matters seem to be referred. Mayor Fitzgerald has been asked if he would not urge a law that the city of Boston should provide suitable quarters and care for these people pending the erection of the Psychopathic Hospital, and this in the face of the fact that the State of Massachusetts has, only two years ago, taken not only the insane from the care of the city and assumed it but has forbidden Boston to maintain any place for the insane.

The reason we are asking the State to care for these people and to stop this almost criminal neglect is because the laws forbid any one else doing it and the State should assume control of the situation, — the taking care of the people who cannot take care of themselves, who cannot demand just treatment, who cannot protect themselves against abuse, restraint or incarceration in our common jails. The State should take charge of these people for the law is right as it stands to-day, but some action should be taken at once not six months hence, not a year and a half hence, not three or four year hence, but at once, for the protection of these people. Clearly a campaign of education is needed to instruct the public as to the proper treatment of their early insane cases.

Again to quote the editor of the "Boston Medical and Surgical Journal:" "A great advantage to come of the care of the local insane under State management would be the establishment of an emergency station and observation hospital, a matter which concerns not only the city but the entire metropolitan district as well. By the report of the State Board of Insanity of 1904 it appears that from one-third to one-half of the patients in Boston committed to insane hospitals are obliged to go temporarily to the House of Detention, the City Prison or Deer Island, prior to their transfer to the State hospitals."

The report of the State Board of Insanity says that on October 1, 1909, the whole number of persons under the supervision of their Board was over 14,000. The average increase annually for the last five years was about 400. For construction and other special appropriations they ask for over $800,000 this year. They have received over half a million dollars a year for the last eleven years for this purpose. They ask for over two million and a half for maintenance this year. The average that they have received for maintenance for the last five years is over two million and a quarter and this has increased last year 10 per cent. On December 1, 1908, the State had invested in these institutions over $12,000,000 and not a cent in any hospital used only for the observation and care of the incipient and early cases as a preventive measure. The State has a debt on account of the institutions under the supervision of the State Board of Insanity of over $5,000,000, with an annual interest charge of about $200,000. Is it not time to do something to stop this ever-increasing burden upon the State? Until recently it has not been the policy of the State to give any medical care and treatment to any of the insane until they were committed by the courts, which means an advanced stage. Recently, they opened their hospitals to voluntary patients, allowing them to go to them if they wished to. Still later, and as it is the law to-day any physician may send a patient immediately to the insane hospital in the incipient stage, there to mingle with the chronic patients in wards, etc., on a seven-day emergency clause, but, under the law, the applicant must remove or cause legal commitment of the patient within seven days or be liable for expenses and a penalty of $50.

In Massachusetts it would seem we are living before the time of Pinel, who over a hundred years ago struck the chains from the insane people in the great hospital in Paris and allowed them the freedom of the hospital and gave them hospital care. To-day we are so far behind those times that we allow the police of our city to go into our houses and take members of our families or our friends to the station house and to cells which are filthy in many instances, and thence to the City Prison, where, instead of hospital care and the treatment that Pinel gave his patients over a hundred years ago, we put them in cells and confine them in a strait-jacket; and if it is considered that they are at all dangerous to themselves or to property, everything is removed from the cells that can be removed and only the four padded walls and iron bar gate and the hard floor are left, and after dark these cells only receive light from a little aperture high up at the back or what light glimmers through the bars from the corridor. If they wish to go to the toilet and are sane enough to make their wants known, they are led out and back again; if they show signs of quiet and want to lie down and go to sleep, a mattress is mercifully put on the floor for them to lie on. If they are very quiet, they are given a stool or chair to sit on, but many have neither of these poor comforts.

Gentlemen, you are told that a law exists whereby these people may be sent direct to the hospitals, but is it practicable? The fact is that only five have been sent from the jails under that law during the last year. Supposing you had pneumonia, what would the community say if you were sent to the City Prison until a Board of Hospital Trustees should examine you and decide whether you had pneumonia or not? If they decided you had pneumonia, what would happen if you were not removed from the prison for from one to four days? You would probably die alone on the floor of the cell, and that is exactly what happens with many of these cases, and any one who asks delay or opposes this bill, directly or indirectly, asks you to allow this. These people are often found dead on the hard floor of their bare cells. The disease of the brain is the only acute disease which is not received by hospitals or harbored by them. If you are taken to some of our hospitals and develop a delirium so as to be noisy or excited, the law allows you to be taken from a comfortable bed and medical care and thrown into the City Prison. This is the state of things to-day in this city and in this Commonwealth.

Dr. Charles W. Page of Danvers Hospital, and a leading expert in the care of the insane, in speaking of seclusion or restraint when patients are once placed in a cell, says: "The argument against mechanical restraint applies in a large measure to seclusion of the insane. While seclusion is, in some degrees, less demoralizing in its effects or its influence upon the nursing staff of an institution, only in rare and exceptional cases can its employment be remedial or beneficial. If, as Conolly said, 'restraint is neglect,' it is doubly true that seclusion is neglect. If used, it should never be prolonged. Next to execution, solitary confinement is the severest doom that legal tribunals can pronounce upon hardened criminals. Solitary confinement is universally considered to be painfully trying to a sane mind. How can it be improving to a deranged man, shut away from associations with human beings, incapable of comprehending the logic of his position, consumed by delusions or burning with revengeful indignation toward the authors of his imaginary wrongs?"

After New York had provided for these persons, Dr. M. S. Gregory, the resident physician at Bellevue, said: "The change from a prison cell to a hospital ward is a great reform, and doctors and nurses in place of coarse and brutal prison guards are a tremendous step in the right direction."

I have here several friends of the bill, petitioners, who would like to speak. On account of the late hour, I will limit them to five or ten minutes apiece.

REPRESENTATIVE KEEFE. I would like to ask you, sir, where you propose putting the hospital?

DR. BRIGGS. That I do not propose. The situation is as it is. I do not propose to dictate to the State Board of Insanity nor to the State of Massachusetts.

REPRESENTATIVE KEEFE. Where would you suggest it be put?

DR. BRIGGS. I would suggest that the shell of a house be hired for a small sum, and that beds be placed in the house for the reception of all these cases. The beds could be removed to the Psychopathic Hospital as soon as it was ready to receive them. If that is impossible, *a provision could be made at the Boston State Hospital that would be better than the present state of affairs.*

Dr. Charles W. Page
An ardent advocate for non-restraint

REPRESENTATIVE KEEFE. Do you think that drunkenness is a disease?

DR. BRIGGS. My bill excludes delirium tremens, so that objection is removed.

REPRESENTATIVE KEEFE. I see you allude to the fact that a person is taken in the patrol wagon with a police officer or police officers. How would you get rid of that?

DR. BRIGGS. To-day a large number of clerks, shop girls, boarders in different houses, are depressed, talk to themselves, or are disturbed; and the people about them become alarmed; they call a physician; he is afraid of a suicide or a homicide, and doesn't dare to leave them. There is at present nothing to do except call the police.

THE CHAIRMAN. It is not intended for common drunkards?

DR. BRIGGS. It is not intended for common drunkards.

REPRESENTATIVE KEEFE. You make mention of the fact that the police stations of Boston are in filthy condition. Who is to blame for that?

DR. BRIGGS. There is a bill before the Legislature now in that connection. It was heard last Friday, and you will hear it later in the Legislature.

REPRESENTATIVE KEEFE. I see you make allusion to the fact that the prison is in a filthy condition.

DR. BRIGGS. The city prison is absolutely clean. But there is absolutely nothing in the cells for the patients. They have to sleep on the hard pine floor.

THE CHAIRMAN. Now, then, Doctor, we want to get through this hearing at 1 o'clock, if we possibly can. We want to avoid all repetition and as long as that is regarded, we will allow you to go on until, we will say, twenty minutes to 1. Then, if there is any opposition, we will give that twenty minutes.

DR. BRIGGS. That only gives me twenty minutes to present a very important matter.

THE CHAIRMAN. Twenty-five minutes really. I think enough can be said in less than that time to satisfy the committee.

DR. BRIGGS. All right. We will see how we get along. I will call upon Mr. Robert A. Boit, president of the Boston Dispensary.

MR. ROBERT A. BOIT. Mr. Chairman and Gentlemen of the Commission: I have but one word to say, and that is that the principles that are involved in this bill seem to have been all determined upon two years ago, or in the neighborhood of two years ago, and, therefore, the only question that remains is whether we shall allow the present condition of things to exist until we have time to build the Psychopathic Hospital. And I see no reason because we, as citizens, have to wait for two years for this, why we should afflict our fellow citizens with the present conditions which exist. Any time in the next two years — to-day or to-morrow or the next day — any member of your individual families or my own, any of your relations or friends, you yourself or I, may be put in exactly this position which has been explained, because we are waiting to-day for something which has already been determined upon; and there is no reason why you or I should be subjected to such a thing.

THE CHAIRMAN. Just a moment. You are subjected to these conditions here in the city of Boston and you are waiting for those conditions to be amended?

MR. BOIT. Yes, sir.

THE CHAIRMAN. What are other people in the State of Massachusetts going to do after you get this here?

MR. BOIT. They have got to do the same thing.

THE CHAIRMAN. They have got to wait.

MR. BOIT. They have got to do the same thing. That is practically all I have to say.

DR. BRIGGS. I will call upon Dr. James Jackson Putman who is neurologist at the Massachusetts General Hospital, and professor in the Harvard Medical School.

DR. PUTMAN. I have been for some thirty-five years in charge of the department of the Massachusetts General Hospital which deals with diseases of the nervous system. The patients come to us every year as out-patients to the number of upwards of a thousand, and among those there are a great many who are insane or in danger of becoming insane. Very often it happens that the cases of these patients have been taken up too late to have them go directly to be disposed of and committed to suitable asylums, and then we are often in great perplexity to know what to do with them. It seems to me entirely wrong, — I don't see how there can be any question about it. What Dr. Briggs describes is an anomalous condition. If it possibly can be remedied, it is certainly very unfair that these patients should be subjected to treatment in the city jails while they are waiting. They ought certainly to have the same privilege that other sick persons have of being taken care of as sick persons. I simply wish to give my testimony as one to whom patients of this class come.

SENATOR NASH. Doctor, you feel it would be your opinion, as a nerve specialist, that these men or women, incarcerated in the prison, were endangered by this form of treatment?

DR. PUTMAN. I think there is no question about it.

SENATOR NASH. That such treatment would be likely to develop an incipient case into a chronic case?

DR. PUTMAN. I should think that might happen unquestionably. They are persons who are subject to terror and suspicion, and anything in the way of harsh treatment would be likely to increase those symptoms and make them serious.

REPRESENTATIVE KEEFE. I would like to ask you, sir, if there is any place they can go to now outside of private sanatoriums or hospitals?

DR. PUTMAN. There is no place that I know of.

THE CHAIRMAN. Couldn't they be sent to the Boston Insane Hospital, the Boston State Hospital, I would say?

DR. PUTMAN. If some provision was made. I don't know as there is any arrangement for sending them there without any commitment.

SENATOR NASH. Wouldn't it seem possible to you that some arrangement could be made?

DR. PUTMAN. I should think it might be done.

REPRESENTATIVE KEEFE. I would like to ask, if you please, sir, if in your judgment, it would not be better to send a person with a nervous breakdown to an insane asylum?

DR. PUTMAN. Well, I think, of course, it would be, without doubt, a great deal better to send them to the Boston Insane Hospital than it is to send them to the jail or the Tombs. But it would be a great deal better still to send them to an intermediate place where they could be examined more carefully and their exact status determined.

DR. BRIGGS. I will call upon Dr. Richard C. Cabot, in medical connection with the Boston Chamber of Commerce.

DR. CABOT. Gentlemen, you want first-hand information here. I want to make a plea that you take one minute's walk from this committee room to the city jail and look at it, — and I have not the least doubt that if you do that you will feel that something ought to be done. I am not an alienist, and I have no expert knowledge as to what should be done at the city jail here, which, as I say, I urge you to visit. You will see, of course, a very large assortment of common drunks, and about as close to them as the cages in a circus menagerie, and under about the same conditions, you will find, on certain days, insane people. Now, the conditions at the City Prison seem to me perfectly good for the common drunkards. It is not a question of sentiment; it is a question relating to an insane person who is not as hardened as a common drunkard is to these conditions. I want to say a word as to those physical and mental conditions and their effect upon persons brought into contact with them.

In the first place, as to the physical condition: as Dr. Briggs has said to you, there is a padded cell a little bigger than the table at which you are sitting, with a perfectly plain wooden floor, with no provision for sleeping whatever. There is no mattress in the place, and the police captain who showed me around said it would be impossible to keep a mattress there on account of the collection of vermin that would inhabit it. There is no provision whatever for the passage of urine, for some of these people. If they are able to go out, that is all right, but the majority of them cannot. So much for the more obvious physical side. The exhaustion of the patient, under these conditions, on the physical side is tremendous.

On the mental side, to be confined in this way in a group of cages, with the drunks across the way calling back and forth, carries with it results that can be imagined. One of the officers there said to me, the drunks bothered the insane and the insane bothered the drunks; and I don't wonder. The drunks don't appreciate any difference between themselves and the insane, and they amuse themselves calling back and forth. Now, the terror, the misery of being confined under those conditions, on the physical and mental sides, seems to me such that if you could see those conditions for yourselves, you would have no doubt something ought to be done. That is all I am concerned with. I don't know what ought to be done. The officials of the prisons seem to be of the same opinion. They are doing their best; there is no scandal there; but they don't like the conditions any better than we do.

REPRESENTATIVE KEEFE. What would you suggest would be the best day to visit that prison, sir?

DR. CABOT. I should say Sunday. You get a more miscellaneous collection at that time than at any other time.

REPRESENTATIVE KEEFE. Would you get the same effect on a Monday?

DR. CABOT. I got a fairly good effect on a Monday, but I think Sunday is better.

DR. BRIGGS. Mr. Spring, corporation counsel of the city of Boston.

ARTHUR L. SPRING, ESQ. Mr. Chairman, I am here on behalf of the mayor of Boston. I have only this to say, Mr. Chairman and Gentlemen, that His Honor is in favor of this proposition that is offered by my friend Briggs, who has certainly made an elaborate argument in regard to it. And as I have looked over these two statutes, it seems to me a sensible proposition. The statute of 1908 said, in the first section, that the city shall not hereafter establish any asylum for the care of these people, or be liable for their board or treatment. Then in 1909, as you gentlemen know, by the subsequent statute, chapter 504, the last part of section 1, it was provided that no county, city or town shall establish insane institutions for them or be liable for their board, care or treatment. And that statute went further; it extended the provisions of chapter 613, 1908, beyond mere insane, and included, as I understood it, the feeble-minded, epileptics, and persons addicted to the intemperate use of narcotics and stimulants. Now, we seem to be in this position: the State has taken our hospital; it has paid us no money for it; and it doesn't seem to establish this new institution, — of course, I don't know why, — that is not for me to comment upon. But two years have passed since its authorization, and there is no insane hospital to take the place of ours, or no new hospital in addition to the Boston plant which they have bought. Now, if this condition of affairs is correctly described, it seems to me there ought to be some temporary arrangement for the care of these people. The financial situation is not one that would particularly favor Boston; it is practically a stand-off; the amount we pay of this $20,000, coming round to our third of the State tax, would about offset what we pay now. That is to say, we have got to pay about a third of this $20,000 if you appropriate anything; now we have to pay the expense of these people down at the different institutions, — so that what we would save on the one hand we would have to pay on the other. So it is not a selfish move. It is one which, except for the ingenuity of my friend Dr. Copp, except for that, it would seem to be a condition calling for this change. If we are not to have this new hospital for some years yet, the city, having entered into this arrangement fairly, should not be required to put people who are temporarily insane into the criminal institutions of the city, but the State should supplement its great work of establishing a new hospital by giving us this detention room.

THE CHAIRMAN. *The present conditions are exactly the same as they were at the time of the taking over of the Boston Insane Hospital?*

MR. SPRING. *As far as these people are concerned, I understand so.*

THE CHAIRMAN. The city of Boston did not take any steps towards relieving the same conditions as at present exist before the State took the institution? These same conditions existed? That is, the patients were taken down to the city jail, — Deer Island?

MR. SPRING. Oh, we had no observation hospital, no.

THE CHAIRMAN. That is, just the same as now —

MR. SPRING. I think they were in the same place then as they are now, Mr. Chairman.

DR. OWEN COPP. As Mr. Spring must go and raise a legal point, may I ask one or two questions to make that clear? If I understand you, you say that the city to-day legally has no right to take care of this class?

MR. SPRING. As I read that statute, it would seem so to me.

DR. COPP. Well, you, of course, are speaking as the legal representative of the city. Now, is that a fact, in your opinion?

MR. SPRING. Perhaps I better read it again.

SENATOR NASH. I would like to ask Dr. Copp a question right here. Didn't you tell me last year that you thought the city didn't have any right to take care of its insane?

DR. COPP. No. I don't think so.

REPRESENTATIVE KEEFE. I would like to ask, if you please, sir, if the assertions in the newspaper are true, — the assertions that about 45 per cent of those arrested for drunkenness are not residents of the city of Boston?

MR. SPRING. I am at home on that. I prepared this for the hearing in the next room, but it will do here just as well. Forty-eight per cent of the cases of drunkenness in the city of Boston are nonresidents, and there are now in our island hotels 338 nonresidents.

DR. COPP. May I follow that up just a moment? Because it is a matter of law. You don't make that statement that the city has not at present a right to do this work? You are not clear upon that point, that is —

MR. SPRING. Mr. Chairman, the statute says that no county, city or town shall establish or maintain an institution for these people, or be liable for their board, care or treatment. Of course that does not say, Mr. Chairman, that we shall not support them. It says that we shall not be liable for their care or treatment. That is to say, if we are taking care of them now, we are doing it voluntarily. That would seem to me the situation.

DR. COPP. Waive that point and say that description included this class — which I think is questionable. Suppose it did, that there was a direct, absolute prohibition against doing that work, in that act. Is it then illegal for the city to do it?

MR. SPRING. I don't know as I would go as far as to say that it is illegal; but we are not obliged to do it. Waive the legality of it; we are doing a thing which no one else seems to undertake. I don't care whether it is legal or illegal, we are doing it, and doing it in the face of an uncompleted duty on the part of the State, as it seems to me. I don't use the word "duty" harshly, but I can't see — without knowing the history of this agitation at all — I can't see why the State should not go ahead and provide these accommodations and take care of these people and prevent this situation, which we have voluntarily undertaken. I don't see why, now, when the State is going to take this whole matter into its hands, why it should not take it into its hands.

The CHAIRMAN. Mr. Spring, this one hundred or two people, that means one hundred or two hundred, that you are taking care of now?

MR. SPRING. Whatever it amounts to — it may be fifty or five hundred.

THE CHAIRMAN. You don't want to tell this committee that those are practically insane or feeble-minded or mentally incapacitated, but simply drunks, you claim?

MR. SPRING. Oh, no, Mr. Chairman. The committeeman over here asked me a question and I answered it. I am not talking about drunken cases or people afflicted with any particular disease at all. I don't know just the number down there of the insane. I said one hundred or two.

DR. COPP. Supposing that was a prohibition. Supposing there had been subsequent legislation which gave that specific right to the State, would the city then have a right?

MR. SPRING. That would make a difference.

DR. COPP. That general law, I may say, was signed by the Governor, June 12, the day after special permission was given for the city to do these acts. That gives a special right.

MR. SPRING. I said, "barring the ingenuity of my friend Dr. Copp."

DR. COPP. Barring the facts.

DR. BRIGGS. I would like to say that my friends here, many of them, have got to go, and I wish we could confine ourselves to the State. The bill provides the State should do this and not the city, or any other person or institution. If this other question is to be argued, I would like to have it argued after the question of the State taking up the matter has been discussed.

I would like to call upon Bishop Lawrence of the Eastern Diocese of Massachusetts for a few words.

BISHOP LAWRENCE. I have very few words to say. The situation is this: a person walking the streets is suddenly bewildered by a nervous breakdown — some phase of insanity. As I understand it, there is nothing to be done but for the police to take that person into keeping and place that person only where the police can place him. He is thereby held, — it might be for eight, ten, twelve or forty-eight hours. We can appreciate the frame of mind in which the person might be, — the critical situation into which he might be brought under those conditions. Now, as I understand it, it is to enable the State Board of Insanity to take that person and put him under proper supervision until he can be handled skillfully that this bill provides, that, as I understand it, is the situation, — and only, perhaps, for the next two or three or four years, until the State Board of Insanity is able to make proper regulations for it. Now, I don't know anything about the regulations of the State and the city, or anything of that sort; all that I am here for is to ask that those cases, — it may be a hundred, it may be fifteen hundred, — in the next three years, should be carefully considered, and that the Board of Health should be put in a position where they may be taken care of with the consideration which belongs to citizens of the State. I think that is all I have to say.

DR. BRIGGS. Prof. William T. Sedgwick of the Institute of Technology, who is about writing a "History of Science," and is familiar with these subjects.

PROF. WILLIAM T. SEDGWICK.   I was, Mr. Chairman, for some years chairman of the Pauper Trustees, the Pauper Institutions' Trustees of the City of Boston, and in that capacity had occasion to see more or less of this abuse which the bill before us undertakes to correct.   Year after year reports were made, if I remember correctly, by our Board and other Boards, urging the city of Boston to take cognizance of this abuse, and speaking with a good deal of knowledge in regard to it.   Nothing, however, was done, and I suppose that the petitioners for this bill, feeling that now that we have a new order of things concerning the treatment and care of the insane, something may be done rather quickly under this bill, — I say, supposing that people have that in mind, I am very glad to appear here and to testify to the need of action and to the practicability of it.   I think it is simply a question of giving the State Board of Insanity authority and money to do the work.   Just what authority and just how much money, I do not know.   It is quite out of my line, — more out of my line to-day than it was ten years ago.   But I haven't the least doubt there is here an abuse which is a disgrace to the State of Massachusetts, and that it ought to be terminated as quickly as possible.   As I understand it, no great sum would be required.   It might even happen that these people could be taken care of in one of the existing asylums in the neighborhood, and that no great length of time would be necessary, because the new Psychopathic Hospital is likely to be ready, I understand, in a couple of years or less.   That is all I have to say.

DR. BRIGGS.   I might say here that Mr. Augustus Hemenway left because he could not longer remain, and said he would like to have his name put down in favor of the bill.   A representative, also, of the Massachusetts Civic League has left word that the council of the Massachusetts Civic League passed a vote endorsing this bill.   I would like to call upon Mr. Thorpe, the President of the Massachusetts Prison Association, who comes in contact with these people.

MR. J. G. THORPE.   The official connection which Dr. Briggs has alluded to, and the experience it has given me, simply gives me a right to say that the present places of detention of the city of Boston, or, in fact, of the State in general, are entirely unfit places to send insane people.   The fact that they are sent is recognized as inhuman and disgraceful by many States of the Union; it has been so recognized by the State of Massachusetts; and I don't see why the cure should be postponed a day longer than it is necessary.   I simply stand up to be counted, and my experience, as I say, gives me a right to be heard upon the subject.

DR. BRIGGS.   I will call upon the Rev. Dr. Elwood Worcester of Emmanuel Church, whose work brings him into touch with the people whom this bill concerns.

REV. DR. ELWOOD WORCESTER.   We come in contact with a large number of persons of this character, — that is to say, with persons who may be called incipiently insane, or with persons who are threatened with insanity.   A certain number of those persons are suffering from true mental disease and will probably become incurably insane.   A large proportion of them, however, are not of that class; they are suffering from conditions that are temporary, and by kindness, by mental care, by occupation, by rest, and by good advice, a great many of those persons can be saved. We saw that very plainly after the Chelsea fire, where a great many persons, owing to the experiences they had gone through, were in a distorted state of mind, and by means such as I have mentioned, all those persons were saved from insane asylums. I am, therefore, very strongly in favor of Dr. Briggs' bill, first, on account of its humanity, and second, because of its economy to the State.

DR. BRIGGS. Mrs. Barrett Wendell, president of the Colonial Dames.

MRS. BARRETT WENDELL. I really didn't feel that I ought to take your time, but I should like to represent many women in the Commonwealth to say how deep an interest we feel in this matter, and how truly Massachusetts has always stood for humanity, and that we have got to stand for that now, and that we can't let such a thing as that go on.

DR. BRIGGS. Dr. McCollom, superintendent of the City Hospital, will perhaps say, in a very few words, why the city of Boston can't, at present, take care of these people.

DR. JOHN H. McCOLLOM. I am heartily in favor of this bill. Certainly it is a bill that should pass, there is no question about that. Some little time ago it was suggested that the City Hospital should take charge of these things. That is manifestly impossible. In the first place, we haven't the room; in the next place, the class of patients we have there would be injured by these other patients; and third, the patients themselves would not derive as much benefit as they would to be sent to a different institution. It would be just as logical to say we should care for cases of smallpox in the City Hospital as to send persons insane or in the incipient stage there. It seems to me there is no question about it, and that the Board of Insanity ought to take care of these cases.

DR. BRIGGS. I would like to call on Mrs. Henry Parkman, who is at present secretary of the Municipal League.

MRS. HENRY PARKMAN. I am not here as a representative of the women; I have not been delegated to attend this hearing. I can only say that personally I, as of course any one with humanity would, feel that it is a bill which should be passed.

DR. BRIGGS. Miss Higgins of the Associated Charities.

MISS HIGGINS. I am the secretary of the Associated Charities, and my society is in favor of it. Don't let medievalism stay with us any longer.

THE CHAIRMAN. Let all those in favor of the bill rise.

DR. BRIGGS. I would like to have a few words from Dr. Evans.

DR. ALBERT EVANS. One hundred years ago this same discussion was going forward in Massachusetts. Dr. James Jackson and Dr. John C. Warren of Boston called attention, in a circular letter, to the need of a hospital for the insane; in these words I quote from the letter of August 20, 1810. "It has appeared very desirable to a number of respectable gentlemen, that a hospital for the reception of lunatics and other sick, be established in this town." What became of that letter? It was the germ from which grew that great and splendid institution, the Massachusetts General Hospital, where there is, night and day, ever-ready aid for all who may be sick or injured in body, while the victim of mental sickness, apparent or real, goes into jail awaiting the movements of soulless committees. One hundred years ago this good seed was planted in Massachusetts. Anything wrong with the soil of Massachusetts, that she could not grow a perfect plant? She has not even grown a hedge about her borders, under the shade of which the insane can find *immediate* relief. Since that time, so long ago, the seed has been sown again and again. A perfect product has not been harvested in Massachusetts. Gentlemen, why are we here, *pleading* for a thing *so* righteous, *so* humane, *so* urgent? We are come here as the spokesmen of those who by disease or injury are incapable of intelligently expressing their own needs. Disregarding, for the moment, the question of our moral duty to those sick ones, the actual results of immediate care and treatment in incipient insanity pays well the State that gives it. A mind may merely "slip a cog" and if taken hold of at once, become geared up into a normal running once more. Gentlemen, the State owes a solemn duty in this matter, and there comes a time in the life of every son and servant of the State when duty becomes high privilege. If it is the duty of the State to care for these unfortunates, it is her duty to care for them in every particular. What stands in the way of the enactment of this bill? Who is it that does not endorse it? Does it lack the endorsement of the State Board of Insanity? Is the chairman of the State Board of Insanity here to-day advocating the rightness and justice and expediency of this bill? I do not know. But this I do know, that in the light of truth and the *facts*, all sane disinterested men endorse this bill. And what are the facts? I'll tell you. Buoyed by hope we have lived on promises. Promises of better things to come. These promises have lacked the assurance and conviction of honest purpose, and politics blocks the wheel of progress. One hundred years! A long incubation period! It's time something was hatched.

THE CHAIRMAN. Are you perfectly satisfied, Dr. Briggs, that you have had all the time necessary.

DR. BRIGGS. Mr. Merriam, the editor of "The Watchman," has one word to say.

REV. EDMUND F. MERRIAM. I simply wish to enforce the point made by Dr. Evans. When I spoke to Dr. Briggs, it hadn't been made, that is, the economy to the State. Of course, I agree with all that has been said as to the humanity and the necessity, and the fact that the State has already provided for this thing in the future, showing that it ought to be provided for to-day. But the special point I wish to make is that from the statistics of the hospitals for the insane in the State at present, it appears that about 70 per cent of the cures of the insane are of those who are taken at once or within three months of the first symptoms of insanity. So that, as a matter of economy to the State, it is wise for them to take hold of these cases at once, and the sooner the better. A day, as any insanity expert, Dr. Briggs or any other, knows, a day may be fatal and may cause the State a life-long care, whereas prompt care might perhaps suffice.

THE CHAIRMAN. You would be in favor of establishing this kind of institution all over the State of Massachusetts just as well as in the city of Boston?

MR. MERRIAM. I am in favor of taking care of the insane, or of those who give any symptoms of insanity. It is a case of utmost necessity.

DR. BRIGGS. I would like to have you ask again that all those in favor of the bill should rise.

THE CHAIRMAN. All those in favor will rise.

Of the thirty-two present, all arose excepting Dr. Copp, Dr. Wentworth and Mr. Whittemore, members of the State Board of Insanity.

THE CHAIRMAN. We will now listen to any remonstrants to this bill.

DR. COPP. Well, I want to say something, but I suppose if you asked me — I am talking in my individual capacity — if you asked me to say "Amen" to substantially everything that has been said, I should do it with both hands raised. We agree as to the need, and substantially as to the conditions, and the only difference is as to the way of doing it, and whose duty it is to do it. Now, as to that point, I am not in any sense taking a position opposed to it. As a State officer I must state to you certain principles of law which must be considered, and then, if this committee and the Legislature wish to have the State Board of Insanity do this, we will do it, and do it cheerfully, and just as quickly as we possibly can. There shan't be a moment's delay. Now, the facts are simply these, that is, admitting everything that has been said here, substantially everything that has been said, — now comes the question, and that has not been discussed at all, how are we going to do it, as the law stands now? Mind you, if we changed the law so that it becomes the duty of the State, why, then, I don't say that I would not support it, I am inclined to think I would, but we have got to deal with this just as it is now, and if there is a violation of principle we must discuss that. And that principle is simply this, — where does the State's duty begin to-day, according to law, and where does the municipality's obligation end? Now, if you will read the statute, it says all these classes, epileptics, etc., who pass into a State institution, into the institution maintained and controlled by the State — those are substantially the terms — that is where it begins. Now, if we, as State Board, recommend anything, it must be in harmony with existing law, or we must come out frankly and discuss why we should change existing law. Now, if we should do this thing purely and simply and alone by itself for the city of Boston, we must do it for Fall River, Springfield, Lawrence, Lowell and all of the cities. Now I am not saying that that is not the best thing to do. I wish that it might be done adequately, and I wish we could put it on a broad basis, and I believe I should stand with these people if we were discussing that issue. But we are discussing something which violates existing law without fully and carefully discussing the principle of it. Now, you will say, that is inconsistent with the fact that you are going to do this work in the Psychopathic Hospital. But when you stop to analyze that, you will see that that is not so. Why do these people go to the State Prison and to the House of Detention to-day? Why do they go? Simply because of the delay in making connections with the State institutions. The State institution is so far away that from a practical standpoint they go to the City Prison. The moment that the State establishes right here, as it proposes to in the Psychopathic Hospital, an institution that will provide for them, they go to that, and the State is doing that work and is glad to do it. We could do it with the existing hospital if it were right here near where they could go to it. The condition for years has persisted because it was not practicable. Now, as regards whose duty it is to do it, or, rather, — I think I have discussed that point enough, — we come to the question of how soon we can do it. Can it be done any faster than we are doing it? We are hurrying as fast as we can to build a psychopathic hospital. It will probably take a couple of years before we shall get into it. We shall get into it just as soon as we can. Now, this matter of temporary provision has been discussed for years and years and years. It was discussed two years ago, and the situation was just as acute then, and that Boston bill was passed. And so it has been to my personal knowledge, it has been discussed for ten or fifteen years before that by the Medical Society. Everybody is interested in it, recognizing the need, and the question is how to do it, and nobody has found a way how to do it. It may be it is the State's duty and it is best for the State to do it. If so, let us take up that question.

SENATOR NASH. Well, Doctor, we went all over that ground last year. Now, what was the ground upon which you came here and asked for this money, and asked us to put this thing all in the hands of the Governor and Council? What were the grounds? You were the first man who ever brought to my attention the wrong imprisonment of these people in the Tombs and in the jail. You came before us and said that was the reason you wanted this (psychopathic) observation hospital.

DR. COPP. You will qualify that by saying "one of the reasons."

SENATOR NASH. Well, it was the chief reason that moved the committee.

DR. COPP. I don't want to minimize the importance of it. I recognize it now just as I did then.

SENATOR NASH. You seemed to think then that the observation hospital could do it. Now, is it —

DR. COPP. At that very time this very thing was discussed. Dr. Briggs knows it. We discussed it, and on every occasion I took exactly the position I am taking now.

SENATOR NASH. How can you do it with your new hospital which you say is to be done in — how many years?

DR. COPP. I should say two years would be a fair time. I honestly think that, though I can't guarantee it.

SENATOR NASH. Well, you don't honestly think that, do you?

DR. COPP. I do honestly think it.

SENATOR NASH. I thought you told me it might take three.

DR. COPP. Three years from the time it passed as a law. I don't say three years from the present time. You said it would take more than three years, I said it might take more than three.

SENATOR NASH. The thing that moved the committee last year, Doctor, is the very thing which these people to-day have asked for. You told us the abuse, not in the officers, but in the conditions, and you said these things ought to be stopped, that these persons ought not to be sent to the Tombs; and you said you proposed to have an institution here for that purpose, one for the metropolitan purposes, and then down in Fall River, and down over the State. You said we ought to have one here, and you said, "We will commence with the metropolitan district."

DR. COPP. You know we discussed various problems — lots of problems.

SENATOR NASH. Not so many but what my mind is clear on that.

DR. COPP. It is easy to confuse the persons responsible for certain ideas. I think, I can prove that I am perfectly consistent in my position when we talked of the Psychopathic Hospital. That is the hospital unit of our State insane system. I hope we shall come in time to doing for the whole State what we are to do with Boston.

SENATOR NASH. Doctor, then for Heaven's sake, do tell us, — and if I am so dull I couldn't understand last year, it is too bad the district has sent me for five years to represent them, — what under the sun, what reason you gave for asking the State to appropriate over half a million dollars?

DR. COPP. We have always maintained, Senator, that there were three main objects for this hospital; that it was a hospital which was a necessary part of our State system; that it had three main objects — the first object of that is to give adequate treatment to our acute cases, and to adequately investigate causes and methods of treatment of the insane.

SENATOR NASH. Then you really tried to work this other thing, to make us establish a million-dollar hospital out here to educate doctors?

DR. COPP. No.

SENATOR NASH. Yes, you did, too.

DR. COPP. That we maintain existed. The second point is, if we are going to cure and prevent mental disease, we have to do it through our general practitioners and family physicians. Now, that object, which is a paramount object, we shall attain when we send out practitioners and family physicians who have some practical knowledge of mental disease, as they see it at the medical schools, as they are taught in surgery and general medicine. We shan't get that result until we have done that. Then the third one was that we shall be here, and we shall obliterate that delay between the person going to that institution and the distance, — the difficulty of getting there, — and as a result of that location we shall do this work, which is very important work; and I entirely agree that it is one of the most important, perhaps the most important, but in matter of principle is not controlling. Now, an effort, Senator, by anybody to place the Board of Insanity and myself in an inconsistent position in this matter will fail. We have done as much, we are willing to do as much, as any living being.   And I believe that our record shows that we have done as much; and we are not letting up one particle; we are just where we stood from the beginning; we shall do it if the Legislature brings up that issue, straight and fair, that it is the State's duty to do this. I am inclined to think I should stand right with that, that the State can do it, but when it does it, it shall do it in a consistent way, if we support it, for Boston, for Fall River, for Worcester, for Lawrence, for Lowell.[1]

SENATOR NASH.   Why didn't you recommend that when you recommended this psychopathic hospital?   Why didn't you recommend one for Fall River and Worcester and all over the State?

DR. COPP.   We discussed that for the future.   The time has not arrived yet.   The demand is not great enough.   The question of taking care of the patients who come into the hands of the police, that is initial work where you have not established insanity.   That is another point that is a part of it. But the Psychopathic Hospital embraces this and embraces the others, and we have got to make those distinctions.   Now, as a practical matter —

REPRESENTATIVE KEEFE.   Doctor, I would like to ask you a question, and the reason is, I am a new member of the committee and am trying to get all the light on it I can.   I would like to ask you, Doctor, if you don't think the time has arrived for this sort of work?

DR. COPP.   If the State will do it.   There are needs which exist to-day which we recognize, which the public recognize, which can be met, and there are those which cannot be met just now.   Now, it is a matter of good judgment to do the thing you can do and move on.   If we ask you to do the impossible and to couple that with the possible, we shall miss the possible and the impossible also.   I think if you will follow the history of the last ten years you will find that the State Board of Insanity has not been backward in demanding things for the insane.   We have spent money enough for that, and done things for that.   We have moved as fast as we dared.   We would move faster if there was a public demand for it.   We have ten things to do —

REPRESENTATIVE KEEFE.   Now, I would like to ask this question.   Don't you believe that this sort of treatment, if it could be furnished now, right away, immediately, would decrease the number of inmates in the institutions throughout the State?

DR. COPP.   When you come to your hospital for nervous breakdowns, you will find me saying everything I can.   And when the Lexington proposition failed, I was the sorriest man to have it fail, and as soon as it can be revived with any possibility of carrying it out, you will find me right at the front with it.   If you discuss this question of taking these cases all over the State, and

---

[1] Special report of the State Board of Insanity, Senate Document No. 358, 1908, says: "Prolonged detention of the insane should be guarded by strict compliance with every technicality of the law; but temporary detention for a few days, to prevent recourse to jail and lockup during the necessary delay of legal procedure, should be governed by the principles of the quarantine. The Psychopathic Hospital should have authority to receive mental patients for a few days without formality." They further say: "It is not less discreditable to the Commonwealth than to the city that one-third of Boston's insane are lodged temporarily in the City Prison and House of Detention."

establish the principle, you will find me fighting hard for that. When it comes as a State policy, to put it forward as a practical and immediate thing, then my judgment does not agree with you. I don't believe we can do it. We are asking this morning to take 700 insane from Tewksbury and provide new quarters; we are asking this year, with plans and specifications, we are asking for an 800-bed increase, in order to have facilities for this work.

REPRESENTATIVE KEEFE. Excuse me for breaking in on you, but I would like to ask this question: The Massachusetts General Hospital was built first in Boston before we had others built in the State. Now, down here, they examine the tuberculosis patients before they send them to Rutland — that is, temporarily.

DR. COPP. We believe persons afflicted with mental disease should be treated just as persons afflicted with any other disease are treated; they should be taken in and have separate wards for temporary observation. We believe that is infinitely better than for the State to do this, but don't believe it can be done now. We have been trying with all the force of the medical profession in Boston for that thing and pushing it, and haven't made the slightest progress. Now the only ray of light in this whole situation was when the Board of Insanity and all the other medical men took up this problem, and put forth the Psychopathic Hospital as established correctly in principle. It is the only thing that has brought that within a gunshot of accomplishment. Now that is two years away. I wish it was not one day away.

SENATOR NASH. Doctor, I wish you would tell this committee frankly just what you asked. I want you to tell this committee absolutely what this Psychopathic Hospital has been established for in the face of the fact that you say — and said last year — of course, everything we say you said last year you say you didn't, or you have some way of changing it.

DR. COPP. You didn't mean that.

SENATOR NASH. Yes, I do, absolutely. We all have poor memories — I have, no doubt; you may have a chance to put me in the insane asylum.

THE CHAIRMAN. You will put me in one if you don't get through this thing.

SENATOR NASH. I want to know what this institution that is going to cost the State $1,000,000, — what it has been established for, *in a few words*. There is no need of taking a long time to tell us.

DR. COPP. It is a matter of law. In the first place, the Legislature has appropriated $600,000.

SENATOR NASH. At your request.

DR. COPP. Yes, to buy the land to build the buildings, to equip a hospital. Now, then, that is to take care of — the bill states — it is for the first care and observation of mental cases. It is for the short treatment of the acute and curable cases. It is for research into the causes and results of incipient insanity.

REPRESENTATIVE HOLMAN. I have sat very quietly through this delay. I want to say to the Doctor that I came here in a judicial frame of mind, and as far as I have been able to make up my mind so far, I have heard the petitioners very fairly, and have heard Dr. Copp until he got taken off on a tangent; and the Doctor, if I understand him aright, thoroughly agrees with the purpose of this bill. Now, that is as far as he got before bull-baiting. Now, I would like to allow him a couple of minutes to carry along my mind logically as to the exact reasons he opposes the bill.

DR. COPP. *There are parts of the bill I do not oppose.* It is only on the question of practicability that I have any question. Now, the first section provides for these cases going directly, as you go to the General Hospital, to this Psychopathic Hospital, — that is, without any formality. That is a very desirable thing. The existing law does not provide for that. If that section can be modified so as to confine the class and confine the work to be done carefully, I don't see why that is not a desirable thing, from my standpoint.

REPRESENTATIVE HOLMAN. That is the first section?

DR. COPP. Yes. Now, let me qualify. In that first section the whole class is referred to. That is, we take in everybody without exception. Mind you, he excepts, but I will deal with that later. It takes in between 40,000 and 50,000 persons under the acute effects of alcohol. Now, of course, this bill does not intend that the whole number shall go to this hospital for diagnosis; he excludes those. I would like to broaden that so as to exclude the cases of delirium tremens and the persons under the acute effects of alcohol, meaning by that drunk. That would leave the mental cases and those cases that have, substantially, been spoken of this morning. But, if you remember, we have always claimed that the alcoholic and the delirium tremens cases would not at this stage be received or treated there.

THE CHAIRMAN. That was the intent.

DR. BRIGGS. I accept that amendment.

REPRESENTATIVE HOLMAN. Does not this first section distinctly say that?

DR. COPP. Yes, we don't differ on that point at all, if we should go further and make it clear that that class of persons shall not go there, except by mistake. In the interest of the patient he ought to go where he will be treated immediately. So that it should be made clear in the statute that he is not to go there for diagnosis; he is to go there directly.

Then that section provides that a person — mind you, it is mandatory — "shall go there." If the friends should come afterwards in order to take them, we should provide for that; and I understand Dr. Briggs would be very glad to have that done. A patient might get there — then it says you shall care for them until they are recovered. That is all right, but I should say "or otherwise suitably provided for." If the friends wanted to take care of them, we would not go against the friends. Making that qualification, I think that first section is eminently desirable.

When you come to the second section there, I should say this — of course the first of May is out of the question — I should think it was out of the question. It certainly, if it is going to be done at all, should be done as soon as it can be done, I don't dissent from that. Who is to do it? The Board of Insanity is not an executive board. The trustees of the hospital are equipped to do this much better, so that the trustees of the hospital should do it under the supervision of the Board, and not the Board directly; that is, if we follow out the analogy of what is done in other cases.

SENATOR PICKFORD.   Is there any reason why the State Board of Insanity cannot recommend to this Board of Trustees, if in your opinion you think that it is really necessary, that provision should be made at the present time for the taking care of these unfortunates for whom I understood last year that everybody that came before us here advocating this measure — and I did for one — did really believe that there was going to be something done long before now?   Is it not possible for the State Board of Insanity at the present time to recommend to the trustees of the hospital, which you mentioned, that they should proceed practically forthwith to do something to take care of a few — I don't expect you are going to take care of every one — but it will show a disposition for taking care of some, and that you intend to do it now?

DR. COPP.   Of course, that comes to the point I have discussed all through — the Board of Insanity is in a position to do exactly what you want.   If you provide means, and the law, the State Board of Insanity will do its level best; if you want the State Board of Insanity to do it, we will if you indicate by law it is your purpose to do this special thing.

SENATOR PICKFORD.   Is it possible for the State Board of Insanity to take part of that money which was appropriated last year for this purpose and proceed?

DR. COPP.   Absolutely not — can't touch it — no law allows the Board of Insanity or any officer of the State to do anything except what has been done.

REPRESENTATIVE HOLMAN.   Have you any objections to section 3?

DR. COPP.   The purpose of this section is all right.   The wording of the section I think you can find difficulty with.

REPRESENTATIVE HOLMAN.   We have struggled through sections 1 and 3, and your opposition is trivial.   Now, won't you try to struggle through the rest of section 2 before I become insane myself?

DR. COPP.   I haven't anything further to say there.   On section 3, of course, I don't know how that could be modified, the intent is to exclude them from penal institutions, which we all want.

DR. BRIGGS.   That section 3 should be modified to exclude the insane now in Bridgewater workhouse, if that is under the head of a penal institution, and at the same time that these people should be taken direct, as soon as it is established, to the temporary or psychopathic hospital rather than that it should be — "taken in twelve hours."   Under this law they can all be taken for twelve hours to the cells.

THE CHAIRMAN.   Taken where?

DR. BRIGGS.   Under section 3, the point has been brought up by the Associated Charities when they endorsed this bill, that it might include the criminal insane in the Bridgewater Hospital, on the ground that that was a penal institution, so that should, perhaps, be excepted.

SENATOR NASH.   Those verbal changes could be made.

DR. BRIGGS. The other matter would be that as soon as this temporary hospital is erected, or, I mean the psychopathic hospital is provided for, or temporary quarters wherever they may be, that people should not be taken directly to the prison and then to the psychopathic or temporary hospital, but to the psychopathic or temporary hospital direct.

REPRESENTATIVE KEEFE. I would like to ask if you feel that you have had the opportunity to present your case here to-day?

DR. BRIGGS. Yes, I think I probably had over twice the number to speak, but I think that enough spoke to convince the committee that there is a demand for the immediate care of these people.

SENATOR PICKFORD. One question I would like to ask Dr. Copp, and that is if it would be possible to amend this bill so that there could be some of that $600,000 taken to provide a temporary hospital.

DR. COPP. It becomes a matter of maintenance, of doing work. If we are going to build the hospital, we need all the money we asked for it, and it would cripple us to take some of that money for this purpose.

REPRESENTATIVE KEEFE. I would like to ask the Doctor, if you please, if you think possibly an arrangement could be made to send them to Foxborough?

DR. COPP. That is too far away — that is the trouble. You see the real difficulty is this: you are getting right into the midst of things. You probably hire a house, and if you have our experience in buying houses, you would probably be held up immediately by protests, and you have got to hear them; and if you start in you will probably have an injunction. This has got to be done right in the midst of the people, and we have had difficulty in getting our location.

REPRESENTATIVE KEEFE. You haven't any place at all to put them now, so I claim any place is better than none, to give them shelter. I am looking for all the information I can get of this, because I am a new member. I want to say that I understand that you have a large number of people in the city of Boston that are here, strangers, and they are taken, for instance, on the sidewalk, and have no place to go. In the city of Fall River or Springfield it is not quite so.

DR. COPP. Not so many, no, sir.

REPRESENTATIVE KEEFE. I am looking for light on this. Why can't you afford a place temporarily right away? I am asking for information.

THE CHAIRMAN. Doctor, of course, we went all over that last year, and the year before. *Why shouldn't some use be made over at Mattapan?*

DR. COPP. We will do everything we can. Every case that comes to us we take. We are very much limited there for provisions. There is tremendous pressure on us. That is why we are asking for so many buildings this year. It is simply a question of room, you know. We are crowded up with patients, and it is hard for us to classify them. We will take everything that comes to us. We never cut out a case that comes to us. We take a lot of emergency cases.

REPRESENTATIVE KEEFE. What is that institution?

THE CHAIRMAN. This is the State institution at Mattapan.

REPRESENTATIVE KEEFE. I didn't know that, Doctor.

DR. COPP. Mr. Whittemore was here and Dr. Howard was to be here, but was called for.

SENATOR PICKFORD. You are empowered by the State Board of Insanity to come here and act for them to-day?

DR. COPP. I am just discussing the matter personally. The *Board of Insanity have not acted on the matter at all.*

THE CHAIRMAN. He is not against the bill as a whole.

DR. COPP. I am simply here to give you, for what it is worth, my ideas on it. It would not be proper for the Board of Insanity to try to influence your action at all, or for me. I would not for a moment. *If it were said that the bill failed because the Board of Insanity was against it, I don't think that would be so.* I never did anything more than I have done this morning.

SENATOR PICKFORD. Then it looks reasonable to me that the State Board of Insanity, as a body, ought to be present.

DR. COPP. The State Board of Insanity is subject to the call of the committee. Other than that it is a question whether it would be proper.

MR. WHITTEMORE. I am a member of the State Board of Insanity. I will answer any question that Senator Pickford wishes to ask, through the chairman.

SENATOR PICKFORD. What I wanted to get at was if the State Board of Insanity has taken any action for or against Senate Bill No. 212?

MR. WHITTEMORE. If I understand Dr. Copp's statement when he began, he said distinctly *he was not here to represent the State Board*, that he was ready as an expert to answer questions and to give any opinion with reference to this bill. Now, directly to your question, I would say that the State Board has not acted upon this bill in any way, and *no one is here in opposition to it.* I supposed from what Dr. Copp had said, that his purpose was constructive rather than destructive. I think he must have conveyed that impression to some members of the committee, at least, if not to all.

SENATOR NASH. Mr. Whittemore, how do you feel — what is your position? He says he speaks simply from an expert point of view. What is your position, and the position of the Board, as to providing temporary quarters? Of course, you as a Board — now, before the committee on insurance, of which I am chairman, the commissioner always appears; we never send for him in the world; and, of course, he makes his suggestions and we listen to him, we tell him no, and he accepts it in a very kindly way. Now, what is your position as regards the practicability of having the *patients carried directly to Mattapan instead of being put into the Tombs? Could not temporary quarters be provided there? Has the Board ever considered it?*

MR. WHITTEMORE. It is a question of expense. I should think the distance would make it a very difficult matter.

SENATOR NASH. As long as the expense does not involve the city, it is a question whether it is practical or not.

MR. WHITTEMORE. I should think it would be a very difficult matter to convey temporary arrests or detentions so far as that.

SENATOR NASH. Senator Pickford understood last year as I did that the chief reason for this psychopathic hospital, which you recommended as a Board, was as a place of observation where persons should be sent instead of sending them to the Tombs, and the chief lever for that bill, Senator Pickford and I understood, was the incarcerating of the insane patients and incipient cases in the Tombs. Now, as far as I can see, you are not planning for it now in your new hospital.

MR. WHITTEMORE. Oh, yes.

SENATOR NASH. I understood you, Dr. Copp, the day we talked downstairs, that did not necessarily imply that an officer had the right to carry them —

DR. COPP. That is the point I made here. We would like that provision in the first bill, to make it obligatory to take them there. That is our desire. Now, they can be received on a physician's certificate, but it is not obligatory.

SENATOR NASH. It ought to be obligatory.

DR. COPP. We surely agree with you.

SENATOR PICKFORD. Does this bill cover the deficiency in the bill of last year?

DR. COPP. It simply means this: this is in the hands of the police of the city of Boston, and this makes it obligatory that they should take this class of cases there rather than to the City Prison.

SENATOR NASH. This bill makes it so, but yours of last year does not, as I understand it. *Why couldn't you have them go to Mattapan until you get the hospital ready?*

DR. COPP. We will do everything we possibly can do, it is our attitude. I think it has always been found impracticable to get them over there. We do it in a good many cases. We had 70 emergency cases last year.

THE CHAIRMAN. What is the length of time it takes to go from the center of the city out to Mattapan?

DR. COPP. It is a $5 coach ride. That is what it means. That is the regular fare, to get a coach. They would probably do it cheaper than that.

DR. BRIGGS. What would be the difference, taking them out to the Psychopathic Hospital and taking them to Mattapan now?

THE CHAIRMAN. Yes, what would it cost to take them there?

DR. COPP. The distance out is about twenty minutes.

DR. BRIGGS. It is just seven minutes in an automobile from one place to the other.

DR. COPP. How far is it from the Psychopathic Hospital to the city?

DR. BRIGGS. I didn't notice. We went from one to the other. It doesn't seem to me that is an objection. It seems to me there are nothing but objections to this bill, as to taking care of these insane people, — nothing but obstacles put in by the State Board of Insanity, or whoever represents it, — for the continual piling up of our chronic insane; and no one comes forward and says, for the State Board of Insanity, "We will help you all we can to take care of these people." They are the ones to do it, as they know.

REPRESENTATIVE CLIFF. Mr. Chairman, I move we adjourn.

The motion was adopted, and the hearing adjourned. The following letters were received just before or after the hearing from Miss Mason and Mrs. Henry Parkman.

1 WALNUT STREET, BOSTON.

DEAR DR. BRIGGS: — Pray pardon my delay in answering your note about the bill you are presenting. I am much interested in it and fully believe in its object.

Sincerely yours,

ELLEN F. MASON.

30 COMMONWEALTH AVENUE,
Boston, February 22, 1910.

DEAR DR. BRIGGS: — Thanks for your letter. I was deeply interested in the hearing. In hearing the testimony I became, however, anxious that someone should dwell upon the necessity of temporary or examination stations being under the same control as the insane hospitals, for the reasons that connection could thus be quickly made without red tape, and the whole field be under the supervising eye of the State. It should be done in every city, as the State has assumed the care of the insane, and I suppose the Psychopathic Hospital will be a State affair.

Truly yours,

FRANCES PARKMAN.

FEBRUARY 23, 1910.

DEAR VERNON: — The hearing seemed to go very well and I hope some good will come of it. There were certainly a good many distinguished people present.

Truly yours,

AUGUSTUS HEMENWAY.

The Rev. Elwood Worcester of the Emmanuel Church wrote:

FEBRUARY 23, 1910.

DEAR DR. BRIGGS: — I thought your bill was admirably prepared and presented, and I hoped that the men and women who spoke for it would produce an impression on the committee. I cannot understand the attitude of the State Board of Insanity, unless it is a mere professional jealousy.

I shall continue to speak on this matter whenever I have the opportunity. Believe me,

Yours sincerely,

ELWOOD WORCESTER.

DR. JAMES J. PUTNAM

A friend of the mentally ill, who during
his life supported all progressive measures for them

109 MARLBOROUGH STREET, February 22, 1910.

DEAR DR. BRIGGS: — My heart and mind will always serve as an ever-ready aid to any cause that is right and just.

In a quiet way my activity in this matter will continue until the objects of your (our) bill are within reach.

Yours very truly,

ALBERT EVANS.

Dr. G. Alder Blumer, superintendent of the Butler Hospital, Providence, Rhode Island, under date of February 23, 1910, wrote:

DEAR DR. BRIGGS: — I am very much interested in your bill. It is a long step in the right direction and I hope it will become a law. The words "in the same manner as other persons afflicted with other diseases are taken to the Massachusetts General Hospital" are happy in so far as they convict insanity as a disease and furnish a justification for the act.

I am

Yours very faithfully,

G. ALDER BLUMER.

On February 24, 1910, Dr. Putman of the Harvard Medical School wrote:

DEAR DR. BRIGGS: — I sincerely hope that your bill will pass. I cannot see why the State should oppose it.

Yours sincerely,

JAMES J. PUTMAN.

The Rev. E. A. Horton of the Unitarian Association, pastor of the Second Church and chaplain of the State Senate, wrote:

FEBRUARY 23, 1910.

DEAR DR. BRIGGS: — I was not able to get to the hearing Monday, but I read the reports carefully. Possibly I can do more for the cause by talking with Senators Evans and Nash, who are part of my "flock." It is evident that you have a righteous reform in hand, and I thank you for calling my attention to it. The attitude of the Board is too much, alas, the way of commissions and boards. Success to your efforts.

Sincerely yours,

EDWARD A. HORTON.

The "Boston Transcript" said:

Dr. Owen Copp of the State Board of Insanity opposed the bill. He said the only difference is as to who is to take care of it (the Psychopathic Hospital). . . . There was more or less sharp colloquy between Senator Nash and Dr. Copp, the Senator expressing the view that the State Board of Insanity is too exacting and too dictatorial in its administration.

Mr. Hartman, secretary of the Massachusetts Civic League, seemed confused at this time, as his letters showed, and it was difficult to know just where he stood.

Following the hearing, conferences were held to perfect the bill and put it in such shape as to be acceptable to the Legislature, with the result that Senate Bill No. 274 was introduced by Senator Pickford on March 3, 1910, as a revision of my bill, No. 212. This bill was immediately reported unanimously by the Committee of Public Charitable Institutions.

SENATE   .   .   .   . No. 274

The Commonwealth of Massachusetts

AN ACT

Relative to Persons suffering from Certain Mental and Other Disorders or Diseases in the City of Boston

Be it enacted by the Senate and House of Representatives in General Court assembled, and by the authority of the same, as follows:

SECTION 1. All persons suffering from the disorders hereinafter referred to, now under arrest or who may come under the care and protection of the police of the city of Boston, and who, owing to lack of suitable buildings or wards, are at present placed in the City Prison, the House of Detention or the House of Correction at Deer Island, pending a medical examination and transference, shall be taken directly to the Psychopathic Hospital for examination when said hospital has been completed and is ready for the reception of patients, in the same manner as other persons afflicted with other diseases are taken to the Massachusetts General Hospital. If, after examination, the physician in charge of the Psychopathic Hospital decides the case to be one of delirium tremens or drunkenness, he shall not be obliged to admit the patient to said hospital, but otherwise said hospital shall admit and observe or care for all persons suffering from delirium, mental confusion or delusions and hallucinations until such persons can be transferred to the hospitals or institutions appropriate in each particular case, unless the patient should recover before such transfer is made.

SECTION 2. From and after the first day of May in the current year and until such time as a psychopathic hospital shall be completed and ready to receive persons suffering from the disorders referred to in section one, the State Board of Insanity shall provide at the Boston State Hospital suitable temporary quarters for receiving and giving medical care and treatment to all persons suffering from sudden delirium, mental disorders or kindred conditions, to which quarters shall be sent directly all such persons who are at present placed in the City Prison, House of Detention or House of Correction at Deer Island, pending medical examination and transference.

SECTION 3. On and after the first day of May in the current year no person suffering from mental confusion, mania, delirium, hallucinations or delusions shall hereafter be harbored or confined in any penal institution within the city of Boston for a period exceeding twelve hours.

The "Boston Advertiser" of March 5 said:

The aftermath of the friction between the Boards of Charity and Insanity, and the reflections on the delinquency of the Insanity Board in failing to take advantage with expedition of the act of a year ago for a psychopathic hospital is seen in the unanimous report of the Committee on Public Charitable Institutions. This report requires suitable quarters to be provided in the Boston State Hospital by May 1 for persons arrested under suspicion of insanity, and prohibiting the incarceration, after May 1, of any such persons in any cell or police station or the City Prison for more than twelve hours. This is reported on the petition of Dr. L. Vernon Briggs.

As the bill progressed, Mary Morton Kehew, who had been a staunch friend, wrote on March 10:

I congratulate you on the success which seems to be not only "in sight" but reasonably assured!

On March 7, 1910, the bill passed the Senate and went to the House, receiving no support from the State Board of Insanity.

The "Boston Traveler" on March 8 said:

Dr. Briggs stated to-day that he had received sufficient assurance to cause him to believe that the anticipations of the past few years are about to be realized.

On March 16, 1910, I received the following letter:

DEAR SIR: — Mr. Pickford of the State Senate has asked me to request you to meet him, if possible, to-morrow, Thursday morning, at 10.30 o'clock, in the Senate Smoking Room. The House Committee on Bills in the Third Reading has made a new draft of the Psychopathic Hospital bill, and Mr. Pickford and Dr. Copp would like to go over it with you. They will come to my office, Room No. 356.

Sincerely yours,

H. C. MERWIN,
Clerk of the Committee on Bills, Third Reading.

This was quite a surprise, and I later understood that a similar notification was equally surprising to Dr. Copp, who had had an executive session with the Committee on Bills in the Third Reading and had made some distinct changes in the bill, which it was possibly presumed might go through without my knowledge of the alterations. I reported, in answer to the above letter, to the State House, where I found Senators Pickford and Nash awaiting me. Dr. Copp did not seem anxious to meet with us, but when he did, Mr. Nash put some questions very plainly to him and he acknowledged having had a hand in the re wording of the bill. The interview between them was sharp and personal. Senator Nash later said that he believed this interview influenced Dr. Copp's retirement from the State.

Senator Nash, Senator Pickford and I then took the bill and changed it to meet the wishes of the Committee on the Third Reading without killing the original bill, which I believe would have been the case but for this conference.

Several people tried to interest Grafton D. Cushing, speaker of the Massachusetts House of Representatives, in the cause, but he was very careful not to commit himself either way.

Roger Walcott, a member of the Legislature, was in the same class as Grafton Cushing. It was difficult for me to tell whether he was working with the State Board or was remaining neutral. In answer to a letter from me, he wrote on March 17, 1910:

> While I am unable to commit myself either for or against this measure until I have heard all the arguments on both sides, you may rest assured that the matter shall receive my careful attention.

Grafton Cushing had already written on March 8, 1910, that he would "give the matter careful consideration."

It was most refreshing to hear from men who really understood the situation as did Dr. G. Alder Blumer, who wrote on March 21, 1910:

> I congratulate you on the passage of your bill. It is a wise and humane measure.

And under date of March 25, 1910, Dr. White of the Department of the Interior, Government Hospital for the Insane, Washington, D. C., wrote me as follows:

> You are to be congratulated for what you have accomplished in Massachusetts. I wish they might do as well in the other States of the Union, here in the District of Columbia, for instance, where medievalism is only too much in evidence.
>
> Very truly yours,
>
> WM. A. WHITE,
> *Superintendent.*

The bill on which they congratulated me became a law under chapter 307, Acts of 1910, and read as follows:

AN ACT RELATIVE TO PERSONS SUFFERING FROM CERTAIN MENTAL DIS-
ORDERS WHO ARE ARRESTED OR CONFINED IN THE CITY OF BOSTON.

Be it enacted, etc., as follows:

SECTION 1. All persons suffering from delirium, mania, mental confusion, delusions or hallucinations, now under arrest or in confinement, or
who may hereafter be arrested by, or come under the care or protection of
the police of the city of Boston, and who, owing to lack of suitable buildings
or wards, are at present placed in the City Prison, the House of Detention or
the House of Correction on Deer Island, pending a medical examination and
transference, shall be taken for examination directly to the hospital constructed under the provisions of chapter four hundred and seventy of the
acts of the year nineteen hundred and nine, when said hospital is ready for
the reception of patients, in the same manner in which persons afflicted with
other diseases are taken to a general hospital. If, after examination, the
physician in charge of the said hospital decides the case to be one of delirium
tremens or drunkenness, the hospital shall not be obliged to admit the patient,
but otherwise the said hospital shall admit, observe and care for all persons
suffering from delirium, mania, mental confusion, delusions or hallucinations
until they can be committed or admitted to the hospital or institution appropriate in each particular case, unless the patient should recover or should
be placed by the physician in charge of the said hospital in the care of his
friends before such committal or admission.

SECTION 2. From and after the first day of May in the current year,
and until such time as the said hospital shall be completed and ready to
receive patients, the *State Board of Insanity shall provide at the Boston State
Hospital suitable temporary quarters for receiving and giving medical care* and
treatment to all persons suffering from the above-mentioned disorders, exclusive of drunkenness and delirium tremens, to which quarters shall be sent
directly all such persons who are now in the City Prison, House of Detention
or House of Correction on Deer Island, pending medical examination and
transference, or who, under the provisions of this act, will be sent to the
hospital constructed under the provisions of chapter four hundred and seventy
of the acts of the year nineteen hundred and nine, when that hospital is ready.

SECTION 3. On and after the first day of May in the current year no
person suffering from delirium, mania, mental confusion, delusions or hallucinations shall be harbored or confined in any penal institution within the city
of Boston for a period exceeding twelve hours. [*Approved March 29, 1910.*]

On April 7 Dr. Evans wrote to me:

I rejoice with you in the signal victory that closes forever a dark and
dismal chapter.

In the name of humanity, I thank you from my heart for your courage
and persistency.

Sincerely yours,

ALBERT EVANS.

The secretary of the Associated Charities of Boston, who had been active in my support, wrote under date of April 8, 1910:

My Dear Dr. Briggs: — I have heard something about the progress of your bill in the Legislature, and have been able once or twice to speak the feeling of the committee for the need of its passage. Please accept heartiest congratulations on your success in getting it through.

May I also take this opportunity of thanking you for the kind co-operation you are giving our district secretaries? I have heard from several of them of the pleasure they have had in working with you and of the great assistance you have been.

Cordially yours,

Alice L. Higgins,
General Secretary.

Mrs. Henry Parkman on April 8 wrote:

Dear Dr. Briggs: — I am delighted to hear that the bill went through, and that, thanks to your efforts, those unfortunate people will have a better chance.

Truly yours,

Frances Parkman.

The then superintendent of the Danvers State Hospital wrote under date of April 17, 1910:

I congratulate you upon your success in pushing this business. You got a very fine class of men and women to aid you. I am surprised the State Board did not openly work with you.

Sincerely yours,

Charles W. Page.

At the same time, Dr. Henry Maudsley of London was endeavoring to establish a hospital for incipient cases in London, and finally offered the Council a "bribe," saying he would give them $300,000 with which to erect a hospital. But on April 8, 1910, writing from 12 Queen Street, Mayfair, he says:

DEAR DR. BRIGGS: — Yes, I tried to bribe the London County Council to erect a hospital. Nominally assenting, they practically did little or nothing. Those who would have acted, I suppose, were impeded secretly and effectively by those who did not wish to spend money.

A new council has just been elected and I don't yet know whether they will take the thing seriously in hand. If not, I shall withdraw my offered bribe. You, I am glad to see, have been more fortunate.

The ordinary Britisher is a very stolid, self-complacent animal, into whose mind you can't get a scientific idea to enter until it has become a practical commonplace and he does not need to think it.

Yours sincerely,

H. MAUDSLEY.

This letter is quoted to show that Dr. Maudsley in England had the same difficulties to contend with that we had here.

On April 18, 1910, the secretary of the Massachusetts Medical Society wrote the following letter:

MY DEAR DOCTOR BRIGGS: — You are to be congratulated most heartily upon your success in getting Senate Bill No. 212 enacted into law. The object was a most worthy one, and the wonder is that the evil was not corrected years ago.

The Massachusetts Medical Society could not do better than to put you upon the Committee on State and National Legislation! You would get there when the rest of us fail! I hope you like the work better than I do, although when things come your way, there is a satisfaction in feeling that you had something to do in obtaining the result.

Again congratulating you upon your success in this matter, I am

Very truly yours,

GEORGE W. GAY,
Secretary.

The editor of the "American Journal of Insanity" wrote on April 19, 1910:

I wish to congratulate you upon the success which has attended your efforts in your campaign regarding the care of incipient cases of insanity.

Very truly,

E. N. BRUSH.

On April 26, 1910, Dr. W. M. Knowlton, then the associate of Dr. Walter Channing who opposed the bill wrote from Brookline:

My Dear Dr. Briggs: — The bill that was passed marks the beginning of better things for the unfortunate person who, becoming mentally ill, falls into the hands of the police.

Why should such a condition of things have been possible all these years in enlightened Boston!

Yours truly,

W. M. Knowlton.

Prof. John H. Gerould of Dartmouth College, one of my former professors in the Dartmouth Medical School, wrote on May 23, 1910:

I am very much interested in the work that you are doing, and I wish that I could get down to Boston oftener and so learn more of it.

Mr. J. G. Thorpe of Boston and Cambridge, under date of April 29, 1910, wrote:

Returning from a trip to California, I find a note telling me of the successful passage of your bill. I congratulate you heartily, and still more heartily the unfortunate ones whom your devoted efforts have so highly served. I am glad to have been counted among its supporters.

The "Boston Transcript" of July 29, 1910, contained an editorial from which the following is extracted:

Thanks to the enactment of a statute proposed by L. Vernon Briggs, which the city authorities did not appreciate was going through at the time, the Observation Hospital for Psychopathic Cases at the Deer Island House of Correction has ceased to exist. Nothing has been more out of keeping with the spirit of Boston's treatment of its unfortunates than its housing in this penal institution of such cases of mental disturbance which have been picked up on the streets by the police. Such cases of mental collapse are now transferred for observation and treatment to a special ward at the Boston Insane Hospital in Dorchester.

In obedience to the law as passed, the State Board of Insanity set aside at the Boston State Hospital the Butler Building, so called, which was just being completed for another purpose; and on May 18, 1910, Dr. H. P. Frost, the superintendent of the hospital, wrote to me:

> We are getting on very nicely in the Butler Building. Have seven men and two women.

The wisdom of the new law had already been demonstrated. The police department were enthusiastic over its working. Dr. Frost, formerly of the Buffalo State Hospital, but then of the Boston State Hospital, who had charge of these observation cases, stated that the patients were delighted with their quarters, and he had great satisfaction in caring for them and giving them first aid and treatment.

In a paper which Dr. Frost read before the American Medico-Psychological Association in May, 1912, at its meeting at Atlantic City, he said, in speaking of the Psychopathic Hospital:

> The hospital is to be something more than a receiving department for the main hospital, though that is one of its functions. In the first place, it will receive without commitment, for temporary care and observation, all patients suffering from "delirium, mania, mental confusion, delusions or hallucinations, who may be arrested by, or come under the care or protection of the police of the city of Boston . . ." This is done under authority given by a law passed in 1910 largely through the efforts of Dr. L. Vernon Briggs of Boston, under the operation of which no insane person is confined in a police station or jail, as had previously been the practice.

Governor Draper sent for me as soon as the bill was passed, and asked me to interpret certain parts of it. I have not the whole history of my interviews with him, as no special notes were made. A few letters passed between us, one of which I quote, as follows:

64 BEACON STREET, BOSTON,
May 5, 1910.

To His Excellency Governor EBEN S. DRAPER, *Boston, Mass.*

MY DEAR GOVERNOR DRAPER: — At your request, as conveyed to me by your private secretary, Mr. Murphy, I would say it was intended by those who are responsible for the passage of chapter 307, Acts of 1910, that all cases of delirium, etc., should be taken to the Psychopathic Hospital when the said hospital is finished and ready to receive such cases.

It was intended by myself and others who drafted the bill that until the said hospital was ready, the same class of patients which would be taken to it, under section 1, should under section 2 be taken to the Boston State Hospital for observation and immediate care and treatment. If, after proper observation, the physician in charge decided that the delirium was due entirely to alcohol, he was not obliged to retain such patients.

It was not intended that the bill should, in any way, prevent the Boston State Hospital from receiving or caring for delirium tremens cases if they chose to do so, for there are many cases of insane men and women who are despondent or suffering so intensely from head symptoms that they take spiritous liquors to cheer or relieve their melancholy or deaden the pain or pressure in their heads. These cases should be especially observed; that is what the hospital is intended for.

There is no one now competent to decide whether an arrested person may be insane or drunk until he has been sent out to the Boston State Hospital. The question in section 2 should be decided by the physician in charge of the said hospital and not by the police officer.

The Commonwealth of Massachusetts has, under chapter 504, Acts of 1909, section 1, assumed the care, control and treatment of "persons addicted" to the intemperate use of narcotics and stimulants. It has taken over Foxborough and laws have been passed for the commitment of alcoholic cases, section 50, chapter 504, Acts of 1909.

Is it not reasonable to suppose that when the group of buildings now planned for at Foxborough are completed the State will take charge of these delirium tremens cases and send them as acute cases of alcoholism to their new group of buildings? If this is correct, it would be very nice if the State would now receive such cases at the Boston State Hospital, thus keeping all cases of delirium under one head and avoiding friction as to where each case properly belongs.

Very respectfully,

L. VERNON BRIGGS.

As I previously stated, the reason why Governor Draper suddenly changed his attitude, bringing up arguments against the taking of delirium cases, was because he naturally went to the head of the Department of the Insane, Dr. Owen Copp, for advice, and was guided by him. This may account for the text of his letter which follows, and which is an answer to my letter above quoted:

THE COMMONWEALTH OF MASSACHUSETTS

EXECUTIVE DEPARTMENT

BOSTON, May 7, 1910.

L. VERNON BRIGGS, M.D., *64 Beacon Street, Boston.*

DEAR SIR: — Your letter of the 5th inst. is received and contents carefully noted. The matter that you speak about is a very important one, but it is a question between the State and the city care. At the present time it is the city's responsibility to care for the people to whom you refer, and if the city has no place to do this, it should immediately provide for one.

In 1908 the Legislature passed a law which had special reference to this matter (chapter 627, section 2), which says:

"Until the time when such a building or wards shall be established the mayor shall have *authority* to direct that such persons be placed for observation and treatment in the care of any general hospital belonging to the city."

The Commonwealth cannot assume to take care of these people, because this not only applies to Boston but to every city in the State, would be an enormous expense, and cannot be entered upon by the Commonwealth without legislative action. The city must for the present and under existing law care for its own.

Yours very truly,

EBEN S. DRAPER.

I was again reminded of the fact that the opposition was still active and was trying to influence the Governor in order to thwart the spirit of the law. A letter similar to my letter to Governor Draper was sent to him by Thomas M. Babson, city corporation counsel. The Governor's answer to him was as follows:

THE COMMONWEALTH OF MASSACHUSETTS

EXECUTIVE CHAMBER

MAY 11, 1910.

THOMAS M. BABSON, Esq., *73 Tremont Street, Boston.*

MY DEAR MR. BABSON: — Replying to your letter of the 9th inst., I do not think it is necessary for me to take any further action in regard to the

matter. I am very sorry if you think anything I have done seems unfair
to the city authorities and should feel very sorry if I thought I had done so
in any way. It seems to me it is a matter for the Legislature to act upon
further. They have taken certain action, which, until it is changed, should
stand.

Yours very truly,

EBEN S. DRAPER.

Of course, there was no reason why Dr. Copp should
not take care of the cases pending any decision, as a
humanitarian measure; but he stood on the law in this
matter in a way that was considered by many as unnecessary. I therefore wrote to the superintendent of
the Boston City Hospital the following letter, which
he placed before his trustees:

BOSTON, May 10, 1910.

Dr. JOHN M. McCOLLOM, *Boston City Hospital, Boston, Mass.*

MY DEAR DR. McCOLLOM: — There seems to be no question but what
something has got to be done with delirium tremens cases until next fall.
I have been in conference with the mayor, the corporation counsel, and Institutions Department and others, and in addition have received letters from
the Governor in which he refuses to relieve the situation.

It would be a pity to go to the Legislature with another bill which might
further mix things up, even if any bill could be put through at this late date,
which I very much doubt. I am therefore endeavoring to make an amicable
arrangement whereby these cases will receive proper care and treatment until
such time as we can try out the present law and conditions and know better
what we do want. At the end of six months I am sure the bill could be intelligently drawn to care for these people. I am sure that the State and its
different institutions will take care of a certain proportion of cases, which
would include the old rounders and the most undesirable cases, and I hope
that you will see your way clear to take care of a few, pending the drawing
and passage of a bill next fall which will settle all our difficulties.

If sufficient assurance could be given you that not exceeding two or three
cases a week would be sent you, and that a rule made by you that if you had
three cases under care you would refuse to receive any more until one of
those was discharged shall be recognized and obeyed, would you be willing to
help out to that extent? The situation is urgent. These people are actually
ill, and we are trying to avoid the repetition of what happened at the steamer
landing where one man was bound, hand and foot, waiting between eight
and twelve hours for transportation to one of our islands in the harbor.
This is too far to send them and the only reason they do well after they get
there, in my opinion, is that only the strongest live to get there.

Knowing that you will look at this in a humanitarian way, and hoping that you and your trustees will see your way clear to help us to the above extent, I remain,

Very sincerely,

L. VERNON BRIGGS.

He answered:

THE BOSTON CITY HOSPITAL

BOSTON, May 13, 1910.

Dr. L. VERNON BRIGGS, *208 Beacon Street.*

DEAR SIR: — At a meeting of the trustees to-day, May 13, I was instructed to transmit to you the following vote regarding the admission of cases of delirium tremens to the Boston City Hospital proper:

"*Voted,* That in the opinion of the trustees, the Boston City Hospital proper is not a suitable place for the treatment of cases of delirium tremens, and the trustees refuse to admit such cases."

In view of the fact that in certain instances, emergency cases arise, the trustees decided that if in a given case a physician of the Institutions Department will certify that it is essential that the patient should receive immediate medical treatment, a limited number of these cases may be admitted to the Relief Station at Haymarket Square. The trustees wish to emphasize the fact that the Boston City Hospital is not the place for the treatment of these cases; but as emergencies may arise, as individuals may be suffering from delirium tremens and at the same time may have a commencing attack of pneumonia, such cases may be admitted to the Relief Station. This is merely a temporary arrangement.

I remain

Yours very truly,

JOHN H. MCCOLLOM,

Superintendent.

Fearing that this would be the outcome of my appeal to the City Hospital, I had written to Governor Draper also on May 10, as follows:

64 BEACON STREET, BOSTON,

May 10, 1910.

His Excellency Governor EBEN S. DRAPER.

MY DEAR GOVERNOR DRAPER: — Your letter of May 5 was received. I hardly see how it is an answer to my letter of the same date, and I cannot believe that it was written after consulting a legal opinion.

I would have gone to you personally in regard to my bill long ago but for the reason that I understood from Mrs. William Tudor, who did go to you to plead for this bill, that you did not intend to in any way interfere, and you did not wish to be consulted about it. That I desired your personal and careful consideration and opinion on many matters connected with the insane before next winter, and that I should have liked to consult you regarding this bill, I can assure you are facts.

The question is so big and involves so much of the State's money that I feel that no one man's opinion should be taken as final; and in going to you for a higher opinion, I understood it was the desire of those who went to get not the opinion you have given, which they have had in almost the same form several times before, but a fresh opinion. As I understand, those who were invited to the conference with you came away with the understanding that in place of your personal opinion, which you did not wish to give, they were going to receive the opinion of the Attorney-General and Mr. Babson.

I am now trying to make some amicable arrangement for the care and treatment of the delirium tremens cases which border so nearly on mine and which mine might be mistaken for. If a broad interpretation could be placed on my bill, allowing doubtful cases to be sent to the Boston State Hospital, and of a reasonable assurance that not more than one or two delirium tremens cases a week should be sent them until next fall, I think that there would be no necessity of any further friction, and that the city of Boston would do its share. I am in communication with the proper authorities to ascertain if they would meet the question more than halfway.

No adequate law could have been drawn this winter and no law could be drawn now which would properly provide for these cases until this whole question has been tried out for at least six months. When the Legislature meets next fall, all parties will be in a position to agree upon a bill which will definitely and permanently settle this question. Mayor Fitzgerald assured me yesterday that if some arrangement could be made temporarily it would be his desire that Boston should have a ward attached either to the Relief Hospital or as an outbuilding to the Boston City Hospital for the care of such cases as should properly go to the city.

I do not believe in the starting of any fight now, one way or the other. I do believe that if we all look at this question from a humanitarian point of view there will be no difficulty in taking care of these people this summer without establishing any precedent of the State or city, and that next fall, as I said before, we shall be able to draw an intelligent bill which could not be done now.

As we already have Dr. Copp's opinion on these questions, in appealing to you we are not asking his opinion. I know that the State Board of Insanity and the trustees of the Boston State Hospital will do anything that you suggest to relieve the condition of these unfortunate people and their predicament. If they took care of two a week at the outside, they would enable us to relieve the present situation, and these people would have the medical care and treatment given them which they otherwise, I am afraid, will not receive.

Faithfully yours,

L. Vernon Briggs.

His answer showed he was not willing to help.   It was as follows:

THE COMMONWEALTH OF MASSACHUSETTS

EXECUTIVE CHAMBER

MAY 11, 1910.

Dr. L. VERNON BRIGGS, 64 Beacon Street, Boston.

DEAR SIR: — Your letter of the 10th inst. has been received, but I do not care to make any further statement in regard to the matter at the present time than I have already made.

Yours very truly,

EBEN S. DRAPER.

The Massachusetts Society of Examining Physicians at this time asked me to read a paper on "The Care of Cases of Acute Insanity," which was to be discussed by Dr. Edward B. Lane and Dr. Charles C. Dewey. After giving the history of the bill I said:

On May 1, 1910, Massachusetts established her first observation wards for the reception of these cases.   Up to May 25, or a little over three weeks, 20 patients had been sent there, of whom only 9 have been committed to insane hospitals.   During the same period there have been 5 cases of delirium tremens coming under the protection of the police of Boston.   One of these was sent to the Relief Hospital, 3 to the City Hospital, and 1 to Foxborough Hospital.   In the same period last year there were 7 cases of delirium tremens sent to Deer Island.

This showed what was being done for delirium tremens cases.   The mental cases had been taken care of, but now the delirium tremens cases were left out in the cold.   Continuing my paper on the subject:

As I said before, it is not clear in my mind what is to become of the delirium tremens cases.   Nothing that I have seen or heard from the State Board of Insanity, from the trustees of Foxborough, or any information I have been able to obtain from those in authority over the State's affairs gives assurance that the delirium tremens cases are going to receive any immediate care.   As many of you know, the bill I introduced into the Legislature last winter for the care of delirium cases does not reach this class directly.   It certainly was not my intention that the delirium tremens cases should be treated and cared for alongside of the mentally ill patients; but the line is hard to draw, and I did have the law so framed that all cases of delirium, including cases of delirium tremens, should be taken to the new hospital for examination by specialists to determine if they were purely delirium tremens cases. The law as passed forbids the delirium tremens cases being taken to Deer Island or any other penal institution. It requires that they be taken to the psychopathic ward of the Boston State Hospital; but the said hospital is not obliged to keep them if it is determined that they are purely delirium tremens cases. I naturally supposed they would be transferred to the several city and State institutions to which they belonged. . . .

Under the Acts of 1909, chapter 504, section 1, I quote: "The Commonwealth shall have the care, control and treatment of all insane, feeble-minded and epileptic persons, and of persons addicted to the intemperate use of narcotics or stimulants, the care of whom is vested in the Commonwealth by the provisions of law in force on the date of the passage of this act, or of any person who shall thereafter be received into any institution or receptacle owned or maintained by the Commonwealth for such persons. No county, city or town shall establish or maintain any such institution or receptacle, or be liable for the board, care, treatment or act of any inmate thereof," but still the Commonwealth refuses to take care of the cases of delirium tremens; they are too acute; the State Board of Insanity evidently wants chronic cases. It has been so with the insane. It was the policy of the State to do nothing for the incipient insane, to do nothing for the prevention of insanity, but to sit still and receive the ever-increasing hordes of insane people and care for them after all hope of saving over 50 per cent of them was passed. Is it any wonder that our insane for the last five years have increased so much that at length we cannot get money enough to provide proper buildings even to house these people and give them board and lodging, much less treatment? Many neglected cases go insane, and every insane person costs the State over $200 per year for maintenance, or the interest on $5,000 at 4 per cent for a great many years. Our insane increased 1,288 the last two years. Just the increase of insane cases the past year has cost the State the income of $2,500,000. Think of this increase each year and nothing being actually done for the prevention of insanity by this Commonwealth until May 1 last, nothing but plans for the indefinite future, and this in face of the fact that our State is paying a net of over two and a half million dollars a year for the maintenance of our insane, with a 10 per cent increase last year and over a half million dollars each year for the last eleven years for construction. With all this expenditure, 1,300 insane patients are now sleeping on cots and beds in day rooms and corridors, owing to the overcrowded conditions of our asylums, for they cannot honestly be called hospitals while the present conditions exist.

I claim that the psychopathic ward of the Boston State Hospital, under Dr. Frost's management, is going to stop the increasing figures from growing larger each year and very soon set them going the other way; but if the Commonwealth refuses to provide care and treatment for these particular alcoholics, they know full well that they are raising another crop of insane patients for their now overcrowded hospitals. Can you conceive of such a short-sighted policy?

In June, 1910, I read a paper before the Section on Nervous and Mental Diseases of the American Medical Association, at St. Louis, Missouri, on "What can be done for the prevention of Insanity by the Treatment of Incipient Cases in General Hospitals, and what has been done in the Past."

In June, 1910, Dr. Frost wrote me concerning suggestions for sending cases to the Butler Building, which was then the temporary observation hospital used pending the construction of the Psychopathic Hospital. In answer to his letter, among other things, I said:

> I was much pleased with the arrangement at the Butler Building. I wish all the day patients could be taken through the side entrance and not have the impressions that are bound to be conveyed to the mind of the incipient cases by running the gauntlet of unpleasant cases.
>
> I wish also that the building was more suited for the medical and other treatment of early cases; but this, of course, will come next year when the Psychopathic Hospital will have, I hope, its observation ward in commission.
>
> I want to thank you for your deep and active interest in the care of this unfortunate class and in furthering and carrying out the provisions of the new law as soon as the patients are placed in your charge.

In the meantime, Dr. Maudsley wrote on June 22, 1910:

> DEAR DR. VERNON BRIGGS: — As I understand that you have now got your hospital program duly sanctioned, I should be much obliged if you would kindly tell me what amount of land you have secured or hope to secure for your hospital. The difficulty in London is to get sufficient land in a suitable locality for the desired site. I want 4 or 5 acres, as a desirable minimum. But I should be pleased to learn what your views and intentions are.
>
> With kind regards
>
> Yours very truly,
>
> H. MAUDSLEY.

CHAPTER VII

CONTRACT FOR PSYCHOPATHIC HOSPITAL. — STILL NO PLACE FOR DELIRIUM
TREMENS CASES. — CITY HOSPITAL LATER OBLIGED TO RECEIVE THEM. —
AFTER PSYCHOPATHIC HOSPITAL OPENS, DR. SOUTHARD ACCEPTS
AND TREATS CASES OF DELIRIUM TREMENS

On November 17, 1910, I received a letter from Dr. Copp in which he said:

I am happy to inform you that the contract for the Psychopathic Hospital has been let and that the contractors are at work upon the excavation. Fortunately, it was not necessary to modify the plans, except in a few minor points of construction.

As regards the suggestion in your letter of November 3, relative to legislation, I heartily reciprocate your sentiments, and should be very glad to coöperate with you and every one to improve conditions.

The Board's recommendations to the incoming Legislature have not been formulated definitely. If you would like to make suggestions to the Board, I am very sure they would like to have you present your views in person at some meeting, or in writing, if you prefer. If it suits your convenience, it would be wise to do this at as early a date as possible.

The important question to be decided by the then incoming Legislature was the care of the cases of delirium tremens. On November 29, 1910, I wrote the following letter to the mayor of Boston:

BOSTON, November 29, 1910.

Hon. JOHN F. FITZGERALD, *Mayor, City Hall, Boston.*

MY DEAR MR. FITZGERALD: — The question of the care of the cases of delirium tremens will come up this year in the Legislature. If you remember, last year temporary provision only was made for them. For a great many years these ill people have been sent to Deer Island, which was against the law.

Last year a law was passed forbidding their being sent to any penal institution. They are just as ill as other people who should have medical care and treatment.

It is difficult for the police to distinguish whether a man is suffering from delirium tremens or whether he is nervous or mentally broken down, or has taken alcohol to brace himself up when mentally ill.

Most of the large cities in this country have an alcoholic ward connected with their city hospitals. In Bellevue Hospital it is so large and so arranged that all persons under the influence of alcohol to the extent of not being able to take care of themselves may be sent first to the alcoholic ward. The police officer telephones for the Bellevue ambulance instead of the patrol wagon.

During our interview last year you spoke of the possibility of an annex being built to the present Relief Hospital to take care of these cases, or some building being added to the City Hospital plant. From a humanitarian point of view as well as to make a "model 1915 city," it would seem that this much-neglected branch of service should be taken care of, and I feel that you are just the man to do it.

I should like to talk it over with you and assist in any way I can in bringing about proper care to this class of citizens. They are unfortunate and should be re-educated and treated medically. Throwing them in jails and prisons has never tended to either reform them or lessen the increasing burden on the city.

Hoping that you will be able to take up this most important matter in the midst of your other important duties, I remain

Very sincerely yours,

L. VERNON BRIGGS.

In answer to this letter, I received on December 1, 1910, a communication from Mayor Fitzgerald, saying that he would "make a study of this important question," and thanking me for calling his attention "to the lack of permanent provision for this class of unfortunates," and expressing the hope "that as a result of the attention which has been given to the subject some place for care and treatment may be provided."

In the meantime, the City Hospital did receive many cases. Mr. Fowler, the institutions' registrar, wrote Mayor Fitzgerald that in his opinion they should all be sent to the City Hospital or to its branch, the Relief Station at Haymarket Square, "because," he said, "these hospitals are centrally located and easily reached and most of the delirium tremens cases come from centrally located police stations. . . . If the City Hospital authorities will continue to receive delirium tremens cases, legislation will be unnecessary, because arrangements could easily be made whereby the police department would send these patients directly to the City Hospital."

About this time, Charles F. Gaynor of the City Institutions Registration Department lent his support. He wrote on December 2 that the mayor had asked for his views concerning the handling of delirium tremens cases, and he sent me a copy of his answer. Mr. Gaynor further said:

> From June 1 to November 30, 1910, 140 patients were sent to the psychopathic ward of the Boston State Hospital. Of this number, 90 were afterwards regularly committed; 29 persons suffering from delirium tremens were sent to the City Hospital; 10 delirium tremens cases sent to Tewksbury; and during the same period of the preceding year, 1909, 129 persons were sent to Deer Island Hospital for delirium tremens and observation: 79 for delirium tremens; and 46 for observation, non-alcoholic.

On December 6 Mayor Fitzgerald in a letter suggested that Mr. Gaynor of the Institutions Registration Department, Dr. McCollom of the City Hospital and myself get together and endeavor to solve the problem of the delirium tremens cases.

Early in January, 1911, the State Board of Insanity promised to recommend to the Legislature a bill providing that "no person suffering from insanity, mental derangement, delirium, or mental confusion, except delirium tremens and drunkenness, shall, except in case of emergency, be placed or detained in a lockup, police station, city prison, house of detention, jail or other penal institution, or place for the detention of criminals, but shall be cared for by the Board of Health of the city or town in which the person may be, Boston excepted; and those in Boston should be sent direct to the Boston City Hospital or the Relief Hospital," and a letter was written to the mayor asking that the Legal Department draw a bill on these lines to be presented to the Legislature.

An inquiry addressed to the Bellevue Hospital, New York, regarding its procedure in transferring cases to the psychopathic wards, brought forth the following:

Regarding the alcoholics: All acute alcoholic mental disturbances, such as alcoholic delirium, alcoholic hallucinosis, etc., are now being transferred by us, because all these conditions are regarded by laymen as well as by all general practitioners as indistinguishable from insanities, and we are therefore notified to transfer them as insane patients. I feel, and I think that you will agree with me, that acute alcoholic conditions are really psychoses, and should be handled in a way not materially different from the real insanities. Of course the acute intoxications — ordinary drunks — are not to be included in the above enumeration. The police are inclined to bring many such drunks to the hospital in preference to taking them to the lock-up for a number of reasons. *First*, it is easier for a policeman to do so, as he escapes the necessity for appearing in court the next day, especially if it happens to be his "day off." *Second*, all these drunkards present, as you know, slight contusions and physical injuries, which, in the opinion of the policeman, makes the patient a hospital case. *Third*, from time to time, cases of pneumonia, bronchitis and fracture of the base of the skull, etc., appear in the alcoholics in jails, which at times cause considerable newspaper criticism, and consequently the police authorities are not willing to run any risks.

We are about to make arrangements to examine these drunkards very carefully on their arrival at this hospital, and if they show no disorder aside from their intoxication, they are to be turned over to the police department to be dealt with by the courts.

In answer to your last question, I would say that the matter of the transfer of an alleged insane person to Bellevue Hospital in our own ambulance by our own nurses is not a law, but merely a regulation, and we must, of course, conform to the conditions imposed by the law.

Very truly yours,

M. S. GREGORY,
Resident Alienist.

On January 3, 1911, I received the following note:

THE COMMONWEALTH OF MASSACHUSETTS
BOSTON STATE HOSPITAL

DORCHESTER CENTER, MASS.
January 3, 1911.

DEAR DR. BRIGGS: — I am sending you a copy of a special report we make on the temporary-care service from the date of its inauguration to December 1, a period of seven months. This will appear in our annual report, but, as that may not be available until next spring, I thought you would appreciate having this information in advance, and I consider that you ought to have it, since you were so instrumental in getting the work under way.

Yours very truly,

H. P. FROST,
Superintendent.

The report referred to follows:

BOSTON STATE HOSPITAL

Temporary Care Service

The last Legislature passed a measure (chapter 307, Acts of 1910) which directed that suitable quarters be set apart at this hospital for the observation and temporary care, pending examination and commitment, of persons suffering from mental disorders who would come under the care of the police in the city of Boston. In compliance with this direction, the Butler Building, containing two wards, each with capacity for 10 patients, was emptied by transfer of that number to other wards, and on May 1 was ready for the reception of these cases, — one ward for men and one for women.

This wise and humane provision for immediate beginning of a portion of the service which the Psychopathic Hospital will render to the community has met an urgent need and has been of incalculable benefit to a large number of sick persons who would otherwise have been, of necessity, confined in a police station or jail for a longer or shorter period awaiting commitment and transfer. Under authority of the above enactment, such patients are now brought directly to the hospital at any hour of the day or night, and receive at once the care and treatment their condition demands. With willing and intelligent co-operation on the part of the police department, this method has worked smoothly, and in only a few instances have we felt called upon to reject as unsuitable cases the patients who were presented.

After an experience of seven months, covering the reception of nearly 200 cases, there can be no doubt that the prompt relief thus afforded operates to cut short incipient attacks, to moderate others, and to shorten the period of treatment necessary in a large proportion, besides protecting the patients from needless suffering and distress.

On December 29, 1910, Dr. Copp wrote me as follows:

DEAR DR. BRIGGS: — I enclose the first draft of two bills which the Board is considering. They are in the rough and not final in any sense. I thought you would like to see them as early as possible. If you have any suggestions, the Board would be glad to consider them.

Yours very truly,

OWEN COPP,
Executive Officer.

The drafts of the two bills referred to follow:

AN ACT RELATIVE TO THE RECEPTION AND TEMPORARY CARE IN CERTAIN INSTITUTIONS OF PERSONS SUFFERING FROM MENTAL DERANGEMENT

Be it enacted, etc., as follows:

The superintendent or manager of any hospital for the insane, public or private, may, when requested by a physician, by a member of the board of health or a police officer of a city or town, or by a member of the district police, receive and care for in such hospital as a patient, for a period not exceeding seven days, any person who needs immediate care and treatment because of mental derangement other than delirium tremens or drunkenness. Such request for admission of a patient shall be put in writing and filed at the hospital at the time of his reception, or within twenty-four hours thereafter, together with a statement in a form prescribed by the state board of insanity, giving such information as said board may deem appropriate. Such patient shall, upon the request of such superintendent or manager, be removed forthwith from such hospital by the person requesting his reception, and, if he is not removed, such person shall be liable for all reasonable expenses incurred under the provisions of this act on account of such patient which may be recovered by the hospital in an action of contract. Such superintendent or manager shall cause each such patient either to be examined by two physicians qualified as provided in section thirty-two of chapter five hundred and four of the acts of the year nineteen hundred and nine, who shall cause application to be made for admission or commitment of such patient to such hospital, or to be removed therefrom before the expiration of said period of seven days. Reasonable expenses incurred for the examination of such patient and his transportation to the hospital shall be allowed, certified and paid as provided by section forty-nine of said chapter five hundred and four, as amended by chapter four hundred and twenty of the acts of the year nineteen hundred and ten, for the allowance, certification and payment of the expenses of examination and commitment.

An Act relative to the Care of Persons suffering from Certain Mental Disorders pending their Admission or Commitment to Appropriate Institutions

Be it enacted, etc., as follows:

No person suffering from insanity, mental derangement, delirium, or mental confusion, except delirium tremens and drunkenness, shall, except in case of emergency, be placed or detained in a lockup, police station, city prison, house of detention, jail or other penal institution, or place for the detention of criminals. If, in case of emergency, such person is so placed or detained, he shall forthwith be examined by a physician and shall be furnished suitable medical care and nursing. Any such person not so placed or detained who is arrested by or comes under the care or protection of the police, and any other person who is in need of immediate care and treatment which cannot be provided without public expense, shall, except in the city of Boston, be cared for by the board of health of the city or town in which such person may be. Such board of health shall cause such person to be examined by a physician as soon as possible, shall furnish him suitable medical care and nursing, and shall cause him to be duly admitted or committed to an institution for the care and treatment of such persons, or otherwise suitably provided for. Reasonable expenses for board, lodging, medical care, nursing, clothing and all other necessary expenses incurred by the board of health, under the provisions of this act, shall be allowed, certified and paid as provided by section forty-nine of chapter five hundred and four of the acts of the year nineteen hundred and nine, as amended by chapter four hundred and twenty of the acts of the year nineteen hundred and ten, for the allowance, certification and payment of the expenses of examination and commitment.

In answer to Dr. Copp's letter, I wrote the following:

Boston, January 3, 1911.

Owen Copp, M.D., *Executive Officer, State Board of Insanity, State House, Boston, Mass.*

My Dear Dr. Copp: — Your letter of December 29, with enclosures, is received and I thank you for the same.

I note that these drafts are rough and not final, so I hope that there will be some changes made. In the bill commencing with "No person suffering from insanity," etc., I would suggest that the New York law be followed more in detail. You undoubtedly have the insanity laws of New York for 1910, as prepared by Hoffman, and I would call your attention to section 88, in article 4: "Nor shall such person be committed as a disorderly person to any prison, jail or lock-up for criminals." In the draft you sent me, the phrase "in case of emergency" seems to be a very broad one; and it seems to me it could be narrowed down, for almost invariably these cases are cases of emergency.

Again, I think as you read on, that when the Board of Health and Institutions Registry Department are called, there should be something like this put in: "Such board of health or institutions registration department shall cause a competent attendant to at once be placed constantly in charge and shall have such person examined by a physician as soon as possible, shall furnish him suitable medical care and nursing, and provide him a safe, comfortable and suitable place, and shall ask the state insane hospital in which district the said patient is at the time to send a trained attendant or attendants to bring the patient to the hospital, or shall hold him until the hospital in the district to which he belongs shall be able to send for him." This places the transportation of this class of persons in charge of nurses instead of officers of the law. I should strenuously object, as I did in my bill, to the phrase "or otherwise suitably provided for." It is too elastic, and while it might prove a good working law, with you in charge, it might be taken advantage of by the local boards of health and others.

The bill headed "The superintendent or manager of any hospital," etc., is, if I read it right, a most valuable and progressive bill. Am I correct in interpreting this bill as making it legal for hospitals to receive cases directly under the seven days' law on the request of physicians, etc., or does the law requiring the usual commitments and legal procedure still remain active enough to prevent the carrying out of what I interpret this bill as intending? I find nothing in the laws of other States; and if I am wrong, I want to be corrected as to the liability of physicians in sending cases to hospitals.

With our laws I agree physicians should be liable for improper cases sent to the hospitals, but I think it is a little severe to pass this law in its present form, although it is corroborative of a law already in force. Why would not your purpose be served and your hospitals protected if the second paragraph in this bill should read as follows: "If such person is received at the request of a physician and the said person proves, after examination, to be not mentally deranged, such physician by request shall remove such patient," etc. This would seem to me to protect everybody. Of course, I would personally like the word "may," in the second line, changed to "shall;" and I should like to know the intent of the phrase, "if no objection is made thereto." I cannot interpret it satisfactorily, and I am wondering if other people could. Of course objection would be made by the patient and objection might be made by the hospital. It seems to me that that needs a little plainer statement as to the intent of the phrase.

Cannot we pass some law this winter that will be an entering wedge to a better class of attendants, and *could not the State Board formulate some printed rules, which they would enforce, which would keep an absolute record, as in the case of Danvers, of all abuse or force used, whether necessary or unnecessary, in the handling of patients; also some printed rules regarding the care of the teeth of the patients, and of the eyes. If the State Board took this up in a businesslike manner and made it obligatory, which they could virtually do by their recommendation, it would seem that no law would be necessary;* but as it is left to-day, I know that the patients do not have proper attention paid to them in these respects.

Very respectfully yours,

L. VERNON BRIGGS.

DR. ELMER E. SOUTHARD
First Director of the Boston Psychopathic Hospital

In answer to this letter, Dr. Copp wrote:

I am afraid that your revision involves certain constitutional objections which would prevent its passage and use thereafter. As you know I should object to compulsory sending for patients as unnecessary, in the first place, and as of questionable utility. . . . Perhaps we had each best present our case to the committee and then try to get together and formulate a suitable bill. I thank you for your kind expressions of good will and shall regret very much to leave my friends and my work in the State. On the whole, it seems to be the best thing to do.

Mr. Henry H. Kendall of Kendall, Taylor & Co., architects, wrote me, on January 11, 1911, after the plans for the Psychopathic Hospital were completed:

I take pleasure in sending you herewith a set of the prints of the Psychopathic Hospital, as suggested in yours of the 10th inst. I am sure that your interest in them is the greater because of the part you have had in making them possible.

Dr. Elmer E. Southard was early appointed a director of the Psychopathic Hospital, enabling him to direct such changes during its construction as his experience suggested.

"Constitutional objections" were something one heard a good deal about in connection with our bills when presented to the Legislature, but when it came to a showdown the Attorney-General never found constitutional objections to our bills. That has been so in recent years. The pessimist is very apt to say, when any new bill is presented to the Legislature, "But you will find there are constitutional objections." Their predictions have not proved true in the case of our bills. Senator Nash predicted that Dr. Copp would leave the State, after the interview with him in the rooms of the Committee on Bills in the Third Reading. In a letter to me dated February 10, 1911, Dr. Copp raised the question of "constitutional objections," and also stated that he was going to leave the State. This in some ways I regretted, as I wrote Dr. Copp, because he had some excellent ideas, constructive and humane; but while he put forth his ideas in the most forceful way, which was a help and inspiration to others, it seemed next to impossible for him to carry out many of them. In so far as suggestions and planning were concerned, he was valuable to Massachusetts, and, on that account, I was sorry for his departure. On the other hand, I think perhaps in view of what followed after his departure, it was as well for the cause of the mentally ill in Massachusetts that he left just when he did, for, though he had his good ideas, he did not seem willing that any one else should put them into effect, even after waiting years for him to do so. He seemed to be afraid that legislation proposed by any one else would somehow interfere with what he was trying to do; and he did not have that clearness of vision which should have shown him that such persons were simply helping him and the cause.

On February 20, 1911, the Public Charitable Institutions Committee held a hearing on House Document No. 79, containing the State Board bills on mental disorders and State care, etc. At that hearing, Dr. Tuttle of McLean Hospital said to the committee:

I think the revised part of this law, concerning early admission of patients to the hospitals, is better than the original. Dr. Copp says that the State Board of Insanity is sensitive about going out and picking up patients and bringing them into the hospital. I myself should hesitate in sending out for patients on telephone call. The attitude of the patient to the hospital when he comes there, is that the hospital simply receives him and he doesn't feel that the hospital sent out and brought him there. I object to sending for patients, and I do not believe the trustees of the hospital would allow me to do it. I would like to suggest one thing to be added to this draft. After the patient comes into the hospital there are two things the superintendent can do. He can send out for physicians to have him committed, or he can send him away.

Dr. McCollom, Boston City Hospital, said:

This bill is a very good bill as far as it goes, but I object decidedly to excluding cases of delirium tremens. He is exactly in the same condition as a person suffering from acute mania. It is very difficult for me to take care of a man with delirium tremens. He is a source of danger to others and to us. You cannot be absolutely sure whether he is suffering from delirium tremens or acute mania. I am also convinced that there ought to be some place to send these cases. It is an acute condition and requires special care and treatment.

Dr. John G. Blake, of Boston City Hospital and trustee of Gardner State Colony, said:

I second Dr. McCollom's remarks. That we should be the last resort of delirium tremens, I should protest. We cannot take care of alcoholics. We have no provision for them except in a general way. Something should be done for that class of patients. They appeal powerfully to my sympathy. There is no class in the community that needs more care than the alcoholics. We are not prepared in our arrangements there, we are not qualified in such knowledge of those diseases. Then I think it behooves you, gentlemen, to recommend some more suitable place for them to be cared for.

Dr. Walter Channing, chairman of the Board of Trustees of the Boston State Hospital during the construction of the Psychopathic Hospital, said:

I should be sorry if the Psychopathic Hospital was made to receive all cases of delirium tremens. I do not understand why they do not like to receive such cases at the City Hospital. For the last twenty-five years we have struggled to have them taken there. In the temporary-care act which makes it obligatory for the Boston City Hospital to receive police cases, quite a number of them are not alcoholic. It is the custom of a great many of the hospitals to have an alcoholic ward. Our hospital is for the first care and observation of acute mental disease. The physicians in Boston have no place to take such cases.

COMMITTEE. Would it disturb the whole ward in the hospital?

DR. McCOLLOM. They do disturb the whole ward. The wards are not adapted for that purpose. Where there are 20 men in the different stages of acute illness and others with typhoid fever, if a man with delirium tremens gets up in the night and makes a big noise, it disturbs the rest.

COMMITTEE.   Why should not the State make provision for such wards in the hospital?

DR. McCOLLOM.   Why not let the State take care of these cases?   I don't see why the city should provide for them because most of them come from outside of the city.

DR. COPP.   But how to do it is a tremendous problem.   It is just as much in harmony with the wards of the City Hospital as it is with our wards.   It is a separate and distinct ward that must be dealt with by itself.

COMMITTEE.   How many would come to the City Hospital during a month, of delirium tremens?

MR. GAYNOR.   Not over ten.

DR. McCOLLOM.   But we are obliged to take them.

After this hearing I had a conference with the State Board of Insanity and members of the Committee on Bills as well as the Committee of Public Charitable Institutions, who insisted on my full approval before they passed on Senate Bills Nos. 409 and 411, which were introduced March 21, 1911.

SENATE   .   .   .   .   .   .   No. 409

The Commonwealth of Massachusetts

AN ACT

Relative to the Care of Persons suffering from Certain Mental Disorders pending their Admission or Commitment to Appropriate Institutions

Be it enacted by the Senate and House of Representatives in General Court assembled, and by the authority of the same, as follows:

. . . No person suffering from insanity, mental derangement, delirium, or mental confusion, except delirium tremens and drunkenness, shall, except in case of emergency, be placed or detained in a lockup, police station, city prison, house of detention, jail or other penal institution, or place of detention of criminals.   If, in case of emergency, such person is so placed or detained, he shall forthwith be examined by a physician and shall be furnished suitable medical care and nursing, and shall not be detained for more than twelve hours.   Any such person not so placed or detained who is arrested by or comes under the care or protection of the police, and any other person who is in need of immediate care and treatment which cannot be provided without public expense, shall, except in the city of Boston, be cared for by the board of health of the city or town in which such person may be. Such board of health shall cause such person to be examined by a physician as soon as possible, shall furnish him suitable medical care and nursing and shall cause him to be duly admitted or committed to an institution for the care and treatment of such persons unless he should recover or be suitably provided for by his relatives or friends. Reasonable expenses for board, lodging, medical care, nursing, clothing and all other necessary expenses incurred by the board of health, under the provisions of this act, shall be allowed, certified and paid as provided by section forty-nine of chapter five hundred and four of the acts of the year nineteen hundred and nine, as amended by chapter four hundred and twenty of the acts of the year nineteen hundred and ten, for the allowance, certification and payment of the expenses of examination and commitment.

SENATE . . . . No. 411

The Commonwealth of Massachusetts

AN ACT

Relative to the Reception and Temporary Care in Certain Institutions of Persons suffering from Mental Derangement

Be it enacted by the Senate and House of Representatives in General Court assembled, and by the authority of the same, as follows:

. . . The superintendent or manager of any hospital for the insane, public or private, may, when requested by a physician, by a member of the board of health or a police officer of a city or town, by an agent of the institutions registration department of the city of Boston, or by a member of the district police, receive and care for in such hospital as a patient, for a period not exceeding seven days, any person who needs immediate care and treatment because of mental derangement other than delirium tremens or drunkenness. Such request for admission of a patient shall be put in writing and filed at the hospital at the time of the reception, or within twenty-four hours thereafter, together with a statement in a form prescribed or approved by the state board of insanity, giving such information as said board may deem appropriate. Such patient who is deemed by the superintendent or manager not suitable for such care shall, upon the request of such superintendent or manager, be removed forthwith from such hospital by the person requesting his reception, and if he is not removed, such person shall be liable for all reasonable expenses incurred under the provisions of this act on account of such patient, which may be recovered by the hospital in an action of contract. Such superintendent or manager shall cause each such patient either to be examined by two physicians qualified as provided in section thirty-two of chapter five hundred and four of the acts of the year nineteen hundred and nine, who shall cause application to be made for his admission or commitment to such hospital, or, provided he does not sign a request to remain under the provisions of section forty-five of said chapter five hundred and four, to be removed therefrom before the expiration of said period of seven days.   Reasonable expenses incurred for the examination of such patient and his transportation to the hospital shall be allowed, certified and paid as provided by section forty-nine of said chapter five hundred and four, as amended by chapter four hundred and twenty of the acts of the year nineteen hundred and ten, for the allowance, certification and payment of the expenses of examination and commitment.

The bills passed satisfactorily.   Thus ended a long fight, which resulted in a ward being set apart at the Boston City Hospital for all cases of delirium tremens, to which obvious cases were sent direct, and to which other cases were transferred from the Psychopathic Hospital when after observation they proved to be delirium tremens.   My original intention was that these cases should be treated at the Psychopathic Hospital, but when objections were raised, I agreed to yield this point, on account of other concessions which were made, and used every effort to have them received at the Boston City Hospital, being satisfied that there they would have medical care.   But my original hopes were realized when Dr. Southard manifested an active interest in treating delirium tremens, and instead of transferring all cases that came to the Psychopathic Hospital to the Boston City Hospital, virtually ruled that all cases of delirium tremens sent to the Psychopathic Hospital should be treated there.   Through his scientific treatment the mortality rate was greatly reduced, — a fact of which he was very proud.

Letters from far and near began to pour in congratulating me upon the results of my work.   Among others was a letter from Dr. Robert S. Carroll of Asheville, North Carolina, as follows:

MY DEAR DR. BRIGGS: — I have for a number of weeks intended to write you to express my hearty congratulations at the practical result of your years of work to secure for your State a psychopathic hospital.   There is such a growing need all over our land for such hospitals, or at least such departments in our hospitals.   You should indeed be most happy to know that yours will probably be one of the first complete ones in operation.

Very sincerely,
ROBERT S. CARROLL.

On June 20, 1912, I received the following letter from the State Board of Insanity:

L. VERNON BRIGGS, M.D., *208 Beacon Street, Boston.*

DEAR DOCTOR: — You are hereby informed that the new Psychopathic Hospital will be ready to receive patients on June 24, and on and after that date cases for temporary care and voluntary patients will be received at the Psychopathic Hospital, 74 Fenwood Road, instead of at Austin Farm.

Very truly yours,
CHAS. E. THOMPSON,
Executive Officer.

CHAPTER VIII

On June 24, 1912, the Psychopathic Hospital was formally opened as a department of the Boston State Hospital. The first great step had been accomplished when the State Board of Insanity gave up the Butler Building of the Boston State Hospital (just completed but never occupied) for an observation or psychopathic hospital. Now came the second great step, — the opening of the new building physically separated from the State Hospital and located in another part of the city. The next step was yet to be accomplished, — that of making this hospital an independent unit, — a real psychopathic hospital and not a department of the State Hospital.

In a letter to Dr. Arthur W. Hurd of Baltimore concerning the establishment of the Psychopathic Hospital (being a contribution to Dr. Hurd's "Institutional Care for the Insane in the United States and Canada"), Dr. Southard wrote:

It took twelve years from Dr. Owen Copp's report as executive officer of the State Board of Insanity, in 1900, before the Psychopathic Hospital became a fact. . . . So far as I know, at the present time (1915) only the Commonwealth of Massachusetts and the municipality of New York possess laws permitting wide uses of a system by which cases can be brought with the greatest facility for temporary care out of the community. New York has gone a step farther than Massachusetts in this regard, since New York officials are enabled to send an ambulance for cases requiring temporary care.

DR. COHOON, DR. FROST, DR. ADLER AND DR. SOUTHARD

On the steps of the Psychopathic Hospital

In referring to the persons who contributed to the success of the propaganda favoring a psychopathic hospital, Dr. Southard wrote to Dr. Hurd as follows:

In this connection it would not be right to omit the name of Dr. L.Vernon Briggs, who was, by his tireless energy and influence with legislative bodies, able to interest various persons who would otherwise have been lukewarm in such propositions as those for the establishment of a temporary-care law and the hastening of provisions for the psychopathic hospital type of case.

On February 7, 1913, when I was unanimously elected president of the medical staff (then composed of 118 physicians) of the Boston Dispensary, I immediately made arrangements for the heads of all departments to send cases of doubtful nervous or mental conditions direct to the Psychopathic Hospital on the three days of the week when there was no mental clinic at the Dispensary. At the mental clinic we were seeing from 20 to 30 cases a day, and we referred many of the new cases to the Psychopathic Hospital for observation.

The first fiscal year of the Psychopathic Hospital ended on September 30, 1913. Besides some readmissions, 1,484 cases was the total for that year. The 110 beds had a daily average of 98 patients. Of the total, 250, or one-sixth, were discharged as not insane; 129 were discharged recovered; 340 were discharged not recovered; and 52 died.

On March 12, 1913, my appointment was confirmed by the Governor's Council (Governor Foss having previously appointed me) as a member of the old State Board of Insanity,[1] succeeding Dr. Herbert B. Howard,

---

[1] Arthur W. Chute, M.D., wrote on March 13, 1913:

MY DEAR VERNON: — I was greatly pleased to see in this morning's paper that the Council ad confirmed your appointment to the Board of Insanity. You merit the appointment and am glad you have been able to put it through. I believe with a great many others that you ill show them that their opposition was unwarranted. Only to-day I heard a man say, speaking of your appointment, that "the Psychopathic Hospital would not have been, had it not been r Dr. Briggs."

who made a long but losing fight to be reappointed. I immediately urged measures of improvement and progress, some of which had been advocated before, but not carried out. Of these activities, I will confine myself to those which had to do with the Psychopathic Hospital.

An interesting experiment in connection with the out-patient department of the Psychopathic Hospital between September, 1912, and June, 1913, was a voice clinic under the direction of Dr. Walter B. Swift and Miss Constance Charnley. Such a project as a voice clinic in connection with a hospital like the Psychopathic was purely experimental, there being at this time but very few such clinics abroad (notably that in Berlin under Gutzmann, a brilliant and original investigator of the vocal process), and in this country only the Vanderbilt Clinic in New York, under Dr. E. W. Scripture, the neurologist. The purpose of the voice clinic was to note the relation of speech defect to physical and mental defect, and to correct the defect, if possible.

In the nine months during which the clinic was open, 66 cases were examined, by far the greatest number — nearly 75 per cent — being stutterers. Only one cure was made in less than ten visits; three cures in visits ranging from ten to twenty; and six in a number of visits greater than twenty, reaching in some cases over forty visits. There were no cures except in stuttering cases. The support for this work was private, but the results were such as to fully justify the maintenance of the clinic. In 2 cases cured, the patients at once obtained better positions; in another, the whole outlook for the patient's future was changed; in another, previ ous constant depression and discouragement were superseded by a more cheerful and pleasant outlook on his life and work. Several children so revolutionized their standing in their classes as to no longer be a laughing stock among their schoolmates. Such work should be maintained at the State's expense and possibly correlated with the work of the schools in speech defect.

In August, 1914, an important step in the training of physicians for State service was taken by the State Board of Insanity, who voted that they would approve of no appointment to the staff of any State hospital unless the appointee had previous experience or had taken special courses in mental hospital work.

In September, 1914, the trustees of the Boston State Hospital voted to approve suggestions of the State Board of Insanity relative to admitting to the Psychopathic Department urgent or selected cases from any part of the State, subject to the approval of the director and the State Board of Insanity; and at the same time voted to approve the plan of giving a course of instruction to candidates for positions of assistant physician to any of the State hospitals, when desired.

Accordingly arrangements were made with the Psychopathic Department of the Boston State Hospital to give such prospective candidates who could not meet the requirements special courses of from three to six months in order to qualify them for the positions sought. Such men were taken as internes, boarded free of expense, and their instruction was free. They received no salary until fitted for their positions and for assuming their responsibilities as members of the staffs. If, at the end of three or six months, it was decided that a candidate would never be able to fill the position which he sought, his hospital was notified and the candidate's connection with the Psychopathic Hospital terminated.

The training course adopted was as follows:

TRAINING COURSE FOR THE STATE HOSPITAL SERVICE, STATE BOARD OF INSANITY, MASSACHUSETTS.

The training courses will for the present begin on the first week days of successive quarters, October, January, April and July, as well as at such irregular times as may be arranged at the Psychopathic Hospital.

Courses of briefer or longer duration may be arranged to fit the previous training of candidates.

Certificates of proficiency will be issued to those meeting requirements.

Special arrangements will be made for candidates for positions as pathologists, clinical directorates, and other special positions, as well as for supplementing the training of those already in the State service.

Special periods, six of a fortnight:

First Period. — Admission of patients under direction; laws of the Commonwealth touching insanity; ward notes on assigned patients; night service as assigned.

Second Period. — Admission of patients; clinical history taking, house and out-patient service; intelligence tests (Binet-Simon, Yerkes, etc.); general mental examinations.

Third Period. — Ophthalmoscopic work; clinicopathological work (blood, urine, feces, stomach contents, etc.); blood pressure; physiological tests (electric sensibility, etc.).

Fourth Period. — Methods of laboratory diagnosis of organic disease; method of obtaining serum and cerebrospinal fluid; principles of Wassermann method, colloidal gold test, etc.; cytology of cerebrospinal fluid. (The laboratory instruction will be given with a view to its value in routine hospital work.)

Fifth and Sixth Periods. — Regular staff work.

The candidates for positions of assistant physicians will be termed internes, and will be lodged and boarded free at the Psychopathic Hospital, so far as accommodations permit.

The director of the Psychopathic Hospital may, with the consent and approval of the Board, terminate a candidate's training at any point.

Advanced Course for Partly Trained Physicians.

General. — Attendance at daily staff rounds, 8 to 9 A.M.; attendance at daily clinical conferences, 12 M. to 1 P.M.; attendance at weekly welfare conference.

Out-Patient Department. — Attendance at autopsies; library work and journal reviewing, as assigned; notes on work of rounds, conferences and other exercises, as assigned.

The State Board of Insanity's general appropriation has, since 1909, contained a sum of $2,500, devoted to the investigation of the nature, causes, treatment and results of insanity, and the publication of such investigation; and this sum was expended, after the establishment of the Psychopathic Department, in work directly connected with that department.

Provision was made that the director of the Psychopathic Hospital should be an officer of the State Board of Insanity with the title of pathologist, and with the duties of supervision of the clinical, pathological and research work of the various institutions in the charge of that Board. The State Board of Insanity, through whose appropriation was paid the salary of the pathologist from 1909 to 1912, resumed payment of the salary of that officer; and the sum formerly paid to him from the appropriation of the Boston State Hospital was now paid to the administrator, appointed August 21, 1915.

Dr. Elisha H. Cohoon began his duties on August 21, 1915, as administrator of the Psychopathic Department. Dr. Cohoon came from an extensive State hospital experience, culminating in work of special interest in the psychopathic ward of the Rhode Island State Hospital. This appointment at once freed the director from multifarious duties which had been carried on to the detriment of more specialized work in classification, treatment and hygiene. The relations of the director to the administrator are amply presented in the regulations of the trustees, as follows:

The psychopathic department shall be managed by the administrator under the general supervision of the superintendent and in accordance with the director's policy and plans. The administrator shall make reports to the director for transmission to the trustees concerning matters of hospital management, and the director shall add such report on matters of treatment, investigation and policy as he may see fit. *Officers shall be appointed by the superintendent, with the approval of the trustees,* on nomination of the director.

The director's report of 1915 stated:

It is worth while to emphasize that these arrangements are proving entirely satisfactory, and may, with few modifications, be likely to serve as a model for future developments in these directions.

A measure of great importance to the proper classification and treatment of many noncommittable cases was the amendment (chapter 174, Acts of 1915) to the temporary-care law, in accordance with which temporary-care cases were admitted for a period of ten days instead of seven days, as under chapter 395, Acts of 1911.

Southard, in his 1915 report, says:

Besides providing facilities for the temporary-care group, the voluntary group and the varied out-patient group of patients, the Commonwealth of Massachusetts has provided facilities which make the Psychopathic Hospital a center of instruction and investigation. The State Board of Insanity has appointed special officers, working largely from the Psychopathic Hospital as a base of operations, which appointments have added much to the scope of the Psychopathic Hospital in mental hygiene, social service, graduate and undergraduate medical instruction and investigation. *In fact, the Commonwealth of Massachusetts has in this regard taken one of the most advanced positions to be found in any State of the Union.* Similar conditions are to be found only in a few States, *e.g.*, New York, Michigan, Illinois and the District of Columbia. In other States, at the present time, the general psychiatric or psychopathic situation is either undeveloped or has been developed more or less irregularly by the enterprise of a few men only.

In 1916, at the suggestion of Dr. Herman M. Adler, chief of staff, the Psychopathic Hospital adopted the method of submitting to psychological examination every candidate for employment as clerk or attendant, the object being to present the results obtained from the examination of the first sixty candidates.

The candidates, both male and female, were referred to the hospital by different employment agencies of Boston, with a few exceptions. The majority of them had attended grammar school, only 28 per cent having advanced to the high school. Their ages varied from eighteen to fifty-five, the average age being twenty-five. After the candidate had applied for work to the superintendent of nurses, and his references had been verified, he was asked to report for a psychological examination. This examination consisted principally of the Yerkes-Bridges point scale, with the multiple choice, and a few other supplementary tests given at the discretion of the examiner. The point scale, devised in 1914 by Robert M. Yerkes and James W. Bridges, is a method for determining the degree of intellectual development. It comprises twenty tests, to each of which a certain credit is allotted. The subject is graded according to his reactions, with full, partial or no credit; when the examination is completed, the sum total of these credits indicates his mental grading in percentage. From February to June, 1915, sixty candidates were examined. With the exception of two, who applied for position as clerk, all of the applicants solicited work as attendants. The following table shows the classification of these candidates according to their degree of intelligence:

	Per Cent.
Normal	63
Slightly subnormal	17
Intellectually inferior	20

In the normal group, which includes only 63 per cent of the whole, are found all applicants who obtained a score about 82 points, that is, who graded above the standard for the mentality of fifteen years. Of these presumably normal candidates —

		Points.
25 obtained .	. . . . . .	82 to 90
9 obtained .	. . . . . .	91 to 95
4 obtained .	. . . . . .	96 to 98

In the second group (17 per cent of the whole), comprising candidates of slightly subnormal intelligence, are included those applicants who obtained between 76 and 82 points credit.

In the third group we find 20 per cent of the candidates. These graded below 76 points, and their reactions indicated intellectual inferiority. According to the norms of the point scale, these subjects did not attain a mental rating equal to that established for the intelligence of a twelve-year-old child, namely, 77 points. Of the subjects included here —

		Points.
7 obtained	. . . . . .	60 to 69
5 obtained	. . . . . .	70 to 75

It is noticeable that a history of alcoholism, immorality or delinquency was obtained from many of these individuals. It is interesting, also, to note that 26.6 per cent of the subjects failed to meet the Binet-Simon requirement for the twelve-year-old mentality.

The following conclusions were drawn from these results by Dr. C. S. Rossy, interne in psychology at the Psychopathic Hospital, in an article on this subject:

1. A high percentage of defective and otherwise mentally incompetent individuals is found among candidates seeking employment as attendants in State hospitals.

2. It is desirable that each candidate for employment

should be submitted to a systematic psychological examination for estimating his general intelligence.

3. These results, though preliminary, emphatically indicate that the Federal and State civil services might well consider the plan of using reliable intelligence tests in their routine examinations.

In the "British Medical Journal," January 8, 1916, there appears an address by Bedford Pierce, M.D., in which he speaks of the activities of the Psychopathic Hospital as follows:

In order to give some idea of the extremely valuable work done at such hospitals of the kind advocated, I will briefly allude to the Psychopathic Hospital at Boston, Massachusetts. On reading the reports of the work done, one is struck with the enthusiasm of the medical staff and the vast field of research undertaken. During the two years, eighteen medical men describe their work covering almost every department of psychiatry: juvenile crime, tests for feeble-mindedness, incidence of syphilis, alcoholism, hydropathy in its influence on red blood cells, treatment of delirium, prophylaxis, analysis of genetic factors, salvarsan treatment, tests of cerebrospinal fluid, errors in diagnoses, and last, but not least, the value of out-patient departments and after-care.

The administrator, in his report of 1916, says:

The somewhat intimate relations between the Psychopathic Hospital in Boston and the municipal court, the juvenile court, the Prison Commission, Industrial Accident Board, the Immigration Bureau, and a variety of semipublic social agencies, are the primary relations of the institution taken as a unit in public service. It is here that our experience is of most service to the country at large, as well as to our own community.

Tremendous pressure is brought to bear to bring a variety of cases from outside the metropolitan district into the Psychopathic Hospital, and the Commission on Mental Diseases has very liberally permitted the hospital to receive special cases from outside the district. The pressure is becoming so great, however, and the appreciation of the Psychopathic Hospital grade of service is such that, no doubt, as above mentioned, an extension of this service to the western part of Massachusetts is only a matter of time and appropriations.

Of the improved attitude toward the mentally ill, Southard in his 1916 report says:

Our attitude to the medical and general public is precisely that of the general hospital, like the Massachusetts General Hospital or the Peter Bent Brigham Hospital, except that perhaps we are inclined to welcome strangers more eagerly, as a matter of hospital policy, on the ground that there has been in the past too much concealment of hospital conditions. No one who goes through our wards fails to inquire where, after all, are the wards for very violent patients. When assured that he has in his ordinarily quiet walk through the wards seen all the violence in the hospital at the time, he is inclined at first to think that our material is somehow milder than that of insane hospitals with which he is familiar. When reminded that the material, particularly Boston police material, and a good deal of the temporary-care group, is as difficult material to manage as any in the district hospitals for the insane, astonishment grows. We have ourselves been astonished at the continued report of voluntary cases to our hospital, when the newspaper advertising which it gets is rather disconcerting than otherwise, for the newspaper entries concerning the Psychopathic Hospital give the perfectly correct, though partial, impression that persons observed to be queer or violent or distraught upon the streets form a leading fraction in our intake of patients.

On April 1, 1917, the first administrator of the hospital, Dr. E. H. Cohoon, left (to the regret of all its officers) to become superintendent of the Medfield State Hospital. His place was filled by Dr. Arthur P. Noyes, as acting administrator.

Although the national reputation of the hospital at this time was such that subordinate positions in the medical service for limited periods were readily filled, so great was the demand for these men in other institutions of this State and elsewhere, that at the salary offered there could be no hope for a continuity of medical policy. Were it not for the extraordinary zeal of certain workers, and for the fact that officers from the Commission on Mental Diseases, notably Dr. Thom and Dr. Solomon, were available to take the place of regular officers in vacations or illness, the hospital would hardly have made so good a medical record. At this time, also, the routine of the hospital was helped by the delegation from the Surgeon-General of a number of

MAJOR ELMER E. SOUTHARD

As Director of the training course conducted at the Boston Psychopathic
Hospital for the United States Army

excellent surgeons who found their best means of improvement in psychiatry to be participation in the routine work of the hospital. The institution was chosen as one of six for special instruction in military psychiatry, and with the consent of the trustees, the director gave a great deal of his time to the instruction of men deputed by the Surgeon-General.

The National Committee for Mental Hygiene sent numerous persons to the Psychopathic Hospital, seeking therein a model for institutions in other States. And there is no doubt that but for the war the Psychopathic Hospital program for the country at large would, by this time, have been in a flourishing state, both on account of its natural worth and on account of its being forwarded by national organizations.

During this period the graduates of Harvard and Tufts Medical Schools began to show an increasing interest in psychiatry, and Dr. Southard says:

> We shall undoubtedly be able to make it possible for Harvard and Tufts graduates to attain, in their sympathy with and understanding of these cases, the same eminence as the graduates of the University of Michigan or of Johns Hopkins Medical School.

Among the new things of an educational nature which the Psychopathic Department undertook might be mentioned the work for technicians, done in the laboratory under the charge of Dr. Myrtelle M. Canavan, assistant pathologist to the Commission, and Miss E. R. Scott. Here, within a period of six years, a score of persons were trained in the difficult special arts of pathological and neuropathological technique.

On May 1, 1919, the organization, objects and purposes of the Psychopathic Department were very materially modified by the action of the Commission on

Mental Diseases (its new name after reorganization) in establishing the Massachusetts State Psychiatric Institute. The functions of the Institute were clearly outlined by the Commission as follows:

The research laboratories heretofore established and now maintained at the psychopathic department of the Boston State Hospital by the Massachusetts Commission on Mental Diseases are hereby continued and shall hereafter be known as the Massachusetts State Psychiatric Institute. Such institute shall be under the general supervision and control of the Massachusetts Commission on Mental Diseases, and shall be maintained by the Commission from appropriations obtained for the purpose.

The object of the institute shall be —

1. To make psychiatric and pathological researches and investigations.

2. To give instruction in psychiatry, neurology, pathology, psychology and social service, with special reference to instruction in the nature, causes, treatment and results of mental diseases and defects.

3. To promote the advancement of mental hygiene.

4. To encourage scientific work in the institutions.

5. To co-ordinate publications of a scientific nature.

6. To carry on the routine and special duties of the pathological service of the Commission.

7. To supervise and correlate the clinical and laboratory work of the institutions under the Commission.

For the purpose of clinical studies, scientific research and instruction, the clinical facilities of the institutions under the Massachusetts Commission on Mental Diseases, including the psychopathic department of the Boston State Hospital, shall be placed at the disposal of the institute.

The director of such institute shall be psychiatrist to the Commission on Mental Diseases. He shall be appointed, together with such other officers and employees as may be deemed necessary, and their compensation shall be fixed by the Commission. The director shall perform, under the direction of the Commission, such duties relating to psychiatric and pathological research under the Commission, and such other duties as may be required by the Commission. He shall have the supervision and control of such institute and of the physicians and other employees therein, subject to the general direction, supervision and control of the Commission. The institutions under the Commission shall co-operate with the institute in such manner as the Commission may, from time to time, direct. Such officers and employees as the Commission may determine shall, if required by the Commission, reside at the psychopathic department of the Boston State Hospital or such other institutions as may be determined, and shall be furnished maintenance in whole or part.

Dr. E. E. Southard, who had been the director of the Psychopathic Department since it was opened on June 24, 1912, resigned under date of May 19, 1919, to take up his work as director of the Institute and undertake the development of the Commission's plans as outlined. This, of course, led to some changes in the plan of organization of the Psychopathic Department. The position of director of the Psychopathic Hospital was abolished upon his resignation.

At a meeting held on June 9, 1919, the Board of Trustees voted to delegate the "supervision, direction and administration of the psychopathic department" to the superintendent of the Boston State Hospital. Under the supervision of Dr. James V. May, superintendent, the chief executive officer was given jurisdiction over the administrative and executive activities of the department, and the chief medical officer was held responsible for the clinical work of the medical staff, as well as the care and treatment of patients. This organization as a result of the establishment of the Psychiatric Institute relieved the Psychopathic Department of all responsibility for scientific research and investigation and left it with purely hospital functions. The organization of the Psychopathic Department as revised includes (1) the ward service, (2) the out-patient service, and (3) the social service. The pathological and psychological laboratories, the hydrotherapy, X-ray work and other necessary adjuncts to the medical service have, of course, been continued and are important corollaries. The readjustments made necessary in the reorganization of the Psychopathic Department imposed numerous additional duties upon the chief medical officer, Dr. Lawson G. Lowrey, and particularly upon the chief executive officer, Dr. Arthur P. Noyes.

Before Dr. Southard had completed the organization and started the work of the Institute, he died. His death occurred in New York City on February 8, 1920, from pneumonia after an illness of but a few days. It was always his hope that the Psychopathic Department of the Boston State Hospital should become an independent unit, — a true psychopathic hospital. A few days before he died, the knowledge came to him that the separation had been authorized by the Legislature, and he expressed great satisfaction.

In May, 1920, the Legislature enacted the following bill:

SECTION 1. The psychopathic department of the Boston state hospital is hereby made a separate state hospital for the care of the insane and shall be subject to all provisions of law applicable to such state hospitals. Its name shall be the Boston Psychopathic Hospital.

SECTION 2. On or before the thirtieth day of November in the current year the governor, with the advice and consent of the council, shall appoint a board of trustees of the Boston Psychopathic Hospital, consisting of seven members, of whom five shall be men and two shall be women. The initial members of said board shall be appointed for terms of one, two, three, four, five, six and seven years respectively from the first Wednesday in February, nineteen hundred and twenty, or until their successors are appointed and qualified. Thereafter as their several terms expire, the governor shall appoint a trustee for the term of seven years, and shall fill any vacancy for the unexpired term. The said trustees shall have all the powers and duties in respect to the Boston Psychopathic Hospital which the present trustees of the Boston state hospital now have in respect thereto, and shall be subject to all provisions of law relating to trustees of state hospitals for the care of the insane.

Thus the objective which we had had in mind for over ten years was, under the administration of Dr. George M. Kline, director of the Commission on Mental Diseases, finally reached; and it is hoped that this is only one of several psychopathic hospitals which

DR. GEORGE M. KLINE

Commissioner of Mental Diseases, whose interest and co-operation in
solving the problems of the mentally ill have done much to extend
the usefulness of the Psychopathic Hospital over the State, and
develop the Psychopathic Hospital Idea throughout the country

within a few years may be established, located to serve the different parts of the State. Dr. Kline was also responsible for the following legislation:

AN ACT TO PROVIDE FOR THE DEVELOPMENT AND STATEWIDE EXTENSION OF THE PSYCHOPATHIC HOSPITAL SERVICE

Be it enacted, etc., as follows:

SECTION 1. The commission on mental diseases is hereby authorized to develop, extend and complete a statewide system of psychopathic hospital service by establishing new hospital and out-patient units in suitable districts in connection with existing or future state hospitals under the supervision of said commission. The administration of the separate new district units and the appropriations granted therefor shall be in accordance with laws governing the state hospitals to which the land, buildings and furnishing of said units shall appertain. The direction of the scientific work in the proposed new units, together with that of the psychopathic department of the Boston state hospital already established under the provisions of chapter four hundred and seventy of the acts of the year nineteen hundred and nine, shall be vested in the commission on mental diseases by means of its duly appointed agents, and said commission shall provide, out of the appropriation for the department, for the salaries and wages of directing and investigative officers and employees and for the expenses of investigation of the nature, causes, treatment and results of mental disease and defect.

SECTION 2. This act shall take effect upon its passage. [*Approved March 29, 1917.*

PART II

ORGANIZATION AND OPERATION

PSYCHOPATHIC HOSPITAL (rear view)

CHAPTER IX

THE ADMINISTRATION PROBLEM

THE PSYCHOPATHIC DEPARTMENT OF THE BOSTON STATE HOSPITAL, BY
'S ADMINISTRATOR, ELISHA H. COHOON, M.D., NOW SUPERINTENDENT
OF THE MEDFIELD STATE HOSPITAL, MEDFIELD, MASSACHUSETTS

't was recognized by all who were interested in
rchiatry in general and those interested particularly
the care of the insane of Massachusetts that much
1 been accomplished when the Psychopathic De-
tment of the Boston State Hospital was ready for
upancy. It was felt that already a great forward
o had been made in the care of the mentally ill.
Those who had the responsibility of opening and
ducting this new hospital realized that as its aims,
poses and general functions were different from
se of the usual State hospital and also different
m those of a general hospital, its administration
ld also necessarily have to be different. Although
y were possessed of some information regarding the
ration of a psychopathic hospital in Europe, there
practically no precedent in this country to guide
m. The only psychopathic hospital in America at
t time was small in comparison and in every way
ctically an integral part of a large general hospital.
thermore, its aims, purposes and functions were
so numerous or so extensive as those mapped out
the hospital in Boston; hence, the working out of
plan of organization and the methods to be used
ts operation were regarded more or less as an ex-
ment. Located several miles from the main part

of the Boston State Hospital, it necessarily had to be considered as a separate and distinct problem from a standpoint of administration, although it had to depend upon the Boston State Hospital for general maintenance and in a legal sense was under the administration of that hospital.

Keeping in mind its special purposes and functions, its initial organization was as follows:

1. Director.
    He formerly had complete charge of all the operation of the hospital and was responsible to the Board of Trustees and to the superintendent of the Boston State Hospital. It was also expected that he would direct the scientific work and other work naturally associated with a hospital of this type.
2. Chief of staff.
    Under the director he had special charge of the medical work and general oversight over the administrative details.
3. Executive assistant.
    This officer was directly under the chief of staff and attended to the more purely hospital routine administrative details.
4. Head of the out-patient department.
5. Head of the social service.
6. Head psychologist.

Dr. Elmer E. Southard was chosen director. In addition to a splendid record of scientific attainments in the field of psychiatry, and especially in neuropathology, he had studied the psychopathic hospital problem in Germany. Dr. Herman Adler was chosen chief of staff. He had behind him a splendid record both in the laboratory and in clinical psychiatry. From a standpoint of general policy both were admirably equipped to occupy their respective positions in a psychopathic hospital, but neither had had experience along purely administrative lines. They were responsible for the above scheme of organization and are deserving of a great amount of credit considering the fact that the operation of a large psychopathic hospital in America was practically a new administrative venture.

At the time of the opening, the amount of work that the hospital would be called upon to perform could not be at all estimated. It was rather felt by those who had been especially interested in promoting the idea of a psychopathic hospital in Boston, and who should have been in a position to have formed a fairly accurate estimate, that the maximum number of patients ever to be received in any one year by this hospital would not exceed 1,500. In 1913, one year after the opening of the hospital, this number had already been exceeded, and the trustees of the Boston State Hospital in the report of that year called attention to the fact that when this estimate of 1,500 admissions a year had been made, it was looked upon by some as "an exaggeration born of enthusiasm for the cause of a psychopathic hospital." The personnel of this organization had been carefully selected, and the hospital opened with excellent heads of every department. The number of admissions increased so rapidly, and there was such a demand for the various uses of the hospital, that it was soon realized that the personnel had to be greatly increased. The fact that patients had to be examined and disposed of within a few days in itself required an unusual amount of work, out of all proportion to the number of admissions. Being located in the city and readily accessible, there was a great number of daily visitors. The various special examinations, the work of the out-patient department, the social service work, the instruction of medical students, visits by outside physicians and others, together with the intensive study of cases that was required, swelled the amount of work to be accomplished beyond all limits of expectation. The extramural activities and relations were very extensive. Fortunately, the inspiring genius of Dr. Southard attracted workers both in the medical and other fields, but it became very apparent that the problem of administration had been very much underestimated and that it was difficult with the present organization to cope with the situation.

In 1913 the admissions had exceeded 1,500, and in the following year reached approximately 2,000. Year by year the amount of work increased as the admission rate went up and as the activities of the hospital became more extended and diversified. In order to meet this situation, the organization scheme was elaborated. This elaboration was well worked out and seemed to arrange for the proper handling of every detail. There were as many as eight medical services, and the officer-of-the-day system was put in use. By this time the hospital had become more or less of a training school. The personnel of the medical staff and of other departments were largely made up of volunteer workers. These remained but relatively a short time, and so there was a continual change. This condition could not be remedied at this time as the budget did not permit the employment of a sufficient number of regular, salaried, medical and other officers. On account of this lack of stability, it can easily be understood that the officer-of-the-day system could not successfully handle the administrative details, especially those of a public service character. Furthermore, the volunteer workers in all departments were interested particularly in clinical work and, naturally, less in routine details. The result was that both the director and the chief of staff had to give part of their time to the proper handling of these ordinary routine details, and in so doing diverted their attention from the clinical and scientific aspects of the work for which they were more properly fitted and trained.

In 1915 it was realized that steps must be taken to remedy this condition, and it was decided to introduce into the organization the position of administrator. The holder of this position was to have charge of the usual ordinary administrative details of the hospital, except the clinical, scientific and research work. The plan arranged for the administrative work to be conducted along the general lines of policy laid down by the director. In certain respects he was responsible to the superintendent of the Boston State Hospital, and took over many of the duties heretofore performed by the superintendent. He was to make a monthly report to the director, to be transmitted to the Board of Trustees. In order that a suitable man might be obtained, it was provided that he be given the salary and practically the standing of a superintendent.

The writer was appointed administrator in 1915. The changes inaugurated by him in the organization scheme did away with the officer-of-the-day system, reduced the numbers of heads of medical services, and in general concentrated the responsibilities. Another administrative assistant was added. The purely administrative part of the operation of the hospital at once became more stabilized, and the director and chief of staff were relieved of many uncongenial duties and were able to give much more attention and time to

scientific and clinical work.   In evolving this modification of the organization, it was kept in mind that
the administration of the hospital must be so conducted that its primary functions — such as teaching,
research, intensive clinical work, and the promotion of
mental hygiene — should not in any way be decreased
or subordinated to the more purely routine hospital
matters but rather should be encouraged and, if possible, improved and increased.   In a relatively short
time many of the difficulties and vexing problems
disappeared, and there was an increased interest and
output along clinical and research lines.

The first holder of the position of administrator
resigned in the spring of 1917, and was succeeded by
Dr. A. P. Noyes.   The advent of this country into the
World War in 1917, with the resultant difficulty in
obtaining personnel, the leave of absence granted
the director, Dr. Southard, to enter the Chemical
Warfare Service, and also the death of Dr. Henry P.
Frost, superintendent of the Boston State Hospital
necessarily affected the administration of the hospital
but in the main the organization as outlined by the
administrator was continued with fair success.   This
organization was not regarded as a perfect one, and it
was admitted that its success or failure largely depended upon the quality of the personnel.

In 1918, under Superintendent Dr. James V. May
of the Boston State Hospital, a slight change was
made in the organization.   The term administrator
was changed to that of chief executive officer, and the
following organization plan was made:

1. Director.
2. Chief executive officer.
     Executive officer.
        Assistant executive officer.
3. Chief medical officer.
     Medical officer.
        Assistant medical officer.
4. Chief of out-patient department.
        Assistant medical officer, out-patient department.
5. Chief psychologist.
6. Chief of social service.

In the year 1919, following the return of the director, Dr. Southard, further changes were made in the organization. Dr. Southard was relieved of the duties of director of the hospital and made director of the Massachusetts Psychiatric Institute, located within the hospital. This Institute was under the general supervision of the Massachusetts Commission on Mental Diseases. A certain portion of the hospital was set apart for its use, and the director confined his activities to research work, instruction of medical students and, in general, the promotion of mental hygiene and scientific work. The administration of the hospital was placed more directly under the superintendent. He was represented by a chief executive officer and a chief medical officer. The chief executive officer was given jurisdiction over the administrative activities, and the chief medical officer was responsible for the clinical work of the medical staff. Both of these officers reported directly to the superintendent. The purpose of this change was to further relieve Dr. Southard and his assistants from hospital responsibilities and cares and better arrange for more intensive work along scientific lines. The death of Dr. Southard in 1920 had its influence, but no further changes were made in the organization until by an act of the Legislature the Psychopathic Department of the Boston State Hospital became the Boston Psychopathic Hospital December 1, 1920.

The present organization is under the control of the director, Dr. C. Macfie Campbell, who is responsible directly to the trustees and the Department of Mental Diseases. The administrative officer, under the title of chief executive officer, has continued to perform duties and functions not unlike those assumed by the administrator in 1915 and later by the chief executive officer when the hospital was a department of the Boston State Hospital.

As a result of my own experiences and from what I know of the experiences of others, I have come to the following conclusions in regard to the administration of a psychopathic hospital:

1. That the administrative problems as found in a psychopathic hospital differ very much from those found in any other type of hospital. It is a specialized hospital dealing in the larger problems of general psychiatry and the care of the insane, including research work, instruction to medical students, training of other specialized workers, and the promotion of mental hygiene, and, hence, requires a different organization plan of administration than is found in the usual State hospital or general hospital.

2. That if the hospital is relatively large and has a great intake of patients, it should not be connected with a parent State hospital or general hospital.

3. That the administrative problem as it affects the daily routine of the hospital is a very important part of the management of the whole hospital and

should be in the hands of a high-grade administrator of considerable experience. Whether or not the hospital should be in charge of a superintendent who would, of course, be the administrator or chief executive officer, and have under him a director, or whether the director should be at the head and the administrative officer subordinate, is perhaps a debatable question. If subordinate to the director, it should be arranged that the administrative officer should occupy a position of considerable importance and be allowed sufficient authority to administer the hospital without interference but along the lines of policy laid down by the director.   In short, he should be a true executive.   It is important that the executive officer should have had good clinical experience and should give evidence of being in sympathy with scientific work.

I feel that I cannot close this short chapter without expressing my appreciation of the late director of the Psychopathic Department of the Boston State Hospital, Dr. Elmer E. Southard.   His high ideals, his broad vision toward hospital matters, his kindness and sympathy inspired all to do their very best, and the success that marked the course of the Psychopathic Department of the Boston State Hospital can very largely be credited to him.

CHAPTER X

THE OUT-PATIENT DEPARTMENT

OF THE PSYCHOPATHIC HOSPITAL, BY DOUGLAS A. THOM, M.D., CHIEF OF
THE OUT-PATIENT DEPARTMENT, BOSTON PSYCHOPATHIC HOSPITAL;
INSTRUCTOR IN PSYCHIATRY, HARVARD MEDICAL SCHOOL; ADVISORY
CONSULTANT, UNITED STATES PUBLIC HEALTH SERVICE; DI-
RECTOR OF CHILDREN'S "HABIT CLINIC," SOUTH BAY
UNION SETTLEMENT; DIRECTOR OF THE SECTION OF
MENTAL HYGIENE IN THE DEPARTMENT OF
MENTAL DISEASES OF MASSACHUSETTS

I

Although the Psychopathic Department of the Boston State Hospital was opened on June 24, 1912, a chief medical officer to have charge of the out-patient clinic was not appointed until January 1, 1913.

In a report from Dr. Southard, the director of the Psychopathic Hospital, to the superintendent of the Boston State Hospital, dated November 30, 1912, he states:

The out-patient department has been especially successful, although not yet formally opened. Social agencies of various descriptions, particularly those dealing with children and adolescents, have hastened to send their problems to the Psychopathic Hospital. . . . There can be no doubt that the work of the out-patient department, upon the diagnoses of various grades especially the higher grades of imbecility, upon juvenile court problems, upon sex problems connected with adolescence, upon incipient cases of insanity and cases of fear of insanity, upon speech disorder, and, most important of all, upon after-care and prophylactic work in connection with house cases, amply justified its existence.

Dr. W. P. Lucas, now professor of pediatrics at the University of California, was the first physician to assume charge of the out-patient work, and he was immediately followed by Dr. A. W. Stearns. It was noted that the department was beginning to attract a large number of voluntary workers, and it was predicted at that time that the social service problems connected with the neuropsychiatric patient would become more highly specialized and the out-patient department would become a center for the students from schools of social service. The total number of cases visiting the clinic from October 1, 1912, to September 30, 1913, was 830. The following summarizes the source of the clinical material covering that period:

Out-Patient Department, 1913

Total cases October 1, 1912, to September 30, 1913	830
Adult males	243
Adult females	205
Adolescent males (fourteen to twenty-one years)	72
Adolescent females (twelve to eighteen years)	83
Total boys and girls	223
Boys	134
Girls	89
Infants (male)	2
Infants (female)	2
Cases referred from public agencies	89
Courts	40
Schools	49
Cases referred from social agencies	163
Cases referred from hospitals	81
Cases referred by physicians	77
Cases referred by individuals	27
Cases referred from Psychopathic Hospital for after-care	184
Cases resorting on own initiative	209

June 13, 1914, Dr. A. W. Stearns resigned and his duties as chief of the out-patient department devolved upon Dr. H. M. Adler. The number of patients increased from 830 for the statistical year of 1913 to ,133 for the statistical year of 1914. The number of visits was nearly doubled, and 338 special reports concerning cases examined and treated were sent to social agencies and courts. The total number of visits for the year was 5,227, this being the first year that the total number of visits was noted in the annual report.

The work in general in the out-patient department falls roughly into four classes:

First. — The out-patient medical, psychological and social examiners have to deal with questions of feeble-mindedness and mental defect, especially in regard to the mentally defective delinquents referred from courts, reformatories or other institutions, including an increasing number of backward children from schools.

Second. — The out-patient department handles psychiatric cases, both patients discharged from the Psychopathic Hospital and from other State hospitals (those who have a residence in or near Boston who can most conveniently resort to the Psychopathic Hospital, out-patient department). Also, there is a certain number of patients who have never been in a hospital, but still require treatment for mild or incipient mental troubles of a noncommittable nature.

Third. — The out-patient department handles a good many somatic cases, cases that require physical treatment of various sorts in connection with diseases of the nervous system. The largest class falling thereunder is that of the neurosyphilitics, a great number of whom are physically fit for ambulatory treatment.

Fourth. — There is a group of cases that are, more narrowly speaking, cases of the social service group requiring aid chiefly from the community's point of view. We here deal with cases suffering from the ef

MAJOR L. VERNON BRIGGS, CAPTAIN DOUGLAS A. THOM AND
MAJOR JAMES V. MAY

At Camp Devens, Mass., October, 1917. Dr. May succeeded Dr. Frost
as superintendent of the Boston State Hospital and its Psychopathic
Department in 1917

fects, pre-eminently, of poor housing, poverty, deser-
tion, and the like, all of which evils are based upon or
laid down upon the background of mental inadequacy.

The men's club for alcoholics as a therapeutic measure was definitely established.   The total number of
new cases reported to the clinic for the fiscal year of
1915 was 1,426.

In 1916 much stress was laid on the value of specialized social service workers for neuropsychiatric cases.
Dr. Southard said, "Instead of two paid workers with
a varying number of volunteers, we require, I believe,
at least seven paid workers."   The total number of
new patients for the year was 1,485, while the total
number of visits was 9,261, the monthly average
varying from 678 to 938.   (It is necessary here to call
attention to the fact that many of these patients came
in for baths and received no attention whatsoever
from physicians, excepting on the first visit.)

In 1918 the director called attention to the fact that
Dr. Abraham Myerson, the chief medical officer, had
stimulated the neurological side of the work, much to
the advantage of the clinic.   During that year close
relations had been established with Dr. Healy's work
at the Juvenile Court and also with Dr. Anderson at
the Municipal Court.   Attention was drawn to the
fact that a very large percentage of all social problems
presented a very important psychiatric side.   It was
during the summer of 1918 that close affiliation was
made between the school of psychiatric and social service work and the social service department of the Psychopathic Hospital, this affiliation having continued
up until the present time.   The total number of new
cases for the year was 1,543, of whom 317 were chil-

dren.   The total number of visits was 7,761.   The
following table is of interest, indicating the number of
patients who made visits and their relative frequency:

Came only once   1,005
Made two visits   226
Made three visits   104
More than three visits   188

In the report for the year ended September 30, 1919,
a summary of the first five years' statistics was presented as follows:

During the five years ended September 30, 1918, 6,532 new cases were reported in the out-patient service, — an average of 1,306.2 cases per year.
Fifty-eight per cent of these cases consisted of adults, 16 per cent of adolescents,
24 per cent of children, and 5 per cent of infants.   Of these, 4.9 per cent were
referred to the out-patient service by courts, 4.8 per cent by schools, 12.6 per
cent by hospitals, 9 per cent by physicians, and 3.5 per cent by other individuals; 12.5 per cent came of their own initiative, 17.7 per cent came from
the wards of the Psychopathic Department, and 9.2 per cent were sent by
the social service.

For the year 1919 there were 1,517 new cases, of
whom 414 were children.   It is of interest to note that,
in a general way, of the clinical material coming to
the Psychopathic Hospital about one-fourth were
children under fourteen years of age, the origin of the
cases being very largely from the courts, schools, hospitals, social agencies, Red Cross, physicians, and the
wards of the Psychopathic Hospital, and about 15 per
cent coming on their own initiative.   The problems
presented were rather varied, including returned sol-
diers, adult offenders, juvenile delinquents, sex offenders, unmarried mother, backward child, unemployment, alcoholism, children to be placed out or
adopted, and the after-care work associated with dis-

charged patients from the various State hospitals as well as the Psychopathic Hospital. The disposition of the 1,577 cases seen at the clinic during the year was as follows:

Sent into the Psychopathic Hospital 131
Committed to feeble-minded institutions 128
Committed to insane institutions 26
Referred to the Psychopathic Hospital, out-patient department . . 590
Referred back to social agency 296
Report made to court 44

In the report for the year ended September 30, 1921, attention was called to the fact that the actual number of hours devoted to medical service was quite inadequate, and although a great deal had been done since the organization of the Psychopathic Hospital in serving the psychiatric needs of the community, all too frequently the actual service rendered the individual, especially in those cases requiring treatment, was far from satisfactory.   It is quite obvious that by increasing the hours of medical service a much higher standard could be set for out-patient psychiatry.   Dr. C. Macfie Campbell, director of the Psychopathic Hospital, had already done much to meet this need by supplying one full-time physician from the house and sending one physician each morning for the out-patient work, so that ways and means are being provided that we may serve the individual needs of the patient more efficiently than we have heretofore.

The examination of school children in the Brookline district was carried on for the year 1921 by Dr. Percy L. Dodge, who reported there were many problems other than those of feeble-mindedness which should interest the psychiatrist.   Not infrequently he referred conduct problems for treatment.

Special attention was given to the reports going out to social agencies, making an effort not only to give a diagnosis of the case, but also to give the prognosis and advice, and, in so far as our study of the case made it possible, what the disposition should be. A rather interesting problem was undertaken as an off-shoot of the out-patient department by establishing a "habit clinic" under the auspices of the Baby Hygiene Association. This clinic is conducted at the South Bay Union settlement house one afternoon a week by the chief of the out-patient department, and has attracted a great deal of attention and interest from those interested in the mental hygiene of childhood. The problems presented at this clinic are very largely those concerning the development of undesirable habits, and the treatment lies almost entirely in the education of the parents.

The total number of patients coming to the out-patient department for the year ended September 30, 1920, was 1,439, of which about one-fourth were children. The total number of medical visits was 2,638. Total number of visits, including those for baths and occupational therapy, was 4,071.

PROBLEMS PRESENTED

Adoption.	Refusal to study.
Convulsions.	Enuresis.
Backwardness.	Destructiveness.
Loss of memory.	Pain in head.
Stealing.	Sees faces.
Worrying.	Truancy.
"Trances."	Family discord.
Sex delinquency.	Dizzy spells.
Insomnia.	Masturbation.
Tempers.	Crying spells.
Pressure on head.	Spots before eyes.

Depression, suicidal.
Seclusiveness.
Somatic complaints.
Trembling of arm.
Fear of death.
Waywardness.
For commitment.
Assault by brother.
Nightmares.
Moodiness.
After care.
Ideas of persecution.
Inability to walk.
Illegitimate pregnancy.
Inability to sit still in school.
Boldness, untruthfulness, out late.
Condition of family syphilitics.
Depression; desire to be alone.
Dizziness and headaches.
Running away; threatening suicide.
For certificate of health.
Involuntary movements of the arms.
Nervous chronic gastritis.
Conflicting ambitions; stealing.

Character change after accident.
For psychometric only.
Lack of concentration; poor motor co-ordination.
Suspected feeble-mindedness.
Delusions and hallucinations.
Turns night into day.
Timid and fearful.
Guidance as to future training.
Question of epilepsy.
As to whether he can work.
Vomiting, headaches, rumbling in ears.
Depression; obsessive ideas.
Twitching; unstable disposition.
Paralysis of left arm.
Stubborn, obstinate, sex delinquent.
Imagines she sees her father.
Easily fatigued; pains.
Lack of concentration; anxiety.
Hypochondriacal ideas.
Incompetent to hold job; alcoholic.
Routine examination for placing out.
Suspiciousness; outbursts of temper.

II

Nothing that has happened in modern medicine during the past decade has been a greater boon to mankind than the movement which transferred medical interest in psychiatry from the insane hospital to the community. The propaganda necessary for the success of such a movement began to bear fruit with the establishment of psychopathic hospitals and the annexation of psychopathic wards to general hospitals. Public interest in matters pertaining to the mental health of the individual was greatly stimulated by the recent war. Psychiatry, ignored for hundreds of years, even as a medical problem, is now receiving a cordial reception in many fields, such as the schools, courts and industry.

In the great scheme of social and preventive medicine, psychiatry is taking its stand in the front line trenches. In every situation, whether it be medical, social, educational, industrial, judicial or military, in fact, wherever two or more individuals are gathered together, the problem of human adjustment must be considered, and psychiatry in its broadest sense must play its part.

The aims and purposes of the out-patient department of the Psychopathic Hospital have been, in so far as possible, to meet the psychiatric needs of the community. How numerous and varied these needs have been has been shown in a brief summary of the activities of the Boston Psychopathic Hospital during the past ten years.

There can be no sweeping generalizations made of the psychopathic cases, either as they concern one large branch of the medical science or as they are divided into their various subgroups. The problems presented are invariably the problems of the individual, intimate and personal; occasionally trivial and a bit humorous, sometimes ugly and sordid, not infrequently strangely pathetic. I say strangely, because so many of the problems presented at the out-patient clinic are of such a nature and so involved that they frequently seem to bear little relation to the ordinary problems of everyday life. Yet, it is because they are the problems of everyday life that they permit us to lend a helping hand. One feels, perhaps, that what has been said is all very vague and ill-defined, and fails to state just what the functions of an out-patient clinic really are. Many of the problems *are* vague and ill-defined and require skill, ingenuity, patience, and an understanding of human nature which can only be obtained by mingling with the masses and studying their habits of life.

The following are typical problems for an out-patient clinic:

(*a*) Boy, 15; sent in by the judge to determine the boy's mental responsibility for repeated thefts.

(*b*) Unmarried mother brought in by a social agency to determine girl's mental age and to what extent she will become socially adjustable and economically independent.

(*c*) Woman, 55; comes in of her own initiative (recommended by former patient). Complains of pain in head, insomnia and depression. (Caused by living with daughter and son-in-law; cleared up completely after change of environment.)

(*d*) Boy, 9; sent in by teacher. Doing poorly in school. Repeated seventh grade. (Intellect above normal; home conditions poor.)

(*e*) Boy, 19; sent in by private physicians because of hysterical convulsions. (Examination reveals syphilis innocently acquired.)

Such are a few of the cases who are in need of the assistance which the psychiatrist can render.

The fact that a comparatively small percentage of the patients coming to the out-patient clinic are recommended for institutional care, does not mean that we are dealing with a group of problems easy of solution. It is vitally important that accurate decisions be made and wise conclusions drawn, so that the ultimate disposition of the case will not inflict an injustice upon the patient or cast reflection upon the institution. A suicidal case must be properly guarded, the retarded boy cannot be treated as feeble-minded, the illegitimate mother whose misfortune is due to environmental conditions should not be classed with the group of psychopathic personalities and potential prostitutes, and the psychoneurotic wage earner must usually be kept at work until we can provide adequate economic relief for the family.

Dr. C. Macfie Campbell in a recent address at the ether day celebration at the Massachusetts General Hospital said:

> The indoor department of the twenty-first century hospital may be a comparatively minor factor in the general health organization, while the main hospital activity may be in an out-patient department. More and more should the out-patient department be used as the admission route to the hospital, and all patients should be discharged through this department in order to facilitate the after-care work.

The wide variation in the problems presented necessarily prevents what might be termed a routine procedure for every case. Regrettable as it may be, time is always a factor with which we have to reckon, — both the time of the physician and the patient.

History taking, important as it is in every medical case, needs particular emphasis in dispensary work. It would obviously be a waste of time to get a very detailed history of a patient that was about to enter the hospital where time is no object when doing intensive work. Delusions and hallucinations and other definitely psychotic symptoms can be passed over hurriedly in dealing with the majority of the cases where mental deficiency or delinquency are the presenting symptoms. In the former group, a detailed history of early life and the psychometric tests need particular stress, while in the latter group a study of personality and changes in personality is extremely important.

In dealing with convulsive phenomena, a special questionnaire should be used in order that no differentiating points may be omitted. This should be followed by a thorough physical examination and such laboratory tests as will exclude or determine the organic basis of the convulsions. In fact, every case should have a physical examination sufficiently extensive and intensive, with all tests necessary to determine the possibility of any organic basis for the mental symptoms. Not infrequently it is not only wise but necessary to utilize the general hospitals for such examinations and to suspend judgment on the case until receiving their report. A Wassermann examination on the blood is justified in every case, and only by this procedure will errors in diagnoses be avoided. Psychometric tests should be done on all cases where the developmental, educational, economic or social history indicates mental deficiency. Frequently in adults, mental deficiency can be determined even if not measured by other means, thus saving the psychologist's time.

The interpretation of the psychometric test, and its relation to the other aspects of the examination, of course is left with the psychiatrist, and is only one of the several factors which he utilizes in making a diagnosis. The roentgenologist, serologist and specialists along various lines are used to meet requirements of the individual cases.

The psychologist will eventually, without doubt, devise tests which will be of considerable value in our psychiatric problems as they relate to industry.

Perhaps the most fertile field is that pertaining to vocational selection. There is no doubt but what a considerable portion of the unemployed psychoneurotics who are now economic liabilities can be rehabilitated and made socially adaptable and economically independent if they come under the observation of those whose training and experience *have equipped them for this particular line of work.*

The most important aspect of the community work is that of social service. It represents the lines of communication between the hospitals and clinics and those to whom we are rendering service. The outpatient department, without a well-organized, intelligently equipped, smoothly running social service machine to aid in the adjustment of the economic, social and educational needs of the patients, is doomed to failure. Too much stress cannot be laid on the selection of personnel for such a service, for the tasks at hand require nice judgment, a keen sense of social values and an unbiased mind that interprets situations not from a moral but from a social point of view.

The social service worker must be diplomatic, resourceful, interested in humanity and humanity's problems, and last, but not least, an individual whose personality is such that she finds pleasure and satisfaction in doing teamwork. The development and progress of the social service department will be considered elsewhere. It is sufficient for me to say that the Boston Psychopathic Hospital has had the good fortune of having a social service department directed, ever since its organization, by the type of individual just described, so much to be desired, yet so difficult to obtain.

There is no part of the out-patient personnel that

contributes more to the efficiency of the organization than a well-trained clinic manager. The position should be filled preferably by a qualified psychiatric social worker, who should devote her entire time to the interests of the clinic. Her duties are numerous and varied. In the morning, while the clinic is in operation, she is the one who makes the first contact with the patient and those accompanying him. By virtue of her training and experience, she should be capable of taking histories if the pressure of work demands it. She is the keeper of the records, and it falls upon her to see that the innumerable details necessary for the reports are correctly and completely recorded.

It is the clinic manager from whom the outside agencies receive such information regarding their cases as can be given over the telephone and who answers innumerable inquiries from the public regarding the clinic. Not only should she be familiar with the organizations referring cases, but she should know intimately every agency or society which is in a position to be of assistance in making the proper disposition of the case. This permits us to bring our patient in contact with those who are best able to render the necessary service.

With reference to these reports, their value as a means of educating the public and the medical profession cannot be overestimated. On the other hand, they are very apt to consume too much of the physician's time which should be devoted to medical service. I feel that with comparatively little effort on the part of the physician, he can summarize the findings on a case, including the diagnosis, prognosis, treatment and disposition, and the clinic manager can compile these reports. Furthermore, she is usually able to present the case in a way that is more satisfactory to the social organization than the average physician can do. All reports and the records are passed upon by the chief of the clinic and signed by him before going to the public. Obviously, one would not desire or permit a nonmedical person to even compile a report on a medical case where the physical aspect was at all important, but in a very large per cent of all the reports sent out from an out-patient clinic, the social aspect predominates.

In a clinic which does not employ a special person to do the follow-up work, the clinic manager can also assume the responsibility for this important aspect of community service. So, frequently, we find that it is the individuals that are most in need of treatment who accept it very reluctantly. Much can be done by a well-organized follow-up system to bring these cases under the care of the out-patient clinic.

The out-patient clinics are comparable to the first aid stations of the hospital organization of the military system. Just behind the lines, well within the hearing and often within the range of heavy guns, the neuro-psychiatric section of the United States Medical Corps pitched their tents and organized under the most formidable conditions, — the most efficient piece of preventive medicine in the history of the great war. The fact that 65 per cent of all the cases sent to these first aid stations returned to active duty within seventy-two hours after their evacuation, is an indication of the importance of early treatment in our attempt to abort mental illness. Yet how difficult it has been to impress upon those whom it should concern the importance of this experiment! Four years have passed since the armistice. We are again back to civilian life, surrounded by a peace and tranquillity of mind, awakened only from our slumbers by some particular atrocious murder or rape, or an inexcusable wreck or explosion, or some unaccountable industrial catastrophe brought about by mental derangement. In many of the legislative halls the cry still rings, "Millions for buildings and custodial care, but not one cent for prevention." Attention is focused on the end result of mental illness, the source of supply is frequently entirely ignored.

I know of no way in which the State can do more to conserve the mental health of its citizens than by means of well-organized out-patient clinics. Not only can the maximum number of patients be treated at the minimum cost, but they make contact with the physician during the early and incipient stage of their difficulties when treatment is most hopeful. The assistance is made available at a time when the patient is still capable of appreciating his own needs. It is rendered in a manner that makes it acceptable and compatible with the patient's social and economic obligations. It permits him to carry on his work, continue to dwell in the family circle, and be rehabilitated in the environment in which he must continue to live in order to play his part in the social scheme of things. This fact is becoming more and more appreciated — that the out-patient clinic is the pivot point from which preventive medicine, so far as it relates to the mental health of the community, is radiating. Ministers, teachers, judges, probation officers, physicians and lawyers are daily turning to the psychiatrist for advice pertaining to the problems of human conduct, but we should not be satisfied in waiting for them to seek us out, we must penetrate and become part of their organizations.

This is perhaps an opportune time to call attention to the importance and the attitude of the out-patient organization, including the physicians, clinic manager and social service workers, towards the patients, their friends and relatives, and others interested in the case.

So frequently one hears complaints from those attending out-patient clinics that they are considered as cases rather than as individuals. They are rushed in and out of examining rooms in a very mechanical way, and no effort whatsoever is made to make the examination less of an ordeal. Such a system, undesirable as it may be, can function perhaps with a fair degree of success when the physician is dealing with the patient's eyes, stomach or kidneys, or, in more general terms, if he is dealing with the patient's organs rather than the patient himself, but a clinic which attempts to treat the individual, and makes this one of its basic and fundamental points in such a dehumanized method, is sure to fail. The necessity of gaining the patient's confidence, and convincing him that his particular troubles are your greatest interest at that moment, must be recognized as the initial step in successful psychotherapy. This can only be done by meeting the patient on his own intellectual level. Time is never wasted which tends to establish a workable relation between the doctor and the patient. It matters not whether one discusses sports and games with the youngsters, the newly arrived baby with the mother, the tipping system with a porter, or perhaps listens to the reminiscences of the aged. It is in this way that one frequently gains an insight into the patient's personality and learns something regarding the individual which is invaluable in the treatment of his illness. It does not take long to learn that more valuable information can be gained by allowing the patient to talk freely and uninterruptedly during the first interview than can be extracted by direct questioning. Invariably they will touch on the subjects around which their conflicts are centered, which would be ingeniously avoided if the attack were made by the physician.

CHAPTER XI

THE SOCIAL SERVICE, 1913 TO 1918

OF THE PSYCHOPATHIC HOSPITAL, BY MARY C. JARRETT, FORMERLY CHIEF OF SOCIAL SERVICE, PSYCHOPATHIC DEPARTMENT, BOSTON STATE HOSPITAL; NOW ASSOCIATE DIRECTOR, SMITH COLLEGE TRAINING SCHOOL FOR SOCIAL WORK, NORTHAMPTON, MASSACHUSETTS

"The need of a social service in the new Psychopathic Hospital became obvious at once when the plans were tentatively discussed in 1909–1910, and the obvious need was expressed in so many words in the State Board of Insanity's report in 1910." This is a quotation from a memorandum written by Dr. Southard, the director. Space was reserved for the social service in the architect's plans, which was an unusual step at that time. The conception of such a department as the architect represented was not, however, carried out. A small room appears in the plans as the "social service office," and a larger room as the "social service waiting room." The vision of a social worker sitting in her office with a waiting room full of patients and friends outside is about as far as possible from a true picture of social work. In the course of time desks took the place of the empty benches of the "waiting room."

It used to be the common practice, and indeed too often it is still, when social work is started in a hospital, to engage a social worker to be useful wherever she is needed and to get as much done as she can, with the expectation that some day another worker may be added, so that twice as much may be done. Thus the work is supposed to grow spontaneously. The director of the Psychopathic Hospital saw that social work, particularly in hospitals, had already developed far enough to have produced a wealth of experience that could be applied in a new social service department. He appointed a director of the department, or "chief of social service," whom he instructed to develop and organize the social work of the institution in close relation to the out-patient department. This was in May, 1913, about a year after the hospital opened.

The attitude of Dr. Southard toward the social service is indicated in the following excerpt from an unpublished paper which he wrote:

Perhaps it is worth while to say that personally I stand to this work as a scribe. As scribe, however, I have the advantage of saying certain personal things about local developments which the workers themselves could not say. As for personal prejudices, I am afraid I must confess to one at least, namely, that psychiatric social work must be dominated far more than certain other branches of medico-social work, and again far more than certain branches of social service at large, by the physician and alienist. This prejudice, if it be a prejudice, does not hesitate to concede to the trained social worker every latitude in the technique of social investigation and almost every latitude in the offering of advice and in the choice of domestic and economic steps to take in the given case. But decisions concerning medico-social therapy, touching (a) the desirability of private or institutional care of an insane, feeble-minded, epileptic, alcoholic, or otherwise psychopathic case, (b) the choice of institution, (c) further tests necessary, are decisions which are, in my opinion, medical decisions. Decisions concerning the relative parts played by heredity and environment in a given case, whether a case is "morbid" or "vicious," how much improved family surroundings might help a case, whether syphilis is to be suspected, whether there is an element of sex-perversion in the case, whether questionable statements of patients are best regarded as truths, lies, delusions, or mixtures of these, — all these decisions and a vast number of similar ones are decisions hardly to be entrusted to such social workers as the schools have yet developed.

The chief of social service, when appointed, first spent a week in visits to persons in various cities from whom ideas might be obtained upon social work for psychopathic patients. Then the first three months at the hospital were spent in a preliminary survey of the situation to determine how social work might best contribute to the medical work. Meanwhile she acted as clinic manager in the out-patient department, since this was one of the best means to get experience of the clientele and work of the institution.

A study of the need for social work in 200 cases was made, upon which plans for the case work were based. It was estimated that eight social workers would be needed to do adequately all the work of the hospital, on the basis of one social worker for every 200 admissions during the year. Further estimates during the year confirmed this opinion.

On the anniversary of the opening of the hospital, in June, 1913, the First Annual Conference on the Medical and Social Work of the Psychopathic Hospital was held, and for a number of years such a conference was held annually. Social problems of the hospital were presented at these meetings by the physicians and by the social workers of the staff. The close relation of medical and social work was fostered by the director in every way. Social workers, students and volunteer workers of the social service were expected to attend the daily staff meetings, where social aspects of the cases were often discussed at length. When the patient to be presented had come through a social agency, it was customary to ask a social worker from the agency to attend the staff meeting. Through these meetings the director consciously guided the education of the social service as well as of the medical staff. Every year a series of social clinics was held to which social workers of the community were invited. The history was read and the patient then came in. Patients for these demonstrations were carefully chosen in order that they should not suffer, and only those who were willing to appear were presented. To many patients it was an agreeable experience, and others were glad to be of help to social workers dealing with such problems as theirs, even though it cost them some embarrassment.

From the beginning, the different functions to be performed by social workers in the hospital were clearly divided. Even if at times one person must perform all functions, it was considered important to keep the different divisions of the social work clearly defined so that each type of work should be duly considered for possible development. It was apparent at once that a clinic manager to look out for social interests in the out-patient department was essential, to get the social history from patients or friends who came with them, to assist in discovering social problems of the patients and their ability to carry out the physicians' directions, to see that patients and others were made comfortable and understood the situation, and to act as a go-between for the physicians and outside social workers. Although it was felt that a trained social worker was needed to fill this position most effectively, as the only assistant social worker available was required for case work, an untrained worker was appointed clinic manager, under the direction of the social service.

The chief function of the social service is, of course, social case work. As our estimates showed that we needed eight social workers and the budget allowed only two, it was clear that only part of the necessary work could be done. A routine social examination for every patient upon admission was stated by the director in his annual report of 1915 to be our ultimate aim. Since it was impossible to deal with all cases thoroughly with an insufficient staff, a distinction was made between *intensive* cases, in which the social service took responsibility for a full inquiry into the social condition of the patient and his family and for a plan of treatment, if necessary, to secure their social adjustment, and *slight service cases,* in which assistance was given without inquiry beyond the apparent facts or responsibility beyond the immediate service.

Cases were referred to social agencies for the special types of social work which they were able to give, and in certain cases social agencies co-operated with the social service in the care of a patient, giving special assistance, while the social service assumed responsibility for social treatment. In other cases the agency assumed responsibility for care, while the social service co-operated by advice or assistance.

It was soon apparent that the social case work of a psychopathic hospital was essentially the same as social case work in a social agency. The same social problems obviously occur among any large group of persons irrespective of the type of disability that brings them to the attention of the social worker. In these social problems the family are necessarily involved, so that whatever member of the family first requires social attention, in the end social case work becomes a matter of dealing with the whole family. Among 100 intensive cases under care of the social service at one time, 65 cases presented family problems. The number of psychiatric problems that confront societies for family welfare and other social agencies is much larger than is generally known.   Certainly it is a conservative statement to say that one-half of all social problems have a psychopathic basis.

The question of giving financial assistance to patients through the social service immediately arose.   Our policy was to give material help, so far as we could, whenever there was no available agency to provide it and such assistance would be of therapeutic value. Small sums of money were contributed for this purpose at first by certain funds and by private individuals, and later the hospital authorized small expenditures of this sort.

Besides the function of social treatment, one of the primary functions of the social service is to secure the social history that the doctor requires to make a diagnosis.   Since the hospital is peculiarly an observation hospital, diagnosis is its first responsibility, and to promote proper diagnosis is one of the most important duties of the social service.   As a rule, to secure a social-psychiatric history for medical diagnosis, the same sort of social examination is required that is made for the purpose of a social diagnosis.   In some cases the medical opinion may hinge upon some special point, which calls for investigation of that point only; but while securing these special data the worker was expected also to discover whether there were other social difficulties in the patient's past or present condition that would have a bearing upon his diagnosis and treatment.

There was undertaken, after clinic management and case work were under way, a *men's club* for alcoholic patients, which is described in another chapter by Dr. Stearns, who first suggested the idea.   The next step was a *follow-up service* for the out-patient department, through which patients who failed to report were communicated with by a routine method in order to make sure that they continued under treatment as long as the doctor considered it necessary.

Prophylaxis for the families of syphilitic patients required more time than could be given to it by the social workers doing case work. Moreover, it was evident that not only cases known to the social service but all cases in the hospital ought to receive this attention. Through the activity of the assistant social worker, an individual was interested who paid the salary of a special worker for this purpose. Later the Permanent Charity Fund granted sums to maintain this work, as well as the employment work, for several years.

A study of the psychopathic employee in industry was begun, which led finally to an investigation of *mental hygiene of industry*, conducted by Dr. Southard for the Engineering Foundation, administered under the auspices of the United Engineering Society. We found at once that many of our patients who were started on an industrial decline were competent and even excellent workmen, and that with a little assistance in adapting themselves to their employment and an explanation of their condition to their employers, they could be refitted into industry. This led to the idea that similar methods of understanding and assistance might keep other employees from falling into the condition of hospital patients, and further to the thought that mental hygiene, necessary for the psychopathic employee, would also be beneficial to all persons in employment, to the end of promoting their efficiency and personal satisfaction. A committee was formed to carry on a special investigation of the subject. A special social worker for psychopathic employees was engaged, and men patients between the ages of twenty-five and fifty-five were selected for the study. This case work was carried on, with short interruptions, until 1919. In addition to the cases assisted, industrial histories over a period of five years were secured in other cases.

In June, 1919, Dr. Southard undertook for the Engineering Foundation an investigation of possibilities in industrial psychiatry, to which he gave the more inclusive name of mental hygiene of industry, covering the contributions of psychiatry, psychology and psychiatric social work. He expected that the inquiry would take shape in a handbook presenting the subject from various points of view. He had written three papers, addressed in turn to the employment manager, the psychiatrist and the mental hygienist, and had three other papers in preparation at the time of his death.

The idea of *research* upheld by the department is that social problems are studied best through attention to the needs of individuals, so that case work and research may be two aspects of the same activity. This is true of the industrial studies just referred to. It was also true of the syphilis service, which contributed to the researches described by Dr. Solomon in another chapter. It was conceived to be a valuable function of the social worker to contribute to medical research either through social treatment or through obtaining social data by inquiry or observation. Plans for another piece of research of this type were stopped by the war. A study of methods of social examination and treatment was planned, to be made by the most thoughtful and experienced social worker who could be found through social case work with a limited and selected group of cases. It was thought that the psychiatric clinic offered unusually good auspices for such a study.

The responsibility of the department for the *training of students in social work* was recognized from the first, and the hospital offered several interneships for social students. As no training courses for psychiatric social work were yet offered in the schools of social work, an apprentice training was offered at the Psychopathic Hospital. This was a six months' course, later increased to eight months. Out of this attempt grew the Training School of Psychiatric Social Work conducted by Smith College and the Psychopathic Hospital in 1918–1919, under the auspices of a committee of psychiatrists appointed by the National Committee for Mental Hygiene, to prepare social workers for service in the neuropsychiatric hospitals of the army. Sixty-three students were selected for the course, of whom 40 were graduated. Most of the graduates carried out their purpose of working in military hospitals, but some of them went to State hospitals and social agencies. The success of the course led Smith College to continue it as a graduate school known as the Smith College Training School for Social Work, offering courses in preparation for the various branches of social case work and community service.

Attention was given to *office organization* and *record keeping*, with a view to enabling the small staff of social workers available to accomplish the maximum amount of work. Until April, 1917, when a second assistant was appointed, there was only one paid assistant for the routine work, with privately paid workers for special functions and students in training. In his report in 1917, Dr. Southard refers to the work of the chief of social service as "the task of *getting something for nothing*, namely, of getting reasonably expert social work performed by numerous workers in training." It was important to simplify the processes so that the energies of the workers might be given as far as possible to the vital work. Workers and students were divided into groups and cases assigned to the groups in rotation, the head of the group being responsible for the case. A case discussion was held for the first half hour every morning, at which all cases were presented on the fourth day and every three months until closed. A social worker or student was assigned as "visitor for the day," to receive messages and deal with emergencies and to cover the routine of the office. A summary of the history of each patient was arranged under the headings of social, physical and mental facts, and every three months progress in the case was summarized under the same headings.

We held that it is the function of any social service not only to develop its particular division of social work, but also to contribute what it can to the general development of social case work. With this object in view, Dr. Southard, in collaboration with the chief of social service, prepared a book[1] which, although it bears the subtitle "Psychiatric Social Work," is essentially a discussion of principles and methods fundamental to all social case work. Dr. Southard said of

[1] SOUTHARD, E. E. and JARRETT, MARY C. "The Kingdom of Evils: Psychiatric Social Work presented in One Hundred Case Histories, together with a Classification of the Main Divisions of Social Evil."

this book: "Concerning the technique of social diagnosis and treatment we do not claim any approach to complete discussion." It is an account of experience drawn chiefly from the intensive group of social cases, and the conclusions presented are suggestive rather than authoritative.

The chief contribution to social work that grew out of the work of the department will probably prove to be Dr. Southard's scheme for an orderly approach in social diagnosis. He presented his classification of social evils, which he named "The Kingdom of Evils," in a paper given at the National Conference of Social Work in 1918, and later discussed it more fully in the book mentioned above. The uppermost idea of social work in Dr. Southard's mind, at the time of his death, was the application of psychiatric social case work to the problems of employment management in industry. The plan for special study of methods of social diagnosis and treatment, which had been laid aside during the war, was still to be realized.

Of the work of the social service as a whole, Dr. Southard said:

We claim no novelty or originality for the social work of the Psychopathic Hospital, but rather we would claim to have created the part that the social worker is to play in the mental hygiene movement and to have given it a name — psychiatric social work.

It was our endeavor to focus existing trends, to outline requirements for special training, and to define the functions and relationships of this new division of social work.

_____

In the above chapter by Miss Jarrett, no statistics are given. I therefore add a few taken from her reports:

In an analysis of the work on the first 500 intensive cases, extending from 1913 to 1915, it was found that 51 per cent could be regarded as community cases requiring supervision and care; 33 per cent required history for diagnosis; 9 per cent required assistance to the family; and 7 per cent required arrangements for admission to other institutions. During the year 1915 there were 961 cases.

In 1916 Miss Jarrett's report showed that the social service department had dealt with 311 individual cases of an intensive nature, besides slight service to 375 cases, and routine reports to social agencies in 488 other cases. Many persons of psychopathic tendencies, who would otherwise be thrown out of industry because of their temperamental difficulties, when properly understood were kept steadily employed.

Another activity was the prophylaxis and treatment of syphilitic patients and their families. During eight months of 1916, 158 new families and 161 relatives were examined, and 115 patients were under treatment.

In Miss Jarrett's report for 1917 she stated:

Our original estimate, that 50 per cent of admissions would call for social attention, is approximately correct; and we are meeting about one-third of the demand.

The report of social service for 1917–1918 brings out the fact that they had, as chief worker, Miss Jarrett, two assistants on regular work, and three special workers privately paid, — on brain syphilis, on unemployment, and on special investigations. In all, 3,283 visits were made, including 749 visits to patients themselves; and 2,161 interviews were held, of which 1,500 were with patients. The follow-up service cases were 1,174 in number. These, together with 659 syphilis cases, bring the total cases dealt with up to 2,412.

CHAPTER XII

THE ALCOHOL CLUB

By A. Warren Stearns, M.D., late of the Medical Staff of the Psychopathic Hospital, now Assistant Professor of Neurology, Tufts Medical School; Chief of Clinic, Department of Nervous and Mental Diseases, Boston Dispensary

The opening of the Boston Psychopathic Hospital had been heralded for some time as an advanced step in the care of mental patients. In 1912 there was a very distressing situation in Boston concerning the treatment of delirium tremens and, for that matter, drunkenness. The Boston City Hospital would not admit these patients because of their mental condition. The State hospitals would not admit them because they were not regarded as insane; and the Foxborough State Hospital, which treated inebriety, excluded those showing mental changes.

For this reason, in spite of definite legal prohibitions, the pressure was so great that a large number of alcoholic cases were admitted to the Psychopathic Hospital at that time. The detail of these cases need not be gone into. Those desiring a more intimate knowledge of the situation will find their curiosity satisfied by the "Notes of a Conference held at the Psychopathic Hospital, Boston, Massachusetts, before the Legislative Commission on Drunkenness, November 24, 1913," published in the "Boston Medical and Surgical Journal," Vol. CLXIX, No. 26, pages 929 to 942.

It was not long before the use of hydrotherapy in the forms of prolonged baths and packs was demonstrated to be superior to restraint or drugs or neglect, as hitherto practiced with this class of patients. An appreciable number of patients was discharged from the house to the out-patient department completely well.

No phase of mental hygiene at that time offered such favorable prospects. The cause, effect and cure of one phase of mental disease stood out in sharp contrast to the rest of the problem. However, second admissions soon appeared, and the problem of after-care was found to be very difficult. Man after man came to the hospital emaciated, tremulous, feeble, apprehensive and hallucinated. In a few days, or weeks, he went out, having gained weight and strength, free from mental symptoms, grateful to the hospital for its efforts, and firmly resolved to abstain forever.

So the problem of after-care consisted not so much in the creation of the right mental attitude, but in the maintenance of one which already existed. Routine visits at the out-patient clinic were requested, but when a man was working, abstaining and felt perfectly well, it was rather hard to take him from his work for such a visit, so some scheme was necessary by which a contact could be kept with these discharged cases, and the cordial relation established at the time of their hospital residence be maintained.

With this in mind, in January, 1915, a group of these men was invited to the hospital for a social evening. One of the requisites of a successful manifestation of the gregarious instinct is the possession of common experience, as well as common ambitions, and it was found that a men's club developed from this meeting spontaneously. A constitution and by-laws were drawn up and officers elected at this meeting.

Refreshments were served. These meetings continued monthly, the membership and attendance varying from a few to a large hallful.

As time went on and a group of men maintained their interest over months, and incidentally their abstinence over years, the club filled a definite place in the lives of not a few, and undoubtedly was a means of enabling many men to sustain their good intentions. Entertainers and speakers of prominence were easily interested and gave their time.

Later on, meetings were held more often, but were less successful. The outbreak of the war in 1917 resulted in a smaller attendance, less time for service on the part of the staff, and so, in October, the meetings were finally discontinued.

Inasmuch as the after-care of patients who have had an alcoholic mental disease is analogous to the treatment of inebriety, the problem is a mixed medical and social one. Certain cases are almost entirely disciplinary and are not amenable to the altruistic methods described above. Others, where the background is almost entirely neuropathic, are more clearly medical; but brief though the demonstration proved to be, it seems a fact that it was shown by the men's club at the Psychopathic Hospital that moral suasion work of value can be accomplished by such means, and that any institution receiving alcoholics is under a moral obligation to set up some such machinery for after-care.

CHAPTER XIII

SURVEY OF THE WORK OF THE DIRECTOR

OF THE PSYCHOPATHIC HOSPITAL, BY MYRTELLE M. CANAVAN, M.D., ASSOCI-
ATED WITH DR. SOUTHARD AS ASSISTANT PATHOLOGIST TO THE STATE
BOARD OF INSANITY; NOW PATHOLOGIST TO THE MASSA-
CHUSETTS DEPARTMENT OF MENTAL DISEASES

Dr. E. E. Southard, A.M., M.D., Sc.D., was director
of the Psychopathic Department of the Boston State
Hospital, now the Boston Psychopathic Hospital, from
June, 1912, to May, 1919. He brought to the position
a well-trained, elastic mind eagerly alert for the mani-
fold duties involved. Having been an officer in the
Danvers State Hospital (pathologist, 1906 to 1909),
the problems of the State hospital were well in mind.
As full professor in neuropathology at the Harvard
Medical School, he was aware of the teaching duties;
as scientist at large in the community, he was in touch
with the foremost thoughts on psychiatry; and as
student of current and collected literature on the
subjects of psychiatry, neuropathology, neurology, and
allied topics, his qualifications for the position were
complete. It would appear almost axiomatical that a
director of a psychopathic hospital should be of professional rank, have university or collegiate connection,
and have well in hand the problems of teaching and
research to co-ordinate the work of departments in the
hospital, stimulate the workers, maintain for the
hospital contact with courts, judges, consulting staff,
social agencies and the Department of Mental Diseases,
and know and stimulate the interests of the staffs in

the State hospitals by personal visits to them, welcoming staff members to the activities of the Psychopathic Hospital, and encouraging the men to elect a period of training in ward or laboratory work.

The relation of the Boston Psychopathic Hospital to the State hospitals was perhaps best preserved and widened by the numbers of the staff members who actually came in and caught the spirit of the place than by turning into the hospital patients who had been here hurriedly diagnosed. The corners of abrupt contact are always smoothed by further understanding, and the spirit of the workers was always very much more enthusiastic after they had had service and absorbed the point of view than it could be by coming to a staff meeting or only seeing the patients at transfer. Any pattern is held up as a target for fruitless remarks, and the Boston Psychopathic Hospital has shared with other patterns in this respect, as will later psychopathic hospitals; but after the initial bombardment, the value of a hospital for acute borderline cases examined by methods used in the best type of general hospitals commands a deep respect. Dr. Southard felt that if each worker had an aroused conscience regarding the work, rules and methods were unnecessary; the consequences of the work were reviewable at staff meetings and subjected to logical analysis, suggestions made and knots untangled, but the individuality of the worker was preserved and indirectly trained.

That the outgoing members of the staff were appreciative was evidenced by the constant inflow of workers, not only from this but surrounding States and from the middle and far West, attracted by the

Dr. Southard

Presiding at the regular daily staff meeting at the Psychopathic Hospital idea that one could come for as *short* or as *long* a period as he chose, to live in or out as circumstances permitted, and secure in the thought that Massachusetts extended her psychopathic training not alone to officers in her own State but, more generously, to all accredited comers regardless of residence. These newcomers were drawn by the interesting accounts Dr. Southard gave of the psychopathic activities in his many trips to scientific, directorate, clinical and mental hygiene meetings, also through recommendations of interested professional friends who sent him their students and associates.

"That the Psychopathic Hospital could be a practical success in the early access of the patient to expert examination . . . was attested by the large fraction of the admissions to this hospital of the total number admitted throughout the State." The far-reaching question of investigation of special patients or conditions, and making the hospital a station for such investigations, was early brought up. It was certainly approved, as the syphilis clinic will avow. How this clinic grew, Dr. H. C. Solomon tells, and the book on "Neurosyphilis" (1918) was a direct product of the clinic.

That this hospital had ever been centered around laboratories and laboratory points of view could not be questioned. Dr. Southard had since graduation never been out of the laboratory atmosphere, — Boston City Hospital, Danvers State Hospital, Harvard Medical School, — and when he came to the Psychopathic Hospital his first care was to *preserve laboratory space* and provide workers. The clinical laboratory units were just off the wards, there were special rooms for bacteriology, for chemistry, for spinal fluid work, for histology, besides the special research laboratory for metabolic studies for the chief medical officer himself (Dr. H. M. Adler), all showing the centrality of the laboratory idea. Besides the usual accepted routine current in all hospitals for cursory tests, every possible avenue was looked upon as showing additional evidence of the bodily processes, normal or pathologic, and extensive use was made of the laboratories for study of kidney function, sugar content, and spinal fluids and the like.

A system providing for graded internes gave pairs of hands for every research activity to prove its applicability for the hospital use, and it was a pleasant experience to have a forest of hands eagerly reaching out to assist in the autopsies on this group of cases. So much stress was laid on the value to the staffs of the hospitals of post-mortem examinations that a part of the duties of the assistant pathologist when visiting the hospitals in the administrative interests to investigate violent or sudden deaths was allocated to demonstrating lesions on section and to securing material for intensive study in the central laboratory, to round out the systematic photography of 1,000 brains. This goal — 1,000 brains — was eagerly sought as a unique basis for selection of suitable cases to illustrate a book on the "Anatomy of Mental Disease," and to direct the interests of the various clinicians toward pathologic basis for these diseases; moreover, the itinerant pathologist could keep very near the anatomical studies of the research men by supply of material for the special groups (Solomon on "Syphilis," Raeder on "Feeblemindedness," Thom on "Epilepsy," etc.).

The first fragment of the monograph on the "Waverley Researches in the Pathology of the Feeble-Minded" appeared in 1918. In the introduction the pathology of the feeble-minded is plumbed.

It cannot be doubted that every physician associated with the pathological laboratory, either in its investigative or its research aspect, gains an insight into psychiatry more quickly than those who remain away from it. "One autopsy worth ten clinical cases," remarks a former associate.

The histopathological laboratory has ever sought to simplify its routine and elaborate its teaching and research values. To this end no heavy technical load for the individual case has ever been attempted, but the smallest amount was done that would give the most information ("section of cords will bring the news from the nervous system"). To this hospital were sent the technical aids to be trained for the hospitals or private laboratories. Here came journeying physicians wanting a method for a piece of research, and usually remaining to perfect themselves for teaching their own technicians or assistants; others came to spend sufficient time both to learn methods and employ them in research problems.

In the hospital it was desirable that besides the daily fluctuation of cases, the wheels of change in staff should be revolving. No one could keep up indefinitely the accelerated pace that rapid turnover of cases means, — hence many workers for a short time and then whisk them out to other and better jobs. "The Psychopathic Hospital is a great springboard," the director was wont to say. What advantage in seeing 4,000 cases if 1,000 contacts demonstrate ability in the staff member, which must ever be the basis for promotion? How many life histories can any one person carry? Of what value are more kaleidoscopic pictures? The country, from the general practitioner to the grade of specialist, is needing men. If the temperament leads to further contact, the man seeks further psychiatric practice and goes forth with connections toward the hospital, a point of view, and aroused enthusiasm to show his prowess. If he has no ability or interest, there is no use staying. The argument is all for leaving after a short, intensive training.

The hospital must have organization which permits work to go on in the absence of the higher officers. Again, like a general hospital, the executive officers attend to all matters below the medical level but are aware of the medical angle. They determine what type of patient may be admitted, except in an emergency when any type is taken. They keep track of the legal matters pertaining to reception, proper blanks for holding the patient, nursing care, board, clothes, visitors, relatives, special permissions, reports to medical examiners and to the Department of Mental Diseases. Provided one can make cheerful allowance for overlapping of authority, this makes an ideal arrangement for relieving the medical service of all but the real medical problems, which are in themselves definite enough. The standard of a diagnosis in five days, allowing time for laboratory returns and disposition of the case in ten days, makes for the activity mentioned. The wheels of psychological, laboratory, hydrotherapeutic, social service and pathology all need to revolve.

PSYCHOPATHIC HOSPITAL STAFF

The Psychopathic Hospital, moreover, was "not merely to permit research but to foster research whether medical, hygiene, or otherwise profoundly social," and to this end a chemistry laboratory worked full time, and psychology attracted students because of its research. Social service grew beyond mere after-care, as is evidenced in the manuscript of "The Kingdom of Evils, a Case Book of Psychiatric Social Service," in which social treatment is evaluated. Also the treatment of syphilis was on a research basis.

The teaching of undergraduates from medical schools was managed by clinics in sections and by lectures at the hospital, though from 1912 to 1920 there was no chair of psychiatry. The hospital stands ready to provide patients for clinics held by visiting professors of medical schools, now as always; and usually as the temperament of individuals determines interest in future activities, some will be attracted to psychiatry if their impatience of results is not too strong. The introduction to psychiatry would be at the Psychopathic Hospital in its most appealing form. The teaching of undergraduates and graduates then was by actual ward work, as were the army officers stationed here in the war time.

A director must be one of the most highly and broadly trained medical men available; alert to advantages in observation, diagnosis, treatment of the patients; keen to teach, stimulate, and co-ordinate staff and student activities; able to utilize the results of treatment or diagnosis, to point out errors or correct methods and speak acceptably about it; but, best of all, have a point of view for a research attack on some broad angle of the psychiatric problem.

CHAPTER XIV

NURSING AND OCCUPATIONAL DEPARTMENTS

BY HELEN B. HOPKINS, TRUSTEE, PSYCHOPATHIC HOSPITAL

The development of the special type of nurse needed for the care of the acute cases of mental disease, for very disturbed cases brought in by the police, and especially for the incipient cases needing special observation and treatment, such as are taken to the Psychopathic Hospital, has always been one of the most difficult problems. In spite of much earnest planning on the part of the director and the trustees, and in spite of devoted service and effort on the part of the several superintendents of nurses, we must regretfully own that this department has made less progress than any other. In his report of 1913 Dr. Southard says:

The problem of nursing is one of our most serious problems. We must distinguish between what may be called negative or vigilance nursing and the more positive or constructive nursing which has the benefit of the patient in mind. Vigilance nursing, or "watchful waiting," is the most that can be hoped for from most nurses and attendants of asylum type. One familiar with general hospital nursing is astonished to find how much of the work in an insane hospital consists merely of watchful waiting.

I believe that, with the asylum type of nursing that was introduced at the hospital, we have done well. But we have not done so well in constructive nursing. For this purpose a new type of training school needs developing, — one that will attract graduates of general hospitals wishing to fill out their training. There is no doubt that we have important things to teach nurses who have had only a general hospital training, notably in the field of treatment of delirium and excitement, as well as in the treatment of various chronic neurasthenic and psychasthenic states. As it stands, we pay just enough to attract persons of the custodial type and are rejoiced when a few of these persons develop higher qualities. Should we, however, be able to offer much new and attractive work to general hospital nurses, we might need to pay them no more than, or not much more than, they are getting as general hospital nurses. Upon some such lines should the Psychopathic Hospital training school be developed. I am not able to report that we have accomplished much more than a fairly successful custodial or vigilance nursing as yet.

In another report he says:

I hesitate to speak with authority about a classical difficulty in handling the insane, — the problem of proper nurses. But one thing is clear: asylum methods will not work when transplanted to a psychopathic hospital. Psychopathic hospital nursing must be more than the prevention of accidents. And, in the absence of hosts of " workers," *i.e.*, chronically impaired patients such as are found in chronic hospitals, the Psychopathic Hospital has to face the necessity of securing persons to carry on such housework as in the chronic hospital is done either by the custodial type of nurse or attendant, or by "workers" under direction.

The ideals expressed in these reports are still far from being achieved. From the first, the desirability of some sort of training school for nurses had been felt, for aside from the opportunities for special training afforded in the Psychopathic Hospital and the great need of the State and the community for nurses having such training, the problem of the economic and humane management of the nursing force within the hospital was no small one without its own school. An early effort was made to establish a training course of two and one-half years. In the annual report of 1915 we read:

Regarding the nursing service: Two pupils of the original training school were graduated during the year, on completion of a two years' course here and six months' course at the City Hospital.

But by this time Dr. Southard's more progressive plan suggested in the report of 1913, already quoted, was under way, and before these two pupils were graduated the impractical idea of continuing to attempt to give an undergraduate course for general nurses had been abandoned.

In the annual report for 1914 Dr. Southard writes:

The endeavor to establish a higher grade of nursing in the Psychopathic Hospital led, in January, 1914, to wholesale discharges and unregretted resignations. . . . After the establishment of the new régime the wards became much better managed and a good spirit was forthwith obtained, with a diminution in the number of accidents which might have been expected. As against 68 accidents recorded during the statistical year 1913, there were 57 recorded in the statistical year 1914, of which 21 occurred during the first stormy quarter of the statistical year. Whatever may be the proper policy for our institutions of chiefly custodial type, with numerous chronic cases to act as "workers," I believe that our experience proves beyond a cavil that a high type of constructive nursing in a situation like that at the Psychopathic Hospital must be performed by nurses having general hospital training, or having somehow attained its equivalent. It must be our task of the coming year to establish this fact still further by concrete work in connection with a training school, — preferably a postgraduate training school for the graduates of general hospital training schools.

The then superintendent of nurses, Miss Mary L. Gerrin, wrote an article, entitled "Impressions of a General Hospital Nurse beginning Work in the Psychopathic Hospital, Boston," which was published in the Psychopathic Hospital Contributions, No. 49 (1914–1915), in which she speaks hopefully of this first attempt to offer a postgraduate course:

The first class of the Psychopathic Hospital Training School for Postgraduates was formed on April 1, 1914. The course comprises demonstrations in hydrotherapy, clinical instruction in the wards, weekly lectures by members of the staff, weekly classes in psychopathic hospital methods by the superintendent of nurses, sixteen clinics in special work and sixteen days in the social service department, under the direction of Miss Jarrett, the chief. Besides the regular lectures, there have been special lectures on the different branches of public health nursing. . . . Judging from the number of letters of inquiry regarding postgraduate work, scientific nursing of the mentally ill is beginning to attract graduate nurses of general hospitals.

This was but one of several efforts made to establish the much-needed postgraduate school, but none of them has been successful for any length of time. There have also been various plans, some of them very carefully worked out under the best advice, to establish an affiliated course for undergraduate nurses from other State hospitals or from general hospitals. The trustees have taken great interest in these plans and have made every effort to see them carried out.

During the World War all of these plans necessarily came to a standstill. The nursing staff was greatly reduced by the call to overseas service. Miss Gerrin's successor, Miss Gertrude P. Garvin, left to join the Harvard Unit, and for months it was impossible to find any one to fill her position. Indeed, there was the greatest difficulty to secure the services of trained nurses of any sort, even for the most responsible positions, and the routine work of the hospital had to be carried on under a very serious handicap. At the end of the war there was nothing left upon which to build a nursing school.

In 1919 the general supervision of the nursing service at the Psychopathic Department was put under the direction of the superintendent of nurses at the Boston State Hospital. There was a general plan that when the nursing school at the main hospital should have been built up, there should be a close affiliation with the Psychopathic Hospital, with a constant rotation of pupil nurses, affording the nurses in training at the main hospital the privilege of the opportunities for experience in the more acute service at the Psychopathic Department and the special type of training which could be furnished there. But this was slow work, and up to the time of the separation of the Psychopathic Hospital, the school at the main hospital had not been sufficiently developed to make such an arrangement feasible. When the separation took place, there were no nurses in training at the Psychopathic Hospital.

But the idea of a special training school for psychiatric nurses which should be of real service, not only to the State and to the community, has ever been in the minds of those most nearly concerned. In January, 1921, Miss Helen C. Sinclair, R.N., was sent by the National Society for Mental Hygiene to make a study of the nursing in the Boston Psychopathic Hospital, as a part of a general study she was making in similar hospitals throughout the country. Miss Sinclair remained at the hospital for a week, and made a most careful study of the situation. She appended to her report recommendations that a four months' affiliated and a six months' postgraduate course for nurses be established at this hospital, followed by a detailed plan of organization and carefully worked-out curricula for both postgraduate and affiliated courses, with a syllabus of instruction and schedules of service. These may be obtained by those interested from the New York office of the National Society for Mental Hygiene.

This study stimulated the new Board of Trustees to take an active interest in a plan for a suitable training school. A committee, headed by Dr. Channing Frothingham, was appointed by Dr. Wm. Healy, chairman of the Board, to study the situation and take up the matter with the present director, Dr. C. Macfie Campbell, and with the Commissioner of Mental Diseases. The trustees were most fortunate in having the advice of such a man as Dr. Frothingham, who had been head of the military hospital at Camp Devens during the war and was on the staff of the Peter Bent Brigham Hospital. After a careful study of the situation, this committee recommended that a training school be established for graduate nurses and for pupils from first-class general training schools who would like a certain amount of training in psychiatric nursing, wisely leaving the details to be worked out by the superintendent of the proposed training school in conjunction with the director of the hospital. They submitted a plan of organization differing only slightly from the plan recommended by Miss Sinclair, with an estimate of expenditure for nursing service practically the same as the budget of the previous year, excepting that the living expenses for the pupil nurses would, of course, be additional, and that it would be necessary to provide extra quarters for them, as the hospital accommodations were limited. It was estimated that these quarters could be provided at an additional yearly expenditure of about $1,000. This matter, as well as the proposed readjustment of salaries, would have necessitated making an exception of the Psychopathic Hospital to the schedule adopted for the State hospitals.

When this plan was submitted to the Commissioner, the question was raised as to its immediate practicability, owing to the difficulty of getting the co-operation of the general hospitals to supply the undergraduate pupils. On account of this difficulty, which the trustees felt might have been overcome in time by a sufficiently capable organizer, authority was not forthcoming to organize the proposed school, and the scheme had to be abandoned, at least for the time being. It is not always easy, under the conditions existing at the Psychopathic Hospital, with its highly specialized work, to conform to the very excellent schedule which has been made for the large State hospitals in general.

But the time is not far distant when some training and experience in mental nursing will be required for all general nurses. Since recent army statistics have shown that about 10 per cent of all disease is mental disease, it seems absurd that the general nurse should not have as much training in psychiatric nursing as in tuberculosis, surgery or obstetrics. The Massachusetts law requires that no physician shall register to practice in Massachusetts who has not had training in psychiatry. These young physicians will soon be calling for nurses experienced not only in the care and treatment of mental diseases, but capable of recognizing early mental symptoms, of caring for difficult nervous cases, and of properly handling those whose physical ills are complicated by mental symptoms. To meet these requirements it will doubtless be demanded that all nurses as well as all physicians shall have a certain amount of training in the care of mental and nervous diseases before registration. Such nurses must receive their training in hospitals where mental cases are treated, i.e., in State hospitals, and the resources of these institutions will be taxed to the uttermost to meet the demand for satisfactory training when the time comes. Where are they to find teachers? There are indeed few in the entire country to-day competent to undertake such work scientifically. The State must develop these teachers to be ready for the call, and the Psychopathic Hospital must be prepared to train them.

Dr. Briggs' vision has been so prophetic in regard to the developments which have been brought about in

the last twenty years in the care and treatment of the
mentally ill, I conclude by quoting from recommendations in a report made by him when secretary of
the then State Board of Insanity, nearly ten years
ago on "A Uniform Curriculum for Nurses' Training
Schools" (Bulletin No. 5, State Board of Insanity,
page 767):

> The possibility of sending nurses from one institution to another, in order
> to learn the special features of nursing patients of the various types, under the
> direction of the Board of Insanity, should be seriously considered, including
> possibly two or three months in the third year of the course at the Psycho-
> pathic Hospital, and certain time in the other years in the schools for the
> feeble-minded and the school for epileptics, as well as at the industrial colonies.

Then, after some suggestions as to the division of
the time of the nurses in the State hospitals, he added:

> It would still seem possible for some part of the nurses' training to be at
> the Psychopathic Hospital, where they may receive intensive instruction in
> preventive medicine, as well as study the earlier cases, border-line cases, and
> other cases which often do not come within their observation at the State
> hospitals.

In regard to the progress of occupational therapy at
the Psychopathic Hospital, I have a more encouraging
account to give.   It is always easier to build up a new
undertaking than to demolish and reconstruct an old
one!   Nevertheless, in the beginning the attitude of
the hospital was negative as to the possibility, or
advisability, of developing any organized occupations
for the patients.   Dr. Southard was a strong believer
in the value of therapeutic occupation in many types
of mental disease, but he was inclined to agree with
his various executive officers that it was hardly worth
while to attempt to organize such work at the Psychopathic Hospital, where the majority of the patients

remained but for a short time, where many were bed patients, and others were occupied with interviews by members of the staff or undergoing various tests and treatments. But volunteer work in this direction was encouraged, and some efforts were made to occupy or entertain patients in the large rooms on the roof. Such work was attempted voluntarily, from time to time, by different members of the staff.

About 1918 the trustees, feeling that occupations, even if they were not absolutely necessary as a part of treatment, were very desirable for the sake of the morale of the institution and especially of the nurses, invoked chapter 649, Acts of 1911, which compelled the trustees of all State hospitals to see that patients and nurses were taught various handicrafts, etc. This law was the result of a bill which Dr. Briggs had only succeeded in putting through the Legislature after a hard fight, the State Board of Insanity and the heads of several State hospitals at that time being strongly opposed. He felt the law to be very necessary as the idea of occupational *therapy* as distinguished from the productive industries of these institutions was only beginning to be recognized. He was accused of advocating "kindergarten methods," and much sarcasm was bestowed upon the proposition by men then considered eminent authorities on mental diseases. On June 18, 1915, when Dr. Briggs was a member of the State Board of Insanity, the Board voted that in the training schools for nurses there should be obligatory courses in occupations and industries. As no salary had been allowed on the Psychopathic Hospital budget for a teacher of occupations, one of Miss Susan Tracy's pupils, Miss Onice E. Carter, was employed as a nurse and detailed to organize occupations on the roof. She worked under many difficulties, having no assistants, but got the work well under way within a year. She was succeeded by Miss Mollie Weinstein, who developed the department, introduced many new kinds of work, and succeeded not only in interesting as many patients as she could possibly handle in various handicrafts, but in winning the co-operation of the physicians, and instituted a regular system of reports to the staff on the progress of each individual patient under her care. Just before the reorganization of the Psychopathic as a separate hospital, Miss Weinstein's health compelled her to give up her work. For some months it was impossible to get a suitable teacher to fill her place, and both physicians and nurses realized what a very important part of the work of the hospital the department of occupational therapy had become. All were glad when, finally, another very competent teacher, Miss Ethelwynn Humphreys, with previous experience at Plattsburg, took up the department and reorganized the work, which had entirely lapsed, in spite of the efforts of one or two enthusiastic volunteers.

In the year that Miss Humphreys has been at the hospital, significant progress has been made; an assistant teacher was soon found to be necessary and two or more pupils from the School of Occupational Therapy as well as volunteer workers are kept busy. During the past winter an average of 40 patients were occupied daily.

The work in the department of occupations is prescribed by the physicians, special blanks being provided for that purpose, and regular reports of progress are returned to them. It is impossible to estimate the value of this work, especially when the patients remain for so short a time, but no one doubts that the creation of this more normal, busy atmosphere makes a helpful background for the patients and simplifies the work of the nurses in caring for them, as well as possibly contributing to the education of the medical students in training at the hospital, for emphasis is laid upon the value of occupations as *therapy*.

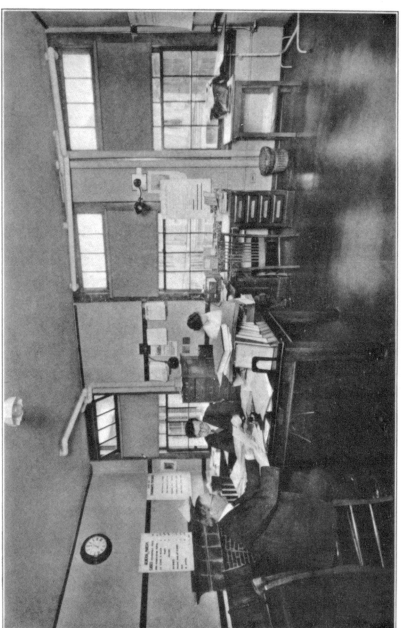

DR. SOUTHARD AND DR. SOLOMON

In the office of the Division of Research in Brain Syphilis

CHAPTER XV

THE WORK ON SYPHILIS

AT THE PSYCHOPATHIC HOSPITAL, BY H. C. SOLOMON, M.D., CHIEF OF THERAPEUTIC RESEARCH, PSYCHOPATHIC HOSPITAL; INSTRUCTOR IN NEUROPATHOLOGY, HARVARD MEDICAL SCHOOL

The rôle that syphilis plays in mental diseases was recognized, and work was instituted to combat this disorder almost at the opening of the Boston Psychopathic Hospital. In 1912, shortly after the publication of the work of Swift and Ellis on intraspinal therapy, the State Board of Insanity appropriated funds to carry out work along this line. Dr. A. Myerson started treating by this method a series of patients suffering from general paresis. He published the results of this preliminary investigation in the "Boston Medical and Surgical Journal" September 18, 1913, and May 7, 1914. While the result of this preliminary investigation was not such that one could become highly enthusiastic, it indicated that there might be certain advantages in treating cases of general paresis. In 1913, this work was discontinued for a time, but it had become obvious that the problem of syphilis was one that deserved consideration in a hospital such as the Psychopathic. It seemed essential to try out the various methods of treatment of general paresis in a systematic and controlled fashion. This work was reinstituted in 1914 under my supervision as an assistant physician. It seemed advisable, in order to get some standard of values, to study the effect of intensive intravenous arsphenamin therapy on cases of general paresis.

At the time this work was started, there were no funds available for purchase of the drug, and it became necessary to collect from the patient or the patient's family a sufficient amount of money to defray the actual cost of the arsphenamin. This limited the number of cases that it was possible to treat. This matter became more acute when, as the result of the blockade against Germany, there occurred a scarcity of the drug. The price of arsphenamin during the latter part of 1914 and 1915 rose to $5 per 0.6 gram. Despite this handicap, it was possible to continue treatment, although under somewhat limited circumstances. The continuation of this work seemed justified as some of the patients treated were apparently benefited.

With the introduction of Canadian arsphenamin and later arsphenamin manufactured in the United States, the cost of the work was greatly reduced, and the State Board of Insanity again came to the financial assistance of the hospital by appropriating a sufficient sum of money for the purchase of the drug. Patients who could afford to pay were asked to do so, and the fund thus collected returned to the State. Patients who had insufficient means were treated at the expense of the State.

While this work was being carried on with the paretic patients, it was seen that the problem of the attack on syphilis in its relation to mental diseases was much greater than that of attempting to treat the patient who had already developed general paresis. Patients with mental disorders caused by syphilis, but of a less malignant type than general paresis, were found to be entering the hospital. More refined methods of diagnosis made it easier to differentiate the paretic and nonparetic forms of neurosyphilis. The results of therapy of the nonparetic type being relatively satisfactory, it seemed that the treatment of these cases was of definite therapeutic interest from the standpoint of good medical care.

As the object of the hospital was and is the prevention as well as the treatment of mental disorders, the problem of diagnosis and treatment of syphilis prior to the development of serious nervous system disorder would seem to come within the scope of the hospital's duties. A number of the patients entering the hospital for difficulties other than syphilis of the nervous system was found to be suffering from syphilis. While being cared for in the hospital, attention to a syphilitic disorder was indicated in exactly the same manner as to a disease such as pneumonia or appendicitis. This at once enlarged the activities of the syphilis division. What was true of the patients entering the hospital as house cases was equally true of the patients attending the out-patient clinic; and as patients were able to leave the confines of the hospital and return to the community, it was necessary to continue their treatment. This led to the development of out-patient treatment of syphilitic patients. When the scope of the work was increased to a consideration of cases of syphilis which had not yet reached the stage of mental disease, the families of our known syphilitics became the subject of investigation. As syphilis is a communicable disease and one which is often transmitted to the offspring of the syphilitic subject, a routine was established for the examination of the mate, children, siblings, and parents of the syphilitic patient who had come to attention. To do this efficiently, machinery was required to follow up and bring in for examination the above-mentioned individuals. For this purpose the social service department placed part of the time of one of its workers at the disposal of the syphilis service. The amount of time necessary for bringing these individuals in for examination, for seeing that the out-patients receiving treatment reported regularly, and for acting as a clinic manager for the out-patient department, soon developed to such proportions that it became necessary to have the full time of a worker. The funds to carry on the work were obtained from benevolent individuals, the idea being that after the value of this type of work had been fairly demonstrated, the Commonwealth would find itself in a position to finance this work.

The extent of the various problems of the syphilitic, namely, the investigation of methods for the treatment of cases with paretic and nonparetic involvement of the nervous system, the methods of diagnosis of syphilis of the nervous system, the examination and treatment of the members of the families of the hospital patients, and the treatment of syphilitic patients at the hospital, became so great that it was found necessary to make arrangements whereby more time of a medical officer would be available than could be given by an assistant physician having the regular hospital duties. With this in mind, the State Board of Insanity created a position of special investigator of brain syphilis, with a salary paid by the Board. With the creation of this position, my services were transferred from the Psychopathic Hospital to the State Board of Insanity. The investigator of brain syphilis was placed in the pathological service of the State Board of Insanity, directly under the pathologist, Dr. E. E. Southard, with headquarters at the Psychopathic Hospital. The duties included the work that had been carried on at the Psychopathic Hospital and, in addition, the duty and privilege of assisting in the establishment of similar work in the other institutions under the control of the State Board of Insanity. With the impetus and assistance offered, the majority of the State hospitals for mental diseases in the Commonwealth became interested in certain phases of the syphilis problem and have continued active work on their own responsibility.

Much credit should be given to the members of the State Board of Insanity for their vision in stimulating the attack on the problem of syphilis as it exists in the institutions under their control. As indicated, a great number of the institutions, after having started this work, have continued it. Credit should also be given to the Psychopathic Hospital for having led the way in establishing the value of such work.

The work of the syphilis service at the Psychopathic Hospital continued uninterruptedly with ever-increasing material and function, although the continuity of service of the workers was broken partly as the result of the war and partly because of the natural turnover that is inherent in institutional work. The out-patient service has continued to grow, and even as yet has not reached its probable peak.

Through the creation of the service under the State Board of Insanity, a number of advantages accrued.

It became possible for the central laboratory at the Psychopathic Hospital to take care of the examination of the cerebrospinal fluids for hospitals which were temporarily without pathologists. It became possible for the medical officer to carry on treatments at the various State hospitals in the temporary absence of a qualified worker at any State hospital, and, further, it afforded the opportunity of establishing a bed service for neurosyphilitic patients at the Summer Street branch of the Worcester State Hospital, where a large group of patients could be hospitalized in excess of those who could be accommodated at the Boston Psychopathic Hospital. The number that could be cared for during any considerable period of time at the latter institution was of course quite limited, but by the establishment of the ward at Worcester, it was possible to transfer patients for treatment not only from the Psychopathic Hospital but from the other State hospitals as well.

The actual treatment of the patients at Worcester was originally done by the assistant pathologist, Dr. D. A. Thom, under the State Board of Insanity, with the assistance of physicians at this hospital.

In 1918, when the Massachusetts Psychiatric Institute was created with Dr. E. E. Southard as director, the personnel which had been under him as pathologist of the Commission on Mental Diseases was transferred to the Institute, and the syphilis work was continued under my direct supervision as director of therapeutic research. This change of organization in no way affected the syphilis work, however.

Again, in 1920, another reorganization took place, whereby the Boston Psychopathic Hospital was established as an entity, ceasing to function as a department of the Boston State Hospital. The director of therapeutic research of the Institute was transferred under the same title to the Boston Psychopathic Hospital. This had the apparent result of breaking off the relationship of this department from the work of the other State institutions, but by this time the syphilis work had been established in the various institutions so that they had no need of practical assistance and had had none for some time. The work of the syphilis service of the Boston Psychopathic Hospital, however, continues to articulate in large measure with the work at the other hospitals. The diagnosis and treatment once established at the Psychopathic Hospital is usually continued if the patient is transferred in the course of events to another State institution, and syphilitic patients whose homes are in the vicinity of Boston, when discharged from the State hospitals, are transferred to the Boston Psychopathic Hospital out-patient clinic for treatment.

The Commonwealth of Massachusetts through its Department of Public Health had the foresight to manufacture arsphenamin for free distribution to properly qualified physicians and institutions. It is thus possible for the Boston Psychopathic Hospital to obtain the drug free of charge for administration. This has been a great boon and has greatly assisted the hospital and other institutions in the performance of this type of work.

From the period of 1914 to 1920 the funds to defray the expenses of social worker and stenographer for the syphilis service at the Psychopathic Hospital were obtained from private sources. During the first part of this period funds were obtained by contributions from private individuals. During the large part of the time funds were made available by a grant from the Permanent Charities Foundation of Boston, a private fund. In 1920 the Department of Mental Diseases established the positions of social worker and stenographer for this service, thus justifying the previous solicitation of private funds in order to establish the value of the work.

It should be borne in mind that in addition to the funds and personnel made available by private endowment and the State Board of Insanity and its successor, the Department of Mental Diseases, much assistance in finance and personnel was given by the Psychopathic Hospital itself. The co-operation and work of the various members of the staff was obtained at all times. In the later years the laboratory work was done by members of the staff. Examination and care of the patients was largely in the hands of the hospital. The hospital staff has always taken care of the supplies and facilities for treatment, the nursing care and hospitalization of the patients.

From 1919 to the present time large grants were obtained from the United States Interdepartmental Social Hygiene Board for research on this subject. The United States Interdepartmental Social Hygiene Board was created during the war to aid investigations on venereal disease. A certain amount of money was made available for institutions properly qualified for research and investigation in methods of prevention and cure of venereal disease and for improving the methods of teaching sex hygiene. The board has accepted the qualifications and the means for investigation afforded at the Boston Psychopathic Hospital and has made several grants.

This financial aid has made possible extended investigations. The fact that this board has felt that the hospital offered facilities and personnel for the conducting of such investigation would seem amply to justify the judgment of the State Board of Insanity and Dr. E. E. Southard, the early director of the hospital and pathologist of the State Board of Insanity, in making possible the establishment of this service.

The methods of treatment of the various types of syphilis at the hospital include —

1. The ordinary systematic treatment, namely, the exhibition of mercury, iodides and intravenous arsphenamin.
2. The intensive use of arsphenamin.
3. Intraspinal injections.
   (a) Of the Swift-Ellis serum.
   (b) Of the Ogiville modification by the addition of arsphenamin to the Swift-Ellis serum.
   (c) By Byrnes' method of mercurialized serum.
   (d) By the direct addition of arsphenamin to the spinal fluid.
4. Intraventricular injections.
5. Cisternal injections.
6. The usage of hyper-tonic and hypo-tonic solutions in conjunction with the other methods.

The types of syphilis subjects treated have included those suffering from —

1. Visceral and latent syphilis.
2. Latent neurosyphilis.
3. Tabes dorsalis and other cord lesions.
4. Vascular neurosyphilis.
5. Nonparetic cerebral syphilis.
6. Paretic neurosyphilis.
7. Congenital neurosyphilis, including juvenile paresis, tabes, epilepsy and feeble-mindedness.

The workers in the syphilis service have always kept in mind that teaching is one of the duties of the hospital. Physicians from other State hospitals have frequently been instructed in the diagnosis and treatment of various types of syphilis. Medical students and practitioners have always been welcomed and many have availed themselves of the opportunities offered. Clinics have been given for the medical public and for the Division of Venereal Diseases of the Massachusetts Department of Public Health.

The co-operation of the Wassermann Laboratory of the Massachusetts Department of Public Health has greatly added to the value of the work. This laboratory, under the direction of Dr. W. A. Hinton, has always met the hospital more than halfway; has been willing to give everything that was desired, especially the titration of spinal fluid Wassermanns; has been willing to repeat tests on patients innumerable times, which has afforded an opportunity for a check on the work that could not have been obtained in any other manner, and all this without expense to the hospital.

No account of the work with syphilis as conducted at the Psychopathic Hospital would be at all adequate without due notice of the work of the pathological service of the State Board of Insanity and later the Commission of Mental Diseases. The very numerous autopsies and the analysis of the material have made possible an understanding of the problem that could have been gained in no other way. Not only have the cases dying at the Psychopathic Hospital, and autopsied there, been available for study, but also large amounts of material collected by the pathological service at other State hospitals have been made available through the pathological services of a number of the State hospitals who have co-operated in the most delightful fashion. This has made possible an extended investigation of neurosyphilis from various phases. Of especial note is the assistance rendered by the late director and pathologist, Dr. E. E. Southard, as well as that rendered by Drs. M. M. Canavan, D. A. Thom and O. J. Raeder.

Finally, a word as to the superior facilities that are made available by the Boston Psychopathic Hospital for the investigation and treatment of neurosyphilis. A thoroughly adequate social service department is available for the follow-up of patients, for bringing in those patients who are desired for examination, for the investigation and alleviation of the social problems arising in connection with the patients and their families, and for the management of the out-patient clinic.

The hospital has all the necessary physical requirements for hospitalization and laboratory work and facilities in the way of operating room for carrying on all complicated treatments. The ease of temporary and brief admission of patients for lumbar puncture and intrathecal therapy and systematic examination and treatment offers facilities to patients and physicians than which there are none superior.

CHAPTER XVI

THE FUNCTIONS OF TRUSTEES

By Albert Evans, M.D., Secretary-Treasurer of the Massachusetts State Hospital Trustees Association

The history of any public institution for the care of the insane, epileptic and feeble-minded in Massachusetts would be incomplete without embodying an attempt at adequate delineation of the functions and an account of the functioning of its Board of Trustees; for from the awakening of legislative reachings toward the light of comprehending the grave question involved in State care of the insane, in 1900, to its present illumination, undoubtedly no single factor has more marked the progress made than public sentiment as focused on this State-wide problem through the several Boards of Trustees.

On December 1, 1920, the Boston Psychopathic Hospital ceased to be a department of the Boston State Hospital, and was made an independent hospital under the Department of Mental Diseases, with its own Board of Trustees, namely, William Healy, M.D., Channing Frothingham, M.D., Dr. Allan W. Rowe, Charles F. Rowley, Esq., William J. Sullivan, Esq., Helen B. Hopkins and Esther M. Andrews. It is a hospital "for the first care and observation of mental patients and the treatment of acute and curable mental diseases, with an out-patient department, treatment rooms and laboratories for scientific research as to the nature, causes and results of insanity."

Powers and Duties of Trustees

Chapter 123, General Laws, which is on the commitment and care of the insane and other mental defectives, provides:

SECTION 26. The trustees of each state hospital shall have charge of the general interests thereof, and shall see that its affairs are conducted according to law, and to the by-laws and regulations established by them.

SECTION 27. The trustees of each state hospital shall be a corporation for the purpose of taking and holding, by them and their successors, in trust for the commonwealth, any grant or devise of land, and any gift or bequest of money or personal property, made for the use of the state hospital of which they are trustees, and for the purpose of preserving and investing the proceeds thereof in notes or bonds secured by good and sufficient mortgages or other securities, with all the power necessary to carry said purposes into effect. They may expend any unrestricted gift or bequest, or part thereof, in the erection or alteration of buildings on land belonging to the state hospital, subject to the approval of the department of mental diseases, but all such buildings shall belong to the state hospital and be managed as a part thereof.

SECTION 28. The trustees of each state hospital, with the approval of the department, shall appoint and may remove from such state hospital:

(a) A superintendent, who shall be a physician and shall reside at the state hospital. With the approval of the trustees he shall appoint and may remove assistant physicians and necessary subordinate officers and other persons. In state hospitals receiving female patients and employing more than two assistant physicians one of them shall be a woman.

(b) A treasurer, who shall give bond for the faithful performance of his duties.

SECTION 29. The trustees of each state hospital shall have the following powers and duties in addition to any other powers given and duties imposed by this chapter.

(a) Except as otherwise provided in this chapter, they shall retain all powers and duties now conferred or imposed upon them by law, and shall maintain an effective and proper inspection of their respective state hospitals, and shall from time to time make suggestions to the department as to improvements therein, especially such as will make the administration thereof more effective, economical and humane.

(b) There shall be thorough visitations of each state hospital by at least two of the trustees each month. Every trustee shall visit his state hospital at least semi-annually, and a majority of the trustees of each state hospital shall visit it at least quarterly. Reports of the visits shall be transmitted to the department whenever matters are observed which need its attention.

(c) They shall carefully inspect every part of the state hospital, either as a board or by committees, with reference to cleanliness and sanitary condition, the number of persons in seclusion or restraint, dietary matters, and any other matters which merit observation.

(d) Upon request of the department, the trustees shall investigate any sudden death and any accident or injury, whether self-inflicted or otherwise, and send a report of the same to the department.

(e) All trustees shall have free access to all books, records and accounts pertaining to their respective state hospitals, and shall be admitted at all times to the buildings and premises thereof.

(f) They shall keep a record of their doings, and shall record their visits to the state hospital in a book kept there for that purpose. They shall transmit promptly to the department a copy of the proceedings of each meeting.

(g) They shall personally hear and investigate the complaints and requests of any inmate, officer or employee of the state hospital. If they deem any such matter of sufficient importance, after determining what, if anything, should be done relative thereto, they shall make written report of their determination to the department.

(h) They may at any time cause the superintendent or any officer or employee of the state hospital to appear before them and answer any questions or produce any books or documents relative to the state hospital.

(i) They shall consider every proposed taking or purchase of land for the state hospital, the site of every new building and all plans and specifications for the construction or substantial alterations of buildings, the grading of grounds and other substantial improvements, and shall report thereon to the department within such reasonable time as it shall fix. No such taking, purchase, construction or substantial alteration or improvement shall be made until it has been submitted to the trustees and until they have reported thereon, or until the time fixed by the department for their report has expired.

The Place of Trustees in the Administration of our Public Institutions

While in the legislative process of centralizing responsibility the powers of trustees have been somewhat curtailed within the department, in no manner are their responsibilities lessened: *they are trustees for the public.* Thus, saving the wisdom of experience in its application to the administration of our public institutions, the law emphasizes the necessity of its comprising both expert *and* lay elements; for without the former it cannot be efficient; without the latter it will, in time, tend to become rigid and narrow and out of harmony with its public object. Each has its own distinctive function, and only confusion and friction result if one attempts the function of the other. Laymen cannot direct experts about methods of attaining results, but they may, and should, indicate results to be attained.

Experience has proved that the nonprofessional board is the most satisfactory body to act as arbiter between the various groups of experts. It is common knowledge that in all educational institutions, to which hospitals for the mentally disabled are closely akin, there is ceaseless struggle between departments, and a decision must be reached as to the relative merits of all unquiet claims; and experts, faithful to good tradition in the fear of error, and loyal to scientific and professional instinct in a zeal for new truths, are more likely to rely on the fairness and wisdom of a well-constituted Board of Trustees, than on one composed of their own number, each actuated, almost unavoidably, by a bias in favor of his particular objective.

With experts, the intellectual deadlock is of all too common occurrence to escape lay notice; hence, their strifes should not fail to arouse and keep active the interest of the lay Boards of Trustees, regardless of whatever "duties" may be disallowed or assigned by statute. As the public is the initiator of the trust, so is the lay Board of Trustees the final authority on every question of results to be attained. The sole object of a Board of Trustees is to aid the hospital staff to accomplish the object for which they are brought together.

Furthermore, once a hospital unit has become organized and is functioning, it is a fact that unless something has happened which, in the infectious language of interest or design, easily translates itself into some form of alleged abuse, the general public is notoriously insouciant to the immediate and remote welfare of its inmates; even relatives and friends perceptibly hardening in the process of being relieved of the day-to-day care of the mentally disabled, to the extent of approaching forgetfulness.

Here the trustees can fulfill a tremendous obligation to the community not merely in allaying public apprehension in the face of some alleged abuse, and in supporting the superintendent through all processes of needed adjustment and discipline, and in advising with him on measures for eliminating sources of like episode, but in awakening and illuminating the public conscience to a just appreciation of the actuating humanitarianism of the administrative genius, permeating its roots and vitalizing the social and scientific activities which go to make up the very life of our public institutions.

Gradually, under the inspiriting influence of public concern exercised through trustee-contact, public institutions for the custodial care of the socially incompetent have developed into hospitals for the treatment of patients, the schooling of nurses and the training of experts in psychiatry.

No longer is the paretic — victim of bureaucratic doom — consigned to his echoless corner in a custodial environment to languish in the shade of official callosity; the treatment of general paresis is now the treatment of a syphilitic infection. In manic-depressive psychosis, no longer is emphasis placed on symptoms, but the high, dominant note is *prognosis*, which in the majority of instances, in spite of the probability of recurrence, is good.

While in our hospitals there are many invalids, under a diagnosis of paranoia and dementia præcox, likely to become permanent patients, *yet they are patients* who, from a practical standpoint, must be studied and treated from a purely mental point of view.

No longer is any ward of the State the outcast of knowledge, and the vernacular of custodial controversy has become displaced by the language of science in art's highest expression, — *service to one's fellows.*

Coincident with the abolition of mechanical, chemical and manual restraint, or their wise use only under expert supervision and accurate record, the mental manacles of the job-secured official have been cast aside and broken, and to-day he welcomes the most searching inquiry into the manner of the application of his own reactions to professional responsibilities; and whereas formerly a superintendent's chief concern was to placate political providence by practicing the most parsimonious performance, to-day he looks upon his charges as human entities entitled to every consideration at the hands of qualified experts, — dietetic, dental, medical, surgical, psychiatric and industrial, inclusive, largely through the instrumentality of the trustees, empowered by the law to "have charge of the general interests" of the hospital.   And a superintendent, disregardful of the relative obligations to his Board of Trustees, can not with safety trust to merit that need of public confidence which alone can sustain him in his hour of trial; sooner or later he will find himself "on the rocks."

Nor may trustees complain if, through their own perfunctory performance or total neglect, the department supersedes them in the promotion of the welfare of the patients and the highest interest of the State.

To quote the late Elmer E. Southard:

It is no longer a matter of the trustees doing something on the side in a dark corner that nobody else wants to do. The high division of psychology and psychiatry has been reviewed.

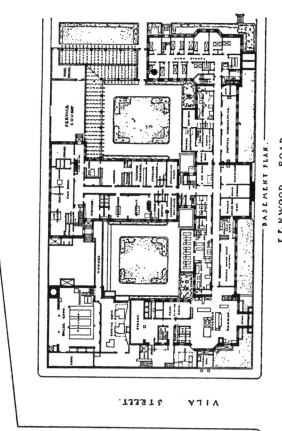

BASEMENT PLAN.

FENWOOD ROAD

VILA STREET.

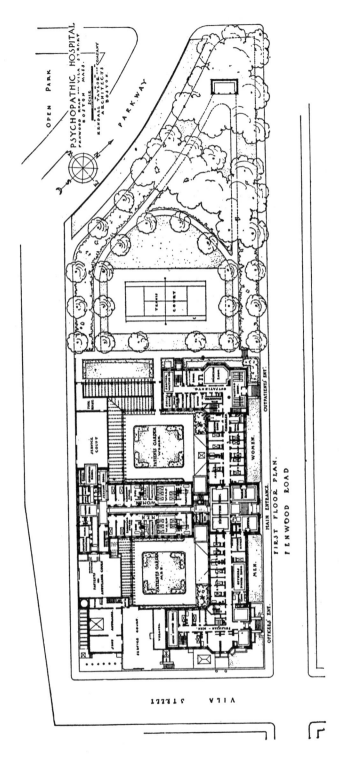

OPEN PARK

PSYCHOPATHIC HOSPITAL
FENWOOD ROAD — VILA STREET
BOSTON MASS.
SCALE
KENDAL TAYLOR COMPANY
ARCHITECTS
BOSTON

PARKWAY

TENNIS COURT

SERVICE COURT

PATIENTS GARDEN
WOMEN

WOMEN

PATIENTS GARDEN

MEN

SERVICE COURT

MAIN ENTRANCE

OUTPATIENTS ENT.

OFFICERS ENT.

FIRST FLOOR PLAN.
FENWOOD ROAD

VILA STREET

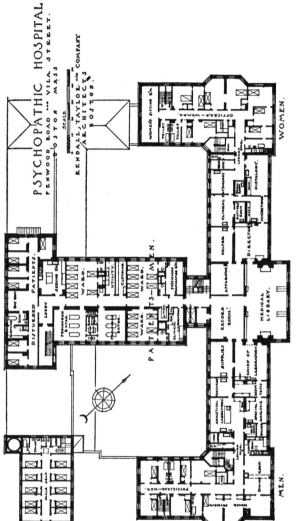

PSYCHOPATHIC HOSPITAL

FENWOOD ROAD AND VILA STREET.
BOSTON MASS

SCALE

KENDAL, TAYLOR AND COMPANY
ARCHITECTS
BOSTON.

SECOND FLOOR PLAN.

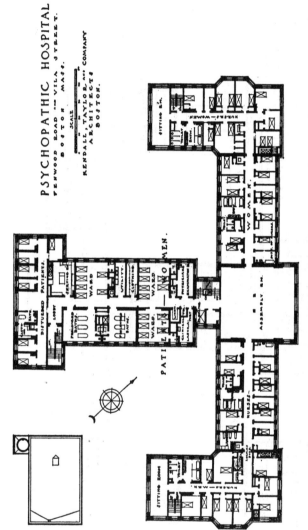

PSYCHOPATHIC HOSPITAL

FENWOOD ROAD AND VILA STREET.
BOSTON MASS.

SCALE

KENDALL, TAYLOR AND COMPANY
ARCHITECTS
BOSTON.

THIRD FLOOR PLAN

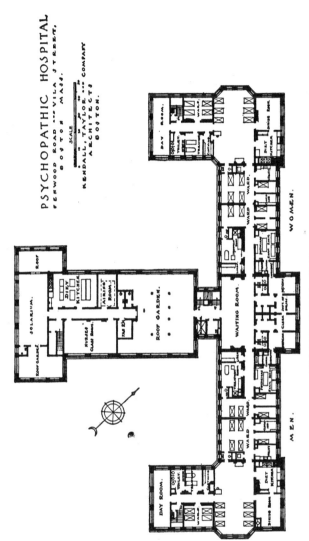

PSYCHOPATHIC HOSPITAL
FENWOOD ROAD AND AVILA STREET,
BOSTON MASS.

SCALE

KENDALL, TAYLOR AND COMPANY
ARCHITECTS
BOSTON.

FOURTH FLOOR PLAN.

MENTAL ILLNESS AND SOCIAL POLICY
THE AMERICAN EXPERIENCE

AN ARNO PRESS COLLECTION

Barr, Martin W. Mental Defectives: Their History, Treatment and Training. 1904.

The Beginnings of American Psychiatric Thought and Practice: Five Accounts, 1811-1830. 1973

The Beginnings of Mental Hygiene in America: Three Selected Essays, 1833-1850. 1973

Briggs, L. Vernon, et al. History of the Psychopathic Hospital, Boston, Massachusetts. 1922

Briggs, L. Vernon. Occupation as a Substitute for Restraint in the Treatment of the Mentally Ill. 1923

Brigham, Amariah. An Inquiry Concerning the Diseases and Functions of the Brain, the Spinal Cord, and the Nerves. 1840

Brigham, Amariah. Observations on the Influence of Religion upon the Health and Physical Welfare of Mankind. 1835

Brill, A. A. Fundamental Conceptions of Psychoanalysis. 1921

Bucknill, John Charles. Notes on Asylums for the Insane in America. 1876

Conolly, John. The Treatment of the Insane Without Mechanical Restraints. 1856

Coriat, Isador H. What is Psychoanalysis? 1917

Deutsch, Albert. The Shame of the States. 1948

Dewey, Richard. Recollections of Richard Dewey: Pioneer in American Psychiatry. 1936

Earle, Pliny. Memoirs of Pliny Earle, M. D. with Extracts from his Diary and Letters (1830-1892) and Selections from his Professional Writings (1839-1891). 1898

Galt, John M. The Treatment of Insanity. 1846

Goddard, Henry Herbert. Feeble-mindedness: Its Causes and Consequences. 1926

Hammond, William A. A Treatise on Insanity in Its Medical Relations. 1883

Hazard, Thomas R. Report on the Poor and Insane in Rhode-Island. 1851

Hurd, Henry M., editor. The Institutional Care of the Insane in the United States and Canada. 1916/1917. Four volumes.

Kirkbride, Thomas S. On the Construction, Organization, and General Arrangements of Hospitals for the Insane. 1880

Meyer, Adolf. The Commonsense Psychiatry of Dr. Adolf Meyer: Fifty-two Selected Papers. 1948

Mitchell, S. Weir. Wear and Tear, or Hints for the Overworked. 1887

Morton, Thomas G. The History of the Pennsylvania Hospital, 1751-1895. 1895

Ordronaux, John. Jurisprudence in Medicine in Relation to the Law. 1869

The Origins of the State Mental Hospital in America: Six Documentary Studies, 1837-1856. 1973

Packard, Mrs. E. P. W. Modern Persecution, or Insane Asylums Unveiled, As Demonstrated by the Report of the Investigating Committee of the Legislature of Illinois. 1875. Two volumes in one

Prichard, James C. A Treatise on Insanity and Other Disorders Affecting the Mind. 1837

Prince, Morton. The Unconscious: The Fundamentals of Human Personality Normal and Abnormal. 1921

Putnam, James Jackson. Human Motives. 1915

Russell, William Logie. The New York Hospital: A History of the Psychiatric Service, 1771-1936. 1945

Sidis, Boris. The Psychology of Suggestion: A Research into the Subconscious Nature of Man and Society. 1899

Southard, Elmer E. Shell-Shock and Other Neuropsychiatric Problems Presented in Five Hundred and Eighty-Nine Case Histories from the War Literature, 1914-1918. 1919

Southard, E[lmer] E. and Mary C. Jarrett. **The Kingdom of Evils.** 1922

Southard, E[lmer] E. and H[arry] C. Solomon. Neurosyphilis: Modern Systematic Diagnosis and Treatment Presented in One Hundred and Thirty-seven Case Histories. 1917

Spitzka, E[dward] C. Insanity: Its Classification, Diagnosis and Treatment. 1887

Supreme Court Holding a Criminal Term, No. 14056. The United States vs. Charles J. Guiteau. 1881/1882. Two volumes

Trezevant, Daniel H. Letters to his Excellency Governor Manning on the Lunatic Asylum. 1854

Tuke, D[aniel] Hack. The Insane in the United States and Canada. 1885

Upham, Thomas C. Outlines of Imperfect and Disordered Mental Action. 1868

White, William A[lanson]. **Twentieth Century Psychiatry:** Its Contribution to Man's Knowledge of Himself. 1936

Willard, Sylvester D. Report on the Condition of the Insane Poor in the County Poor Houses of New York. 1865